Google AdSense For Dummies™®

Cheat Sheet

Signing Up for AdSense

Before you can begin using AdSense, you need to have an AdSense account. Creating an account is a simple process — waiting for approval can be nerve-wracking though, so create your account first thing:

1. **Go to** www.adsense.com **and click the Sign Up Now button.**

2. **Fill in the Website URL, Website Language, Account Type, Country or Territory, Payee Name, address and telephone number, Email Preference, and then choose your referral.**

3. **Agree to the AdSense program policies and then click the Submit Information button.**

4. **Select your e-mail account option.**

   Use a Google account if you have one, or create a Google account if you don't and then click the Continue button.

5. **Wait for approval.**

   The approval could take up to two weeks, so be patient. When you do receive the e-mailed account confirmation, click the link in the message to go to your new AdSense account.

Creating Content Ads

Content ads are the most used ads in the AdSense program, and they're easy to create. These steps have you ready to place an ad on your Web site in no time:

1. **Sign in to your AdSense account from** www.adsense.com **and go to the AdSense Setup tab.**

2. **Select AdSense for Content.**

3. **Select either the Ad Unit or Link Unit radio button and then click the Continue button to proceed to the next page.**

4. **Choose a format as well as colors and corner styles.**

5. **Select the desired options for alternating your ads and then click the Continue button.**

6. **(Optional) Select or create a tracking channel to be applied to the ad and then click the Continue button to move to the next page.**

7. **Confirm or change the name you want to attribute your ads to to go to the next page.**

8. **Copy the code that appears on the new page and paste it into your Web site.**

D1530828

Google AdSense™ For Dummies®

Cheat Sheet

AdSense Do's

- Do target your Web pages specifically to your desired topic.
- Do blend your AdSense ads into your content to make them feel like an extension of your site.
- Do populate your site with fresh, interesting, and original content.
- Do target your site to your site visitors with the intent of filling a need for those visitors.
- Do use a combination of ad styles on your Web pages to ensure maximum audience coverage.
- Do experiment with ad placement on your Web pages to figure out what works best for your specific Web site.
- Do place your ads in the zones on your Web site where they're most likely to gain attention from visitors: top, right, and above the fold.
- Do place ads between or within blog posts.
- Do color your ads so they don't stand out awkwardly on your Web site.
- Do remember that your site visitors change over time, so update your ads occasionally, too.

AdSense Don'ts

- Don't build your Web site with only AdSense in mind.
- Don't cut corners in building your Web site.
- Don't hide your ads on your Web pages.
- Don't click your own ads.
- Don't change the AdSense code.
- Don't fill your Web site with taboo content, such as information about drugs, weapons, or alcohol.
- Don't use automated clickbots to generate false click-throughs.
- Don't hold clicking contests in which the person who clicks your ads the most receives a payment or a prize.
- Don't use cloaking, duplicate content, keyword stuffing, or doorway pages to disguise your Web site for the intent of artificially increasing your AdSense revenues.
- Don't pay other people to click the ads on your Web site.

For Dummies: Bestselling Book Series for Beginners

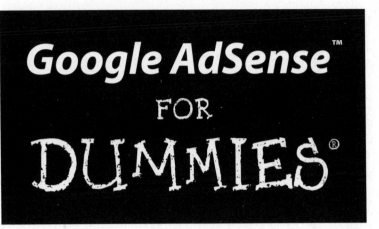

Google AdSense™
FOR
DUMMIES®

by Jerri Ledford

WILEY

Wiley Publishing, Inc.

Google AdSense™ For Dummies®

Published by
Wiley Publishing, Inc.
111 River Street
Hoboken, NJ 07030-5774

www.wiley.com

For general information on our other products and services, please contact our Customer Care Department within the U.S. at 800-762-2974, outside the U.S. at 317-572-3993, or fax 317-572-4002.

For technical support, please visit www.wiley.com/techsupport.

Wiley also publishes its books in a variety of electronic formats. Some content that appears in print may not be available in electronic books.

Library of Congress Control Number: 2008930527

ISBN: 978-0-470-29289-1

Manufactured in the United States of America

10 9 8 7 6 5 4 3 2 1

WILEY

About the Author

Jerri Ledford has been a freelance business technology writer for over 15 years. During that time, she's written 14 books, and over 700 of her articles, profiles, news stories, and reports have appeared online and in print. Her publishing credits include: *Intelligent Enterprise, Network World, Information Security Magazine, DCM Magazine, CRM Magazine,* and *IT Manager's Journal.*

She develops and teaches technology training courses for both consumer and business users, including courses on security, customer service, career skills, and various technologies.

When she's not writing for a consumer audience, Jerri also produces corporate collateral — white papers, case studies, Web content, templates, help documents, and presentations. Her corporate clients include: Microsoft, Switch & Data, The World Health Organization, FujiFilm, Coca-Cola, and NaviSite.

In her off-time (which is infrequent), Jerri spends hours reading, gardening, and playing with her electronic gadgets. She's fondly referred to as "tech support" by friends and family members.

Dedication

For James because you always believed in me, and for Sean, Jennifer, Kyle, and Brandi because a Mom couldn't ask for better kids. I love you all ceaselessly.

Author's Acknowledgments

Above all else, I thank God for giving me the ability to string two sentences together coherently (sometimes). Because I only reach my full potential sometimes, I thank the team at Wiley that helped make this book what you expect it to be. Paul, Jen, Paul Chaney (acting as tech editor), and all the people in production that put in as much time as I have — thank you. Your input is more valuable than I could ever express.

A huge thank you also goes out to Steve Olechowski over at Google. Steve, your last-minute save made you nothing short of a superhero in my book. Thanks so much.

My biggest thanks go out to you, the reader. Thanks for reading this book. I hope it helps you realize all the potential of AdSense.

Publisher's Acknowledgments

We're proud of this book; please send us your comments through our online registration form located at www.dummies.com/register/.

Some of the people who helped bring this book to market include the following:

Acquisitions and Editorial

Senior Project Editor: Paul Levesque

Acquisitions Editor: Amy Fandrei

Copy Editor: Jennifer Riggs

Technical Editor: Paul Chaney

Editorial Manager: Leah Cameron

Editorial Assistant: Amanda Foxworth

Sr. Editorial Assistant: Cherie Case

Cartoons: Rich Tennant
(www.the5thwave.com)

Composition Services

Project Coordinator: Kristie Rees

Layout and Graphics: Carl Byers, Laura Pence, Christine Williams

Proofreaders: Laura L. Bowman, Jessica Kramer

Indexer: Potomac Indexing, LLC

Publishing and Editorial for Technology Dummies

Richard Swadley, Vice President and Executive Group Publisher

Andy Cummings, Vice President and Publisher

Mary Bednarek, Executive Acquisitions Director

Mary C. Corder, Editorial Director

Publishing for Consumer Dummies

Diane Graves Steele, Vice President and Publisher

Composition Services

Gerry Fahey, Vice President of Production Services

Debbie Stailey, Director of Composition Services

Contents at a Glance

Table of Contents

Introduction

· ·

*T*he Web is big business, and you probably picked up *Google AdSense For Dummies* hoping to tap into some of the money that's available online. Good choice. I wrote this book to help you to make more money online.

I'm not talking the *get rich scheme* of the decade, though. AdSense is serious business and requires serious effort. This book is designed to give you an understanding of AdSense and how to make the most money possible using it with your particular Web site. Not everyone is destined to be an AdSense millionaire, but using the principles I lay out in the pages that follow should help you at least add enough money to your budget to enjoy a nice dinner out now and again.

About This Book

Google AdSense For Dummies is an introduction to Google AdSense and how to use it to add a revenue stream to your Web site or blog. I explain every-thing you need to know in order to get started with AdSense, from signing up for the program to creating various types of ads, including ads for content, mobile Web sites, and video ads. The book includes dozens of tips to help you get up to speed with AdSense faster than you can down your allotment of caffeine.

If you know nothing at all about AdSense, this book is the user's guide that you won't find in the online AdSense Help pages. If you're already somewhat familiar with AdSense, you can depend on this book to show you how to optimize your AdSense efforts and start making money with your ads.

Conventions Used in This Book

The alphabet soup that accompanies anything technology is enough to make you gouge out your eyeballs in an attempt to massage your aching brain. I avoid as many of those acronyms as possible. I even try to keep the jargon that's always associated with technology to a minimum.

As with all specific technologies, however, some level of geek-speak is involved. If I absolutely have to use techno-mumbo-jumbo to make a point, I add a clear explanation along with the offensive words, just so you're clear on what you're reading.

Also, I'm a geek, and I have a geek's sense of humor. Still, I lighten up the seriousness of the topics covered where I can. Keep in mind though, it's still technology, and you'll still find that some parts are as exciting as sorting paperclips. Like I said, I'm a geek.

Foolish Assumptions

My dad used to remind me often that the results of making assumptions were often not pretty. Still, I had to make some assumptions about you, the reader, and your understanding of technology. Those assumptions are

- ✔ You have a Web site or blog that you want to earn money from.
- ✔ You're familiar with how that Web site or blog works.
- ✔ You have a basic understanding of technologies associated with making your Web site or blog work.
- ✔ You have a desire to make more money with your Web site.
- ✔ You want to make more money with AdSense.

How This Book Is Organized

Every software program has a structure and a progression. AdSense is one of those programs, and I designed this book to follow that natural structure as closely as possible. The book is broken into parts, and each one covers a different aspect of AdSense. The chapters within each part cover different details of each aspect.

Chapters are designed to stand on their own, so you have two options: You can read the book straight through, or thumb through and read the chapters that are most appealing to you. Here's more information on what you'll find in the sections of the book.

Part 1: AdSense Basics

This first part gets you up to speed with all the information that you need to know, even before you begin using AdSense. If you're going to use an advertising program, you need to have something to use it on, so most of the chapters in this section cover creating and preparing your Web site for AdSense. Of course, I provide a detailed explanation of what AdSense is, too.

Part II: The Major Players: AdSense for Content, AdSense for Search

The way the AdSense program is broken down, you have separate mini-applications within the main application. In this part of the book, I cover two of those mini-applications: AdSense for Content and AdSense for Search.

The first chapters here have everything you need to know when it comes to building ads for your content. (Just to be on the safe side, I also fill you in on how to get great content on your Web site in the first place!) I then go on to tell you how you can use AdSense for Search to make money. (Here's the shorthand version — you place access to search engines on your Web site and get paid when users search and then click the ads that are displayed in search results.)

Part III: Other Types of AdSense

AdSense isn't just about placing ads in your text content. You can monetize your Web site in many other ways, and this section details the different capabilities that AdSense gives you. From placing video ads, to placing ads in your video (they really are two different things), to placing ads on mobile Web sites, you find the information you need in this part.

Part IV: AdSense Administration

No software program or application works without some tweaking from you. If you want to know how to tweak AdSense to get the best performance possible or where to find information on how well your ads are performing and how much money you're making, you can do so in the Administration section of the application. In this part, I show you how to tweak AdSense and how to make the most out of the administrative tools that are available to you.

Part V: The Part of Tens

In this section of the book, you find quick lists to help you use AdSense better. Check out ten (plus two) tools that you have to have if you want to take full advantage of AdSense, ten things you should never ever ever do with AdSense, and ten ways to improve your Web site traffic (because it's all about exposing your ads to more people, right?).

Icons Used in This Book

This *For Dummies* book is formatted just like the other ten gazillion out there, so you'll find icons in the margins to help you identify information you should pay special attention to. The icons used throughout this book are:

I use the Tip icon to alert you to shortcuts and other tidbits of information that you might find useful when you're using AdSense and the other programs that I discuss.

The Warning icon alerts you to use caution when performing tasks or following a set of instructions. The icon indicates information that can cause problems with software or hardware if you're not careful about how you proceed.

Okay, this is the really geeky stuff. Read on if you want to get under the hood a little or just skip ahead if you're not interested in all the gory details.

This icon highlights an important point that you don't want to forget because it just might come up again.

Where to Go from Here

Google AdSense is a great program to help you start monetizing your Web site. In this book, you can find all the information you need to get started using it and using it well. All programs change over time though, and new information becomes available for AdSense almost every week. Keep up with the changes at the Google AdSense blog (http://adsense.blogspot.com/) and keep this book handy as a reference for the basics of using the program.

Part I
AdSense Basics

"Tell David to come in from the hall.
We can make up the shortfall using
AdSense."

In this part . . .

*E*very book starts somewhere, and this one starts with the basics. Here you'll get the information you need to know before you even begin using Google AdSense, as well as tips on how to better use AdSense after you *do* get started.

This part introduces you to Google AdSense and then gets you ready to use AdSense. Not only that, but you also find out how to create a Web site that's designed well for showcasing your AdSense ads. Along the way, I discuss Search Engine Optimization as a way to increase traffic to your Web site — optimizing your AdSense earnings in the process, by the way — and I close by discussing how to install that pesky AdSense code.

Chapter 1

Understanding Google AdSense

Since the Internet first began in the early '80s, it's grown like kudzu in southern Alabama — faster than anyone can keep up with. The adoption of the Internet has been so rapid, in fact, that some companies are spending millions of dollars trying to find ways for third-world countries to have Internet availability.

Closer to home, however, it's probably safe to say that the majority of people already have Internet access. It's probably even safe to take that one step further and say the majority of Internet users also have a Web site, a blog, both, or multiples of both. The Internet Economy has taken over.

Many of the people who use the Internet see it as a path to the business they always wanted to own but couldn't because of the business ownership costs. Setting up a Web site is relatively inexpensive — add some e-commerce capabilities and then connect a blog to it to advertise the existence of the site and the products or services offered on the site.

Even people who aren't necessarily looking to start their own businesses are looking for a way to make money online. And that's where Google AdSense comes into play.

Introduced in June 2003, AdSense offers anyone with any type of Internet real estate the ability to generate at least a small income from their efforts.

This chapter is for *publishers* — those who are interested in using AdSense to advertise on their Web sites. I cover the basics of what AdSense is and how to use it to generate income from your Web site.

Understanding AdSense

AdSense is an advertising program that anyone who publishes a Web site can use to generate income for their Web site. But there's one small condition — Google must approve your site before ads are shown on your site.

A longer explanation is that *AdSense* is an ad-placement program that utilizes Google's proprietary search capabilities to determine the best placement for ads that are purchased through the Google AdWords program.

AdSense is *contextual advertising,* or ads that appear in the context of surrounding content. What this means for you is that AdSense ads are related to the content of the pages on which those ads appear.

It sounds complicated, I know. And really it can be very complicated, but the bottom line is that with AdSense, you can place ads on your Web site that are targeted to the content of your site. So, if your site is about Chinese Crested dogs, ads for Web-based human resources applications don't show on your site.

AdWords: The flip side of AdSense

AdSense is one-half of an advertising duo that Google has cooked up. The other half is Google *AdWords,* a pay-per-click keyword advertising program. (How smart is that? Having both advertisers and publishers as your customers!) In a pay-per-click advertising program, advertisers place ads based on keywords that are related to their content. (*Keywords,* in this context, means key terms or words that are commonly associated with a given subject, topic, service, or product.)

In pay-per-click advertising, advertisers create short, text-based ads that are very closely related to chosen keywords, and then allow those ads to be shown on other people's Web sites that feature (in some way or another) the chosen keyword. The advertiser agrees to pay *up to* a certain dollar amount — called a *bid* — each time a Web site visitor clicks on the ad. Thus, the term *pay-per-click.*

The bid amount an advertiser placed on a keyword is usually determined by two factors:

the budget and the popularity of the keyword. The advertisers themselves set the daily budget for each advertisement — one built around how much they are willing to pay if someone clicks the ad. The bidding process itself sets how much a keyword is worth — clearly, more popular keywords are going to cost advertisers more.

The bidding process works much like any other auction process, with one minor change. Advertisers bid for placement of their ads by keyword, but more than one advertiser can win. The way it works is that the advertiser that has the highest bid has their ads shown in the most desirable places (both on Google and other Web sites). Bidders with lower bids will still have their ads shown, but in somewhat less desirable places. The "less desirable" places can still perform very well, and in fact are sometimes more coveted because they cost less, which means advertisers can afford to have their ads shown more often.

In return for placing those ads on your site, you're paid a small amount each time one of your site visitors clicks an ad, and in some cases, even when site visitors just see the ads.

Money Makes AdSense Go 'Round

Okay, so AdSense is (in essence) an advertising program. But why would you want to use it? Well, for the money, of course. AdSense is an easy way to generate income from your Web site, even if you're not selling anything on the site.

And while creating income is the most likely reason that publishers use AdSense, it's not the only one. Some publishers use AdSense as a means of making their Web site more valuable to site visitors.

Anyone who displays an AdSense ad is considered a *publisher,* whereas anyone who purchases the ads that are displayed through AdSense is an *advertiser.*

Now, this is where a lot of debate usually begins. *Experts* (who are usually people who know a lot just about a given subject) tend to disagree about the value of any type of advertising on your Web site. Some experts say that any advertisement that takes people away from your Web site is a bad thing. Others say that ads are okay, in the right places. You can read more about ad placement in Chapter 3.

When placed properly, AdSense ads can add value to your Web site by pointing users to other resources related to the topic of your site. This means they'll probably surf away from your site at some point. But if your site is well built (which is essential if you intend to grow traffic over time), it's likely that users will come back to your site again in the future.

The value here is that users not only get what they're looking for, but you get return traffic; and because you're using AdSense to help those users find the information they need, you're also making a little extra money in the process.

Deciding Whether AdSense Is Right for You

Even though there are a lot of benefits to using AdSense, it's not for everyone. Just like not everyone likes the idea of eating chocolate, there will be some who aren't willing to risk that AdSense ads push (or draw) traffic away from their Web sites.

One good example of this is if you have an e-commerce Web site that features products on every page. Many e-commerce site owners aren't willing to include advertisements on their pages because the ads can cause site visitors to surf away before they complete a purchase.

What it all really comes down to is to know how badly you would be hurt if a site visitor surfed away from your site. If the damage would be like cutting off your left hand, you probably don't want to include AdSense on your site.

If, on the other hand (the right hand because it's not been cut off yet), the possibility of a site visitor surfing away wouldn't cost you any money, AdSense is probably worth considering. To be clear, a certain percentage of site visitors click an ad on a site and then don't come back, either that day or at all. But that percentage is likely to be very small. If you won't lose money if they don't come back, why not try to make a little money?

Jenn Savedge, the owner of the blog The Green Parent (www.thegreenparent. com), doesn't use AdSense. She says, "I want to have complete control over the products that are advertised on my site. I don't want it to appear as though I am endorsing products when I am not." And that's a valid reason to decide against using AdSense.

A good rule of thumb is generally that all content-only sites can afford to have AdSense ads displayed on some, if not all, pages on the site. Sites that sell stuff? Well, that's a little trickier, but if you have pages that don't contain links to purchase products (like product review pages, or articles that extol the value of a particular product or group of products), you can probably feel pretty secure about including AdSense ads on those pages.

Common AdSense Questions

If you've read to this point, you know just enough to be dangerous, which means you probably have a ton of questions about AdSense. Other chapters answer most of those questions for you, but to keep you focused, I answer a few of the more pressing questions now.

What follows are answers to a few of the more common questions that are usually asked about AdSense (which incidentally are probably the ones that you want the answers to the most).

How much money can I make with AdSense?

There's just no easy answer to this question. Well, okay, there's an easy answer — it depends. But that easy answer isn't really useful. The problem is that several measurements impact your daily revenue from AdSense ads, such as

- ✔ **Unique visits:** A visitor is considered *unique* when she visits your Web site the first time during a given period of time. Depending on the *metric* — the measurement used to track visitors on your Web site — that's used, a visitor might be considered unique the first time he visits your site in a 24-hour period, the first time in a week, or the first time in an hour. For AdSense, the unique visits measurement is used to help determine the click-thru rate for ads.

  Click-thru rate (CTR) is the number of people who click an ad and are taken to the Web page designated for the advertisement. This page is usually a larger, more colorful ad, the opening page of a Web site, or a page that displays more information about the product or service featured in the ad.

- ✔ **Average click-through-rate (CTR):** The *CTR* is the actual number of visitors who click through an ad on your Web site. This is important because you're paid when users click your AdSense ads.

- ✔ **Average cost-per-click (CPC):** The *CPC* is the amount that advertisers pay each time someone clicks one of their ads. This number varies widely and is dependent upon the cost of the keyword to which an ad is related. For you, as an AdSense publisher, the CPC is the basis for how much you're paid.

Using these three measurements — measurements which are highly variable — you can estimate how much you *could* make based on some hypothetical numbers. For example, assume that your Web site gets 1,000 unique visits per day and that the average value of the ads that are displayed on your site each day is $.25 per click (that's the CPC). Finally, assume that about 2 percent of your 1,000 visitors click through the ads on your site each day. Now, you have numbers that you can work with.

With those hypothetical numbers in place, you can use this equation to estimate how much you might make from your AdSense ads on a given day:

```
(unique visits x average CTR)average CPC = potential revenue
```

so

```
(1,000 x .02)$.25 = $5.00
```

Using that equation and the hypothetical numbers I've defined, you could estimate that you'd make $5.00 per day, or $150.00 per month. Again, however, that's assuming your numbers are exactly what I've defined here, and they probably won't be — these are completely fictional numbers used solely for the purpose of example.

Any change in those numbers — more or less visitors, higher or lower CTR, or more or less average CPC — results in different numbers.

I can hear you wailing in frustration — "So what can I realistically expect to earn with AdSense?" I understand your desire for solid numbers, but the truth is, I can't give you an exact figure. More accurately, I can tell you that if your site is well-targeted and has high traffic levels, you can expect to make pretty good money (at least enough to get a check every month). And if your site traffic is slower or your site isn't as highly targeted, you might be lucky to make enough to pay for your Web site hosting each month.

In an effort to keep costs down, Google doesn't release payments until you've earned $100 or more in ad revenues. If you make less than $100 in a given month, your earnings will be held until you reach the $100 minimum. So, if you're not making enough money, you'll get your payment eventually, just not right away.

Fortunately, there are ways to optimize your Web pages so that you get the most possible return on your AdSense ads. I cover those strategies throughout the rest of this book.

How much does AdSense cost?

Easy question, easier answer. AdSense doesn't cost you a thing. Well, it doesn't cost you a thing unless you consider the time that it takes to implement the ads on your Web site. But even this step isn't overly time-consuming, so even labor costs should be minimal.

What kind of ads will show on my Web site?

The advertising kind.

Okay. All jokes aside, the ads that show on your site are determined by the content of your site. Google uses a search algorithm to determine what ads are best suited for your site — an algorithm that's quite similar to the one Google uses when you run a search query from the Google search pages or through a Web site-based search box.

That said, it's possible that the ads that show on your site might have nothing at all to do with the content of the site. Here's why: If your site content isn't very focused, the algorithm gets confused and isn't sure which ads are appropriate. So, it makes its best guess, which may or may not be correct.

The best way to ensure that the ads are highly relevant to your content is to have well-focused, keyword-rich content. You can find guidelines for putting together the best content for your site in Chapter 3.

Can 1 control ad content?

No one wants ads from their competitors on their Web site. Even if you're not selling anything from your site, it's likely that some ads you just don't want shown on your site.

Fortunately, Google's made it possible to exclude some companies from showing their ads on your site. It's not too difficult to do; simply ad your competitors' URLs (*Uniform Resource Locator,* the Web address) to your ad filters, and the competition is then blocked from advertising on your site.

You can find more information on filtering the ads that are shown on your site in Chapter 5.

Can 1 use AdSense on more than one Web site?

Sure you can, and here are a couple ways to do it. First, you can use the same AdSense code on all your sites, and the *metrics* — the tracking measurements, like number of clicks and payment for clicks — are all collected in the same report with no way to differentiate the Web site.

The other way you can track multiple sites (or even different pages within the same site) is to use Google channels. *Channels* simply allow you to track different sites or pages on a site by using code that's written to indicate each separate channel you set up.

You can set up channels by URL or by custom-defined differentiators. You can find out about the fine art of using channels effectively in Chapter 14.

Can I have more than one AdSense account?

Having more than one account might seem like a good idea in certain situations. For example, if you run multiple Web sites, you might want to have a different AdSense account for each of those sites.

Google doesn't think that's such a great idea.

You're limited to a single AdSense account per payee. You can differentiate between ads on your various Web sites with the channels that I mention earlier in the preceding section, but having two accounts is a no-no.

Google's very sensitive about the ways in which publishers use AdSense capabilities. Reading through the AdSense program policies before you even being to set AdSense up for your Web site is a very good idea. Google won't think twice about banning policy violators from using AdSense.

The Potential of AdSense

Okay, AdSense seems relatively simple, so what's all the fuss about? Well, the easy answer to that is *money*. Publishers use AdSense because it's a potential revenue stream that might not otherwise be available to them.

In some rare cases, you may have heard of AdSense publishers making $20,000 or more each month. Those are rare cases, but it's possible to build a decent revenue stream with AdSense if you manage the use of the ads carefully on sites that are very well designed. Is it likely that you'll get rich? No.

What is likely is that you might be able to make enough to cover your Web site hosting or even enough to cover your mortgage. AdSense definitely has the potential. How you manage the program combined with how well your site is designed and the amount of traffic that your site receives determine how much you make.

In the coming pages, you can find out about all the tips and secrets that will help you maximize the potential of AdSense for your Web site. It all starts in Chapter 2, where I walk you through how to sign up for an AdSense account and get it set up on your site, so keep reading. Plenty more information is to come.

Chapter 2

Getting Started with AdSense

· ·

In This Chapter

▶ Signing up with AdSense

▶ Understanding Google's policies

▶ Creating your first ad block

▶ Using public service ads

· ·

*I*f you want to find out what AdSense is, check out Chapter 1. (Too busy to read Chapter 1? Here's the barebones definition — *AdSense* is ad space on your Web page or blog that you lease to advertisers.) Now, I think definitions are all well and good, but it's time to get started using AdSense to generate a little income from your Web site, don't you know? Before I get too deep into the hows, though, I need to address a few whys.

Probably one of the greatest reasons to use AdSense is to tap into the growing Web advertising market, a market expected to reach about $18.9 billion dollars by 2010 if you can believe the folks at Jupiter Research. (You can read all about it at `www.jupitermedia.com/corporate/releases/05.08.15-newjupresearch2.html`.) And if you could have a fraction of a percent of that market, wouldn't it be worth a few minutes of your time to set up an AdSense account?

Of course, you're probably thinking to yourself, "Self, if that much advertising revenue is available on the Web, why don't I just go straight to the source and cut out the middle man?"

You could. After all, why in the world would you want to give Google a portion of the income that you can generate selling advertising space on your Web site?

Okay, okay. I give. The question was a setup. The truth is I can think of a few (very good) reasons that it might be worth losing a small portion of your advertising revenue to allow Google to handle the logistics:

✔ **Ease of advertising sales:** You could find out which advertisers are putting their ads on your site and go straight to them to cut a deal for advertising that would cut Google right out of the picture. But would you know who to contact? And would you know how to go about convincing the advertiser to put his ads on your site? Probably not. Instead, Google handles those sales issues for you, and that alone justifies the premium that Google gets from connecting advertisers with ad publishers.

✔ **Availability of time:** Think of it like this: You can make and bake home-made bread to go along with your dinner every single night, but it's time-consuming and bread's available on the grocery store shelves that you don't have to knead, let rise, or bake. And that bread is just as good as anything most people could make at home (and in a lot of cases, much better!). AdSense is the same. You could track down the sales, negotiate the deals, design the ads, and then connect your site to the advertiser's site. But why would you spend time on that when you could let Google do it, place a couple lines of code in the design of your Web site, and then sit back and wait for the clicks to happen? Time is at a premium, and you have better ways to spend that premium than on the time-consuming activities that go along with selling, designing, and implementing advertising on your Web site.

✔ **Avoidance of technological frustrations:** Those ads that are placed on your Web site when you sign up for AdSense are created by someone. Usually that someone is a tech geek of some kind who not only knows what works in online advertising but also knows how to program pages or sections of pages to see, display, and update advertisements regularly. Are you that someone? Most of the time, the answer to that question is no, you're not the tech guru. If you were, you'd be in advertising and wouldn't need this book. It just makes more sense to allow someone who knows how to handle the situation to handle it. That frees you up to do tasks that are more essential to making money.

Setting Up for AdSense

One misconception that I had when I wanted to start using AdSense was that it would be difficult and time-consuming to set up. Boy, was I wrong! Setting up the account doesn't require your first born child or your signature in blood. Setting up the account takes only a few minutes and a minimum of information. But how you set up the account is determined by whether you already have a Google account.

Having a Google account isn't a requirement, but it can be useful. If you don't have a Google account, you're missing out on other Google applications, like *Gmail* (Google's Web mail program), possibly *AdWords* (the other side of AdSense; it's a pay-per-click advertising program in which you only pay for ads that users click), and *Google Analytics* (a Web site traffic measurement program that tells you all kinds of cool information about who visits your site and what they do while they're there). A Google account makes connecting all these applications considerably easier, too.

If you're going to use AdSense, you most definitely want to have some kind of Web site analytics program. A *Web site analytics program* tracks the number of visitors to your site and some of their behaviors while they're on your site. You can use a program like AWStats or ClickTracks, but those programs are nowhere near as easy to use as Google Analytics.

Google Analytics is free, and it integrates with AdWords and AdSense, so it makes it easy to track your efforts in those programs. You may also want a program that's easy to understand and use. Google Analytics fits that bill, too. And did I mention the program is free?

But I digress.

One reason that many people choose not to have a Google account is because they don't like the way that Google collects personal information. People fear that because Google's claim to fame is its ability to analyze the heck out of online information, it'll use its expertise to dredge up all the personal information that it can about them. To some people it just feels far too much like Big Brother is watching.

AdSense only Web sites

You need to know one more detail before you even start to set up your AdSense account. Many people set up AdSense strictly to build Web pages with the singular purpose of enticing users to click the ads. You've seen these pages on the Web; they're all similar to the one shown below. The pages contain a small amount of text and lots of links, ads, and search boxes — all of which are usually linked to AdSense or a service like it.

If this is the type of page that you're planning to construct and connect to your AdSense account,

don't bother. The page may stay up for a few weeks or even a couple of months, but Google will find it, and when they do, that's it. Google will ban you from the AdSense program.

If you're truly interested in making a little money with AdSense, don't try to cheat the system. Working within Google's guidelines is a perfectly profitable way to make some extra cash that you can depend on for a long time to come. It's also not as difficult as it might seem when you first read through the guidelines and program policies.

(continued)

(continued)

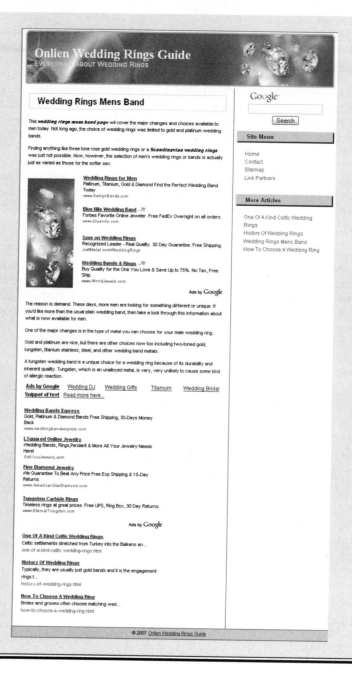

In my experience, however, Google hasn't used my personal information for anything more than what I want it used for. I have a Google account, multiple Gmail accounts, a Google Analytics account, and accounts with Google AdWords and AdSense (and a couple dozen other Google applications and accounts that I won't list here). Not once in the past decade has Google used my information inappropriately. And I'm pretty careful about who I give my information out to. If you're still not convinced, Google has a pretty rigorous Privacy policy in place to protect you. You can find that policy at www. google.com/privacy.html.

If, after reading that document, you still don't want to register with Google, you can jump to the instructions for opening an AdSense account if you don't have a Google account. Otherwise, you can set up a Google account while you're setting up your AdSense account. And if you already have a Google account, you're one step ahead of everyone else.

One more note about setting up a Google AdSense account: Some experts suggest that you should have an AdSense account that's separate from your other Google accounts. The purpose behind having them separate is so that there are no repercussions should you accidentally end up in Google's bad graces with your AdSense efforts. I think that caution is unfounded.

Unless you plan to use your AdSense account in a manner that's prohibited by Google, you should run into no problems at all. And I find that it's much easier to have an AdSense account that's as easy to access as all the other Google applications that you use. One difficulty that I've discovered is the frustration of not having your AdSense account connected to other accounts, especially Google Analytics and AdWords.

You have to decide what you're most comfortable doing: using your existing Google account, creating a new Google account, or not using one at all. But no matter what your preferences are, you can still get started with AdSense (even if not effectively) as soon as you get the approval from Google.

Taking the Plunge

If you have a Google account that you want to use when you set up your AdSense account, here are the steps for setting up the account:

1. **Point your browser to the AdSense Web site at** www.adsense.com.

2. **Click the Sign Up Now button, as shown in Figure 2-1.**

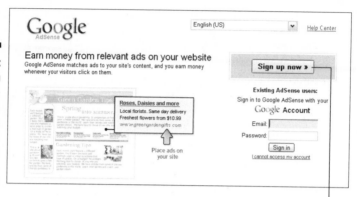

Figure 2-1:
Use the Sign
Up Now but-
ton on the
AdSense
front page
to create an
account.

Sign Up Now button

3. **Fill in the requested information on the form that appears (shown in Figure 2-2) and then click the Submit Information button.**

The information you'll be requested to enter includes

- *Your Web site URL:* Google will check the site to ensure it's appro-priate for ads to be displayed.

- *Your Web site language:* To ensure that AdSense is available to your site visitors and that any ads placed are properly targeted to the main language of your site.

- *Type of account:* Use this drop-down menu to select whether you're creating a personal account or a business account. (If the account is for you, it's personal, and if you plan to use it as part of a busi-ness that you own, it's a business account.)

- *Country or territory:* You do know where you live, don't you?

- *The payee name:* This is the name under which you want your payments issued. If you're creating a personal account, it should be your personal name. If you're creating a business account, it's best to use the business name, but you can also use your personal name if you prefer.

Payments are made electronically or by check, but you set that information up after you've created your AdSense account, so for now all you need to know is to whom and where payments should be sent.

- *Address and telephone number:* Use the address where you would like to have your payments sent, and be sure to include a working telephone number in case the good people at AdSense need to con-tact you concerning payments. You also need to select the I Agree that I Can Receive Checks Made Out to the Payee Name I Have Listed Above check box. This just ensures that you're aware that the name you have selected in the Payee Name portion of the form is the name your checks will be made out to.

- *Email preferences:* If you want to receive the AdSense newsletter and surveys about AdSense, place a check mark in the In Addition, Send Me Periodic Newsletters with Tips and Best Practices and Occasional Surveys To Help Google Improve AdSense check box.

- *Who referred you:* Use the drop-down menu provided to tell Google how you heard about AdSense. This information is likely used to help them effectively market the AdSense service.

- *Agree to AdSense program policies:* The last part of the form is where you register your agreement or disagreement with the AdSense program policies. Be sure to read these policies completely (a link to them is provided on the form). If you don't agree to the program's policies, you will not be approved for an AdSense account. Two of the four check boxes on this list are the most important points in the program policies. The third check box is your agreement (if you agree) and the fourth check box is just confirmation that you don't already have an AdSense account. (You're only allowed to have one, so don't try registering another because it will be refused.) All four of these check boxes must be selected.

Don't blow off the Policies section. You need to read the policies and make sure you understand them because Google strictly requires that *publishers* (AdSense users) adhere to these policies. Slip up, and Google will strip your AdSense capabilities so fast you'll wonder if there's some capability-stripping super power out there that you've never heard of.

4. **In the new page that appears, confirm your payment information, and then choose either the I Have an Email Address and Password (Google Account) option or the I Do *Not* Use These Other Services option.**

   If you select the first option, you can jump right to the next section.

   If you select the second option, a new form appears, as shown in Figure 2-3.

5a. **If you select the second option, choose a new e-mail address for the account, designate and confirm a password for the account, and then enter the verification word. When you're finished, click Continue.**

   A Gmail account will be created for you, using the e-mail address you select.

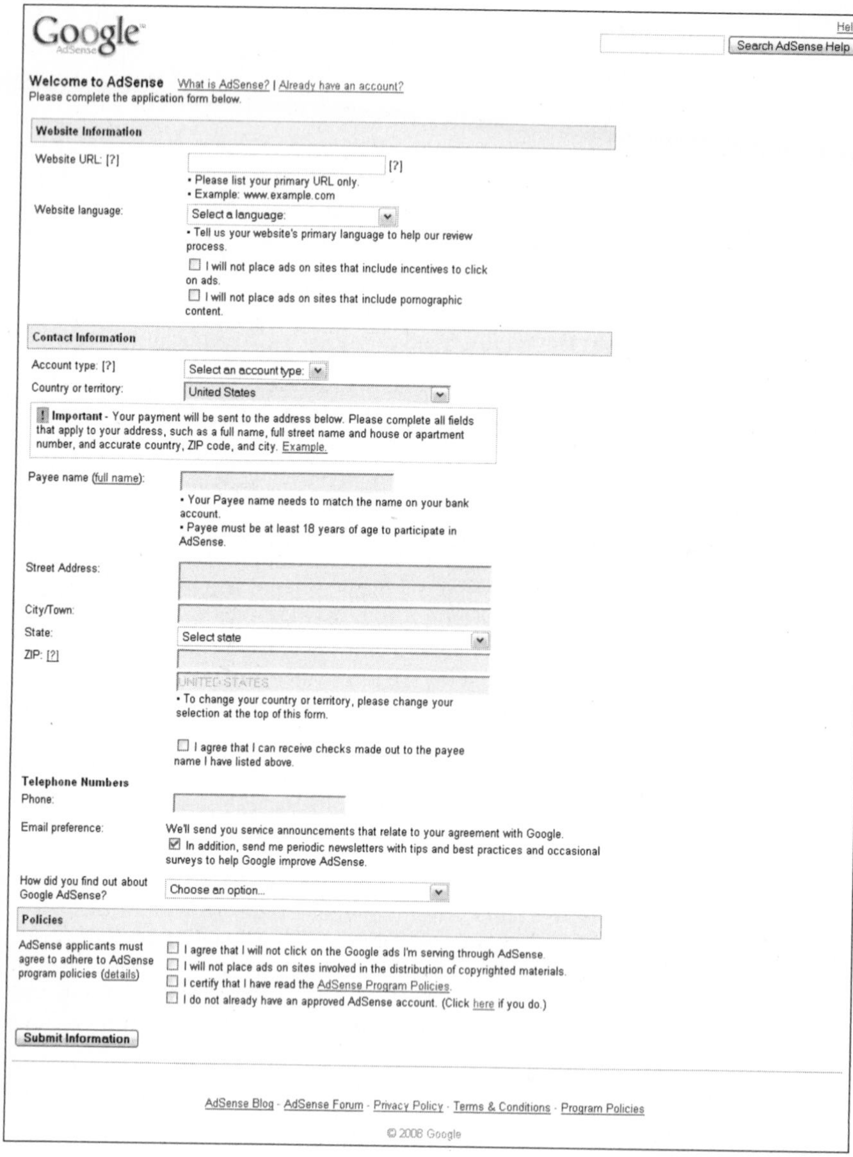

Figure 2-2:
Provide the
requested
information
to regis-
ter for an
AdSense
account.

5b. If you choose the I Have an Email Address and Password (Google Account) option, then you have to choose one of the other two options on the page: I'd Like to Use My Existing Google Account for AdSense or I'd Like to Choose a New Login Name and Password Just for AdSense.

If you choose to use your existing Google account for AdSense, a form like the one shown in Figure 2-4 appears. Enter your active e-mail address and password and click Continue.

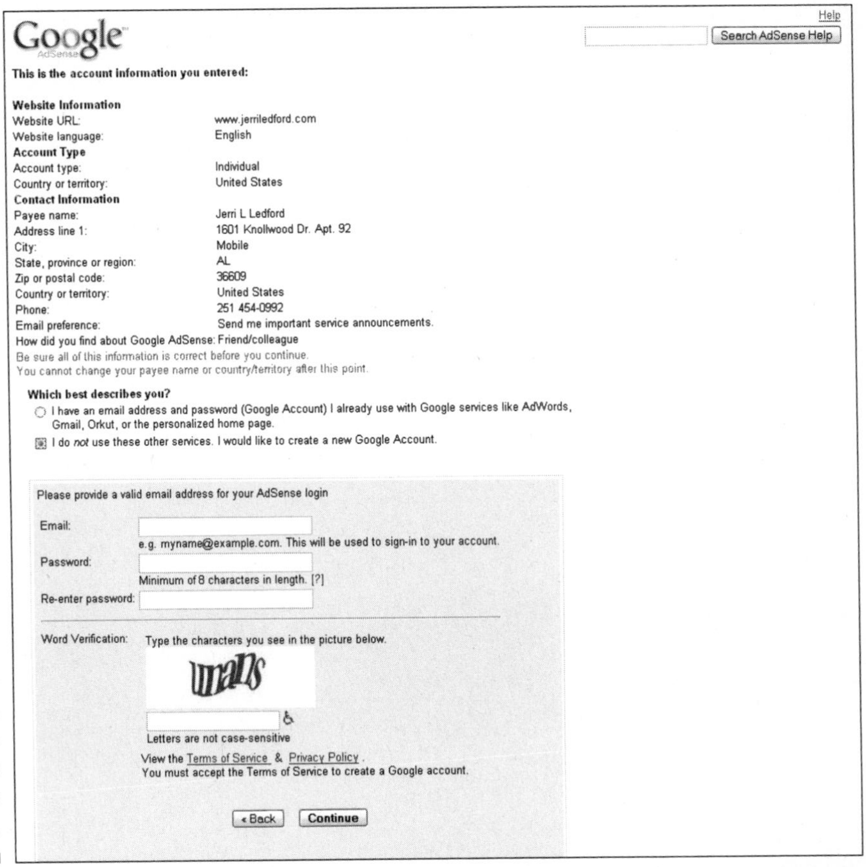

Figure 2-3:
If you
don't have
a Google
account,
you need to
create one
to access
AdSense.

The other option you have is to set up a new login name and password just for AdSense. If you select that option, a form like the one shown in Figure 2-5 appears. Create a new e-mail address for your username, add a password (and confirm it), and then enter the verification word and click Continue.

6. **Wait.**

First you have to wait for an e-mail confirmation from AdSense. That should arrive in your e-mail Inbox within a matter of minutes.

After you've confirmed your e-mail address, you have to wait a little longer for approval of your account. But don't wait too long. Google should only take a few days to approve or deny your application for an AdSense account.

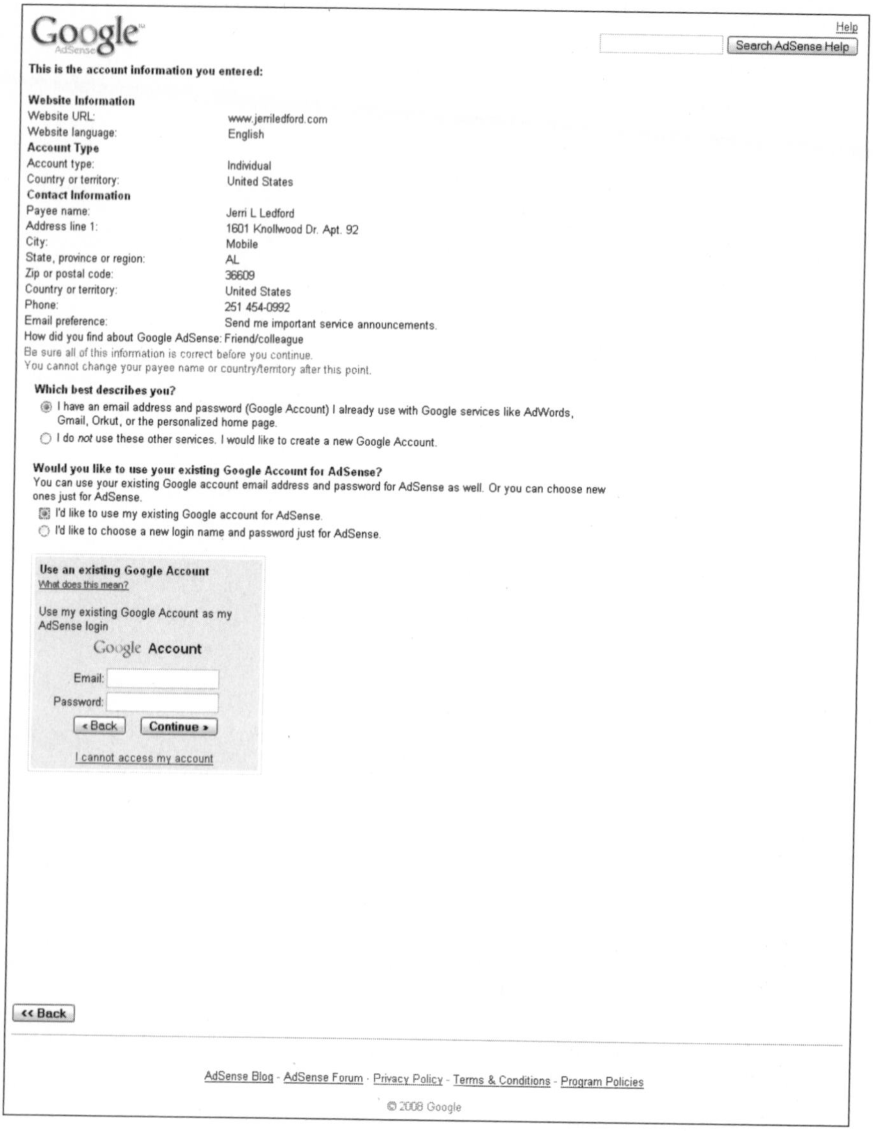

Google™
AdSense

This is the account information you entered:

Website Information
Website URL: www.jerriledford.com
Website language: English
Account Type
Account type: Individual
Country or territory: United States
Contact Information
Payee name: Jerri L Ledford
Address line 1:   1601 Knollwood Dr. Apt. 92
City: Mobile
State, province or region: AL
Zip or postal code: 36609
Country or territory: United States
Phone: 251 454-0992
Email preference: Send me important service announcements.
How did you find about Google AdSense: Friend/colleague
Be sure all of this information is correct before you continue.
You cannot change your payee name or country/territory after this point.

Which best describes you?
⦿ I have an email address and password (Google Account) I already use with Google services like AdWords,
   Gmail, Orkut, or the personalized home page.
○ I do *not* use these other services. I would like to create a new Google Account.

Would you like to use your existing Google Account for AdSense?
You can use your existing Google account email address and password for AdSense as well. Or you can choose new
ones just for AdSense.
☒ I'd like to use my existing Google account for AdSense.
○ I'd like to choose a new login name and password just for AdSense.

> **Use an existing Google Account**
> What does this mean?
>
> Use my existing Google Account as my
> AdSense login
>
> Google **Account**
>
> Email: [   ]
> Password: [   ]
> [‹ Back] [Continue ›]
>
> I cannot access my account

Figure 2-4:
You can use
an exist-
ing Google
account to
create an
AdSense
account.

[‹‹ Back]

AdSense Blog · AdSense Forum · Privacy Policy · Terms & Conditions · Program Policies

© 2008 Google

One question you may have is whether you really need a *Gmail* address to complete the AdSense application. The answer is no. I can sing the praises of Gmail — Google's Web mail program. I've had an account since the program was in beta testing, and it's the best Web-based e-mail program you'll find. But it's not necessary to have one. Any e-mail address will suffice. Just be sure it's an e-mail address that you have access to because that's where Google sends your communications from AdSense, and you must be able to access those communications to verify your account.

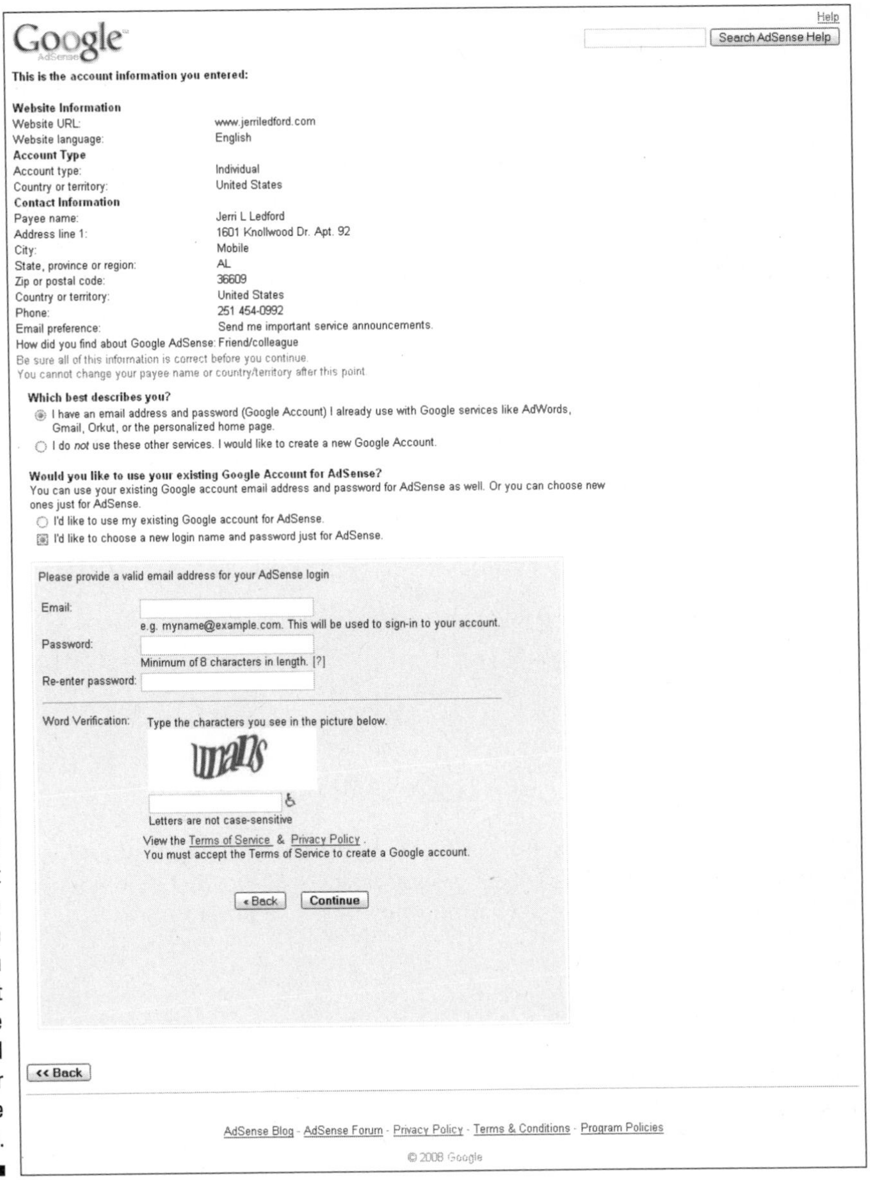

Figure 2-5:
Creating an
account just
for AdSense
is an option
if you
don't want
AdSense
connected
to other
Google
accounts.

Understanding Google's Policies

If you've read anything at all online about AdSense, you've probably seen the phrase "familiarize yourself with the AdSense Program Policies" at least as many times as you've seen the moon. There's good reason for that.

Google is very strict about AdSense users (*publishers*, in their jargon) following the guidelines set forth in the AdSense Program Policies document. If you don't adhere to the program policies, Google reserves the right to disable your AdSense account. And Google will — faster than you can say "What did I do wrong?" They're that serious about the guidelines because the appearance of your site and your adherence to their guidelines determine how people view the advertisements. Google wants to be in users' good graces, and your cooperation helps to accomplish that.

The program policies aren't filled with quite as much legalese as you might find in other policy documents, but you'll encounter ten-dollar words like *pursuant.* Here's a quick list of what you'll encounter in the policy document:

- ✔ Legalese
- ✔ Invalid clicks and impressions
- ✔ Encouraging clicks
- ✔ Site content
- ✔ Copyrighted materials
- ✔ Webmaster Guidelines
- ✔ Site and ad behavior
- ✔ Ad placement
- ✔ Competitive ads and services
- ✔ Product-specific policies

In the next few sections, I deal with each of these points in greater detail. (***Remember:*** This is just an overview. Read the document completely before you agree to the policy requirements of the program.)

Legalese

The document starts with an explanation of Google's legal rights. Basically, the Google lawyers are telling you that you need to be nicer and follow the guidelines Google sets forth or Google can — and will, if it becomes necessary — disable your AdSense account. The rub here is that after your account is disabled, you're just finished. You can't use AdSense anymore. (Yes, you could try to cheat fate by creating a new account, but if Google finds out it's you, they'll just shut you down all over again.)

Invalid clicks and impressions

"Clicks on Google ads must result from genuine user interest."

That's the first line of the most highly debated section of the program policies. This section of the policy lays out the guidelines for what constitutes a valid click. If you click your own ads, those clicks are invalid. If you program (or purchase) some piece of software to click your ads, those clicks are invalid. And these types of invalid clicks are click fraud. *Click fraud* is fraudulently clicking your own or someone else's ads with the intent of affecting AdSense revenues or AdWords costs and is enough to get you banned from AdSense completely, no questions asked — and please don't re-apply.

A valid click or impression has these qualities:

- It's initiated by a real user to your Web site.
- The actual click is performed by a real, live person.
- The click is the result of genuine interest in the content of the advertisement by the real, live person.

Any clicks that don't meet these requirements can be (and usually are) considered invalid clicks. Clicking your own ad even *one* time could get you banned from AdSense. It's not worth it.

You don't have to say it. I hear your objection: How are you supposed to know how the ads apply to your site if you can't follow them? Or how will you know how the ads will look or how they will integrate into your Web site?

Well . . . it's half about trust and half about testing. Trying to view every single ad that's shown on your Web site probably isn't prudent. Because ads rotate constantly and each site visitor might see a different ad set — also called an ad *group* or an ad *block* — you probably couldn't view all the ads, even if you wanted to.

Instead, AdSense has a testing capability — the *AdSense preview tool*. It's a small application you have to download and add to your computer's registry, which allows you to see what the ads look like and how they behave without having to click your own ads.

Download the preview tool from the AdSense Help Center at `https://www.google.com/adsense/support/`. In the Help Center, search for `preview tool`. You should be taken to a search results page where the top result is a link to the page from which you can download the preview tool. The directions on the page walk you through downloading and installing the preview tool.

Here's one catch: If you're a Firefox user, the preview tool won't be much help. It only works with Internet Explorer. For the purposes of previewing your AdSense ad blocks, it might be wise to keep Internet Explorer as a backup browser. You don't have to use it all the time — just when you want to preview your AdSense ad blocks.

Encouraging clicks

The next section of the AdSense Program Policy document addresses the kinds of things you shouldn't pull in an attempt to encourage people to click on your ads. I know this is a little negative, but it's important that you pay attention to these no-nos because ignoring them could have dire consequences.

You can't point out ads. You can't pay people to click your ads. You also can't use any kind of misleading titling around the ads (for example, using a Favorite Sites title when the ads really are just advertisements), and you must be cautious about the graphics you include around ad blocks. If they're at all misleading and appear to be associated with the ads, that's more fodder for the banning machine.

In short, all you can really do to encourage ad unit clicks is to place the ads in the best possible locations. Make them appealing with the design tools that Google provides and then leave them alone. Much more than that and you run the risk of landing on Google's black list.

Site content

Here's where the program policies begin to get interesting. Okay, not really. There is rarely anything interesting about program policies. But a lot of meat is in this section of the program policies, and you should pay close attention to what's here.

Google's requirements for site content are basic: no violent content, no adult content, nothing related to gambling, and nothing associated with any type of illegal activities. But that's not all. Google also frowns on Web sites that are related to anything that could be construed as controversial — tobacco, alcohol, prescription drugs, and weaponry of any kind. Google stops just short of disallowing ads on political pages, though that might not be a bad idea.

Think of it this way: If you were Google, what would you *not* want your name associated with? Just about anything you come up with will probably be on the restricted list that Google's created. Read the list closely. Google doesn't accept *I didn't know* as a good excuse for violating the policies.

Copyrighted materials

This should really go without saying, but plagiarized content will ensure that Google pulls your AdSense access. Copyright infringement is a serious crime; one that's more prevalent on the Internet than grains of sand on a beach. Many people mistakenly believe that because articles and other content on the Web are on the Web, they're free for anyone to use. That's not the case, and Google is a bulldog in the copyright protection arena. The *Google crawler,* which is the program that looks at your Web site to determine the main topics, or keywords, that are relevant to the site, can determine if the content on your page is original or if it appears in another place on the Web. If it's not original and you can't prove you have permission to use it, you'll pay the price. So, be kind; use original content.

Take the time to read about the Digital Millennium Copyright Act and Google's stance on that piece of legislation. The details are on the Web at `www.google.com/adsense_dmca.html`. Not only will copyright infringement and plagiarism get you banned from AdSense, but they can also get you thrown in jail, so use original content. You not only protect your investment in AdSense, but your Web site will probably rank better in search results, too, because search engines — and site visitors — love fresh, original content. Having fresh, original content would naturally make your site more popular.

Webmaster Guidelines

Google's Webmaster Guidelines tell you everything you need to know about what the company expects from the design of a Web site. The document is pretty complicated, but it can be summed up in one word: simplicity.

Keep your Web site simple, easy to use, and relevant to your site visitors, and you shouldn't run into any problems with Google where site design is concerned. Of course, it still doesn't hurt to familiarize yourself with and follow the Webmaster Guidelines. Read them here:

```
www.google.com/support/webmasters/bin/answer.py?answer=35769#quality
```

A more in-depth discussion of Google's Webmaster Guidelines can be found in Chapter 3. There's even a bonus to using this set of guidelines — Google is *the* search engine to rank in. Following these guidelines helps ensure that you rank well in its search results.

Site and ad behavior

Need a few more guidelines for how your site should be designed? Not necessarily? Well, tough because Google's giving a few more anyway. In this section of the program policies, Google outlines yet more no-nos. You can't use pop-ups or pop-unders in your site design. (*Pop-ups* are those annoying little windows that pop up out of nowhere when you click a link leading to a Web site or when you click away from the site. *Pop-unders* are the same except the window appears under your Web browser so you don't see them until you close the browser window.)

You also can't try to deceive your visitors into clicking through ads by disguising the ads or hiding them within text, behind graphics, or in the background of the Web page. The ads must appear as ads and not as sponsored links of any kind.

And to take it all one step further, Google also has Landing Page Quality Guidelines to help ensure that your *landing page* — the first page that site visitors land on when they click into your Web site — is designed well and adheres to the AdSense Program Policy requirements. These guidelines ask the following of you and your site:

- ✔ That you have relevant and original content on your site
- ✔ That your site is clear in your intent and the nature of your business (if that's relevant)
- ✔ That it's clear how your visitors' information will be used
- ✔ That users can find their way around your site, or navigate the site, easily

I recommend checking out the full set of Landing Page Quality Guidelines at `https://adwords.google.com/support/bin/answer.py?answer=46675&hl=en`.

The real key to staying in Google's good graces (for both search engine ranking and the AdSense program) is to design your Web site with the end user in mind. If you're designing a site strictly to collect ad clicks, you might get a high number of visitors for a short time, but that number will fall like a penny dropped from the Empire State building as soon as users figure out what you're up to. Or worse, Google will figure it out first and ban you from AdSense and probably from search engine rankings, too.

A much better idea is to design your site for site visitors. Provide the information that visitors are looking for. They'll spend more time on your site, which means more exposure to AdSense ads, which means ultimately more clicks. And Google will leave you alone to make your money. Not a bad trade for doing things the right way instead of trying to deceive site visitors.

Ad placement

In case there was any doubt, Google set up guidelines for how and where ad units can be placed on your site. The policy document lists the particulars, but it's safe to say that Google wants ads tastefully displayed and in context.

Google also doesn't want visitors overwhelmed by the number of ads on a page, so, you'll also find guidelines for how many ad blocks of each type you can have on any given Web page.

More information about how to actually place ads on your Web site — as well as information about creating appealing ads — can be found in Chapter 5.

Competitive ads and services

This isn't about your competition; it's about Google's competition. Like any good contender, Google doesn't want competitors competing for its share of the prize money. So, you can't display ads from any competing services that could be confused with AdSense ads.

For example, it's okay to include ads on your site from Amazon or other retail services. And you can even include other pay-per-click ads, as long as they don't mimics AdSense ads. Ads that look like they belong to AdSense but do not are a real no-no — that could really stir Google's pot!

Google stops just this side of saying you can't use other advertising services, but only because denying your freedom to use any program without thought of how it could be misconstrued as a Google capability is creating a monopoly. And monopolies draw the attention of Big Brother. He's a sibling no one wants to spend time with.

Product-specific policies

AdSense has a few different divisions, such as Internet ads, video ads, radio ads, and a massive variety of content ads. Google is slowing working into many other types of advertising as well. Because there are so many different types of media in which you can use AdSense, and all those media differ in some way, there have to be policies that directly address some of the differences for each medium. You can find those guidelines at `www.google.com/adsense/support/bin/answer.py?answer=71600`.

The AdSense Program Policy document seems pretty tame on first glance. But as you look closer at the contents of the policy, you can quickly see that there are additional bits and pieces about those program policies scattered behind several different Web links. And after you start getting into those links, you can truly see how complicated Google's policies get.

Don't skip anything, though. Read through all the policy documentation and then read it all again. And read it again as you need to, to stay on the right side of Google's good graces, because if you get booted, it's hard to reestablish your presence on the Web.

Creating Your First Set of Ads

You created your account, waited, and were approved. Now AdSense is active. Now you can fill that blank space on your Web site with money-generating ads. But first you have to set up your ads.

Log in to your new AdSense account by using the username and password that you set up during the registration process. The page that appears at login is the Reports tab (AdSense always opens to this), which features a quick overview of your earnings and the reports that are available for AdSense. Because you don't have any data to be reported yet, you'll have a big, fat zero on that page, much like the one shown in Figure 2-6.

If you want to change that big fat zero into something a bit more lucrative, you need to set up a few ad blocks. Here's how:

1. **If you haven't already done so, log in to your AdSense account.**

2. **Click the AdSense Setup tab, immediately to the right of the Reports tab.**

   A page like the one in Figure 2-7 appears.

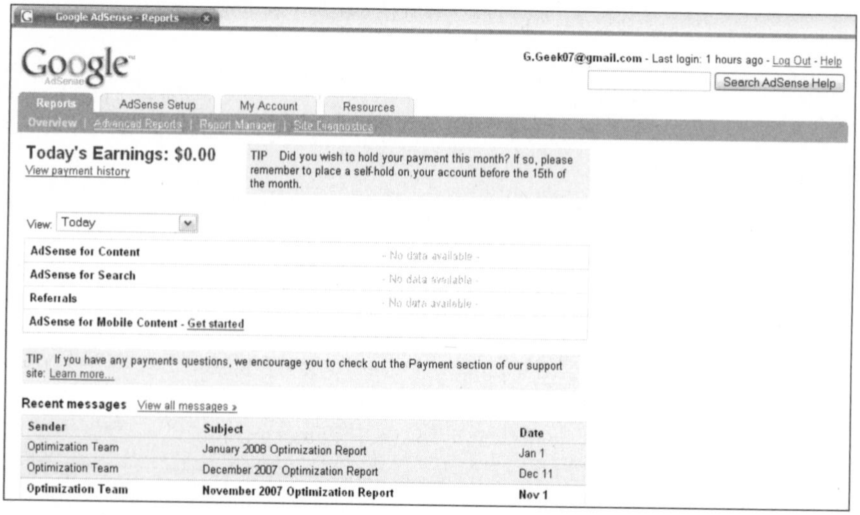

Figure 2-6:
This will always be your starting point when you log in to AdSense.

Figure 2-7:
The AdSense
Setup page
is where
you choose
which type of
ad you want
to create.

3. **On this page, select the type of ad block you want to set up.**

   For this example, go ahead and select AdSense for Content. The other options are covered in later chapters.

   The page that appears is the first step in the Ad Wizard, which walks you through setting up your ad.

   If you prefer a single-page form instead of using the wizard, click the wizard's Single Page link. The information you're asked to enter is the same, but on the single-page form, you just scroll down the page instead of clicking a Continue button.

4. **Choose your ad type and click Continue.**

   Your choices here are

   - *Ad Units*: A graphical text box (as shown in Figure 2-8) inside of which linked ads are displayed.

   - *Link Units:* A set of linked keywords (as shown in Figure 2-9) that lead to advertisers' pages.

   Just to keep it simple for now, select Ad Unit.

Figure 2-8:
A graphical
ad unit.

Figure 2-9:
A link ad unit.

5. **In the new page that appears, choose the size of ad you want to have appear on your Web site.**

   Google offers a variety of different shapes, sizes, and types of ad formats. The format that works best for you depends on the space you have available, the content of your Web site, and the design of the page on which the ad appears. For now, select 234 x 60 Half Banner from the Format drop-down menu. (I give you all the details about ad styles and formats in Chapter 7, when I cover designing the perfect content ad.)

6. **On the same page, choose a color scheme for your ad.**

   Google has several pre-made color schemes available in the drop-down list to the right, or you have the option to specify border, title, background, text, and URL colors by hexadecimal number. This is useful if you know the exact hexadecimal numbers of your Web page design and want to match them.

   For your purposes, select Seaside from the drop-down list.

7. **Still on the same page, choose Slightly Rounded Corners from the Corner Styles drop-down list.**

   The other options available here are Squared Corners or Very Rounded Corners. Visually, each has a different appeal to people in different situations and on different Web sites.

8. **For the last option on the page, choose Show Public Service Ads from the drop-down list and click Continue.**

   What's this about public service ads? Well, Google shows public service ads when your site is so new that it can't be properly populated with paid ads and when your site content doesn't match ad content. You can choose to have these ads displayed, to have ads from another service displayed, or to have a solid color displayed as a placeholder if either of these situations applies.

9. **In the new page that appears, click Continue.**

   This page of the wizard gives you the option to assign the ad to a channel, but you have not yet set up channels. I show you how to set up channels in Chapter 14. For now, channels aren't an aspect of AdSense that you need to worry about. They're for tracking your ads, but before you can track them you need to know how to create them and get the highest percentage of clicks possible. After all, tracking nothing — which is exactly how many clicks you'll have if you do your ads wrong — still leaves you with nothing to track.

10. **In the new (and final) page that appears, enter a name for your ad unit in the appropriate field and then click the Save and Get Code button.**

    When the page appears, a default name is already filled into the Name text box. I recommend renaming the ad unit something useful, but if you want to leave the default name, that's fine.

    The page shown in Figure 2-10 appears with the code for your ad unit.

11. **Copy the code provided by AdSense and paste it into the HTML code of your Web site.**

    How you access your HTML code depends on how you got your code in the first place. If you're using an HTML Editor/Web Page Creation program to design your Web site, you may need to dig around the menus to find out how to get the raw HTML code on-screen. If you're writing your code from scratch, though, all you need to do is pull up the Web site code and paste the ad code into the spot on which you want AdSense ads to appear.

Creating the ad for your Web site is an easy process. Getting it to appear on the right spot on your Web site might be a little bit like landing a jumbo jet in the median of the New Jersey Turnpike. It'll take a little practice, and in the beginning, it could get a little hairy.

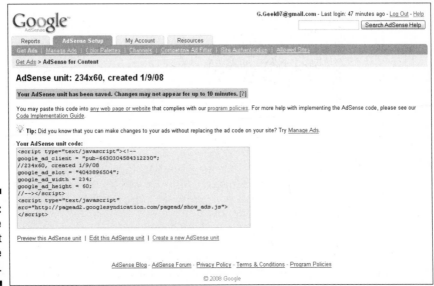

Figure 2-10: The code for your first AdSense ad.

A note about public service ads

The subject of public service ads has come up once in this chapter already. Here's the scoop on public service ads.

Basically, a *public service ad* is an ad that Google places in an AdSense ad block when there are no appropriate ads to be displayed in that space at that time. One time when you're likely to see public service ads is when you've first added the AdSense code to your Web site.

In order to serve ads to your Web page that match the content of the page, Google periodically examines — or *crawls* — the site to determine the content of the site. Then ads are pushed out to your Web site based on that content. When you've first put the AdSense code on your site, it takes a few hours (and sometimes even a couple of days) for Google to crawl the site to examine the content. Until that happens, the company wants *something* displayed in the space that you've made available, so public service ads are the filler.

The problem with public service ads is just that — they're part of a public service, which means you don't get paid when they're viewed or clicked. So you don't want to have those ads hanging around any longer than necessary —

you do want to start making money as soon as possible, right?

If public service ads display for more than a few days, contact Google to make sure that your site is being crawled regularly. You can't ask the company to specifically crawl your Web site (well, you can ask them, but they won't do it), but you can find out if there's something that you can do to speed up the process.

It's possible that your site design is causing the public service ads to be displayed, too. If Google's Web crawler can't determine the topic of your Web page, the public service ads remain in place. This happens when pages are largely graphical in nature or when the content on a page isn't coherent enough for the crawler to determine the overall theme of the page. If the crawler can't understand your site design, it can't target the right ads to your site. And that's all the more reason to familiarize yourself with Google's policies and guidelines and apply them to your site design.

If everything is in order, after a few hours or maybe even a couple of days (or whenever Google crawls your site), the ads are replaced with actual paid ads and you can begin making money.

One resource you may find helpful during the implementation process is the AdSense help page for code implementation:

```
www.google.com/adsense/support/bin/answer.py?answer=44511&sourceid=
                aso&subidww-ww-et-asui&medium=link#3
```

The one thing you need to remember is that this is just an exercise in creating your first ad block. There are more details to implementing ads that work than there are quills on a porcupine. So maybe you do have an ad that you think is ready to go online, but it might not be. You can put it online now, and tweak it as you have time. Or, flip through some of the more detailed chapters about creating specific types of ads. Putting a basic ad on your Web site probably won't hurt you, but your time might be better spent figuring out how to make that ad really sing to your site visitors.

Creating ads seems easy enough. Even getting the ads to display isn't all that difficult. However, getting site visitors to take note of those ads is a completely different tale. One way that you can get users to click your ads is to ensure they appear in the right context on your Web site. In Chapter 3, you find out about building content-rich Web sites and how you can optimize your Web site content for AdSense. Use those tips to help create pages that are complemented by the ads Google dishes out to your site.

Chapter 3

Building a Content-Rich Web Site

Content is the main draw to your Web site. I say this even though I'm the first to admit that pictures can be very cool and that you can do some pretty amazing (and some not-so-amazing) stuff with your pages using Flash animation. When I'm being charitable, I can even see the rationale for all kinds of other electronic bling some folks insist on adding to their pages. All that's beside the point, though; what brings users to your site and draws them deeper and deeper into your pages is content.

Admittedly, one could argue that *content* is more than merely words — it's all the elements that make up your Web site, even the bling. But it's the *words* that help visitors find your site because words can be strung together to form information — and finding the right information is the goal of nearly every person who surfs the Web.

So having the right kind of content is one key to AdSense success. There's such a thing as having the wrong kind of content or even having too much content. Having the right amount and the right kind of content is a balancing act. With careful attention to detail, you can keep all your plates dancing on their assigned poles.

The Big Deal about Content

Content is king! Bet you've heard that a few times before, right? It's an overused phrase that's lost some of its impact. It's still true though — content *is* king. And without enough content (and enough of the right kind of content) on your Web site, you might as well toss the keys to your Web domain down the nearest sewer drain because the domain will be worthless.

Think about what's really motivating you when you surf the Internet. Go ahead — pay close attention to what you do the next few times you go online. To help you remember, keep a list of the Web sites you visit and what you do while you're there. I bet the search for information is the unifying theme to all your Internet sessions. Information is *content* — words, pictures, audio, and video — that relay the information you need when you're online. That's one of the reasons why search engines like Google have grown exponentially in size and popularity. People want information, and they want the best possible way to get to exactly what they need in the least amount of time.

You can tap into that desire for information and use AdSense to generate a decent income, but only if you have the content that draws visitors to your site in the first place. Your site visitors care about content (or information), and you should, too.

Content draws visitors to your site, and keeps them on your site or causes them to return. Content equals traffic — but here's the catch. Content only translates to traffic if the content is relevant and fresh. Old content or completely unrelated content doesn't do you any more good than old fish — it stinks up the place and makes people want to be somewhere else.

Good content is a good thing — I think we can all agree on that. You may ask how good content ties in with AdSense and your desire to turn your Web site into a handy little income stream. It turns out that content is also what Google uses to target ads on your Web site. In fact, Google uses the same technology to target AdSense ads that it uses to create search results. A software program — called a Web *crawler,* a *spyder,* or a *bot* — literally counts the number of times different words are used on your site and examines the words surrounding them (the so-called *context*). Then, using a mathematical equation that would probably take an entire ream of paper to write, the program determines the probability that the site is related to the words used most frequently on the site — the site's *keywords.* (Smaller, common words, such as a, an, the, and, nor, or, but, and etc., are completely ignored by the crawler.)

Then the content on your site — broken down to the keyword level — is used to determine which ads are appropriate for your site. The keyword *value* — how much someone is willing to pay to have their related ad shown in your ad space — determines how valuable the ads for your site are to you, how appropriate they are, and how valuable they can be to your site visitors. Run a site that's largely graphical in nature — lots of images, in other words — and Google has a hard time placing the right ads on the site. What you end up with instead are public service announcements, which are nice enough, I suppose — if you're not interested in making money, because they take up space but generate no income.

My sense is that your interest in AdSense might be tied up with making a bit of green on the side. If that's so, keep the following mantra in mind: "Content is a big deal. Content is king. Content is site traffic. Content is money in your pocket if it's done right." Content done right starts with building the right type of Web site.

If You Build a Content-Rich Web Site . . .

You probably already have a Web site to which you want to add AdSense — and that's a good move. Honestly, any site that's well designed can probably benefit from AdSense. If you're just building your site for the first time, you can do a number of things to optimize your site so that you get the most from your AdSense investment.

The next few sections walk you through some optimization strategies designed to get your Web site working harder for you. I start out with some site-building basics and then move pretty quickly into some AdSense-specific recommendations.

Don't think that all is lost just because your site exists already. Some of the optimization strategies I cover can be tweaked in ways that let you transform an already existing Web site into a site that gets more mileage from your AdSense efforts. A great idea, I'd say.

Site-building basics

Site design is critical to increasing your AdSense revenue. Both Google (the Brains Behind It All) and AdSense users (Average Janes and Joes working in the Web trenches) have tested different combinations of content, ad placement, and ad design to see what works best. There are some clear leaders — site design is important, and it all starts with the site name.

Name and address, please

Okay, it's time for the Obvious Tip of the Week: The name of your site should be closely related to the topic of your site. There's also more to your name than just a name; a well-designed site has a Uniform Resource Locator (URL) — fancy talk for a Web site address — that reflects the site name.

The *URL* is the address that you see in the address bar of a Web site. For example, you don't want a Web site named TheKittenPalace.com if your target topic is dogs or tropical fish. If you look at Web sites, you'll find that the content on the site is usually closely related to the site name.

Domain names come in two flavors: free and premium (or not free). A free domain name is usually used with Web pages that are hosted in a Web site community, whereas a premium domain name is usually hosted all by itself. Think of domain names like a neighborhood. An apartment in a complex at the end of the street usually has to share the same address as several other apartments (those in the same building), the only difference being the apartment number. Houses, on the other hand, have the luxury of their own address.

Free domains are available from a number of sources, including

- **Google Pages:** (www.pages.google.com): A free service you can use when you create your Web pages with Google Page Creator.

- **Geocities:** (http://geocities.yahoo.com): This free Web hosting provider has been around for a while. If you don't mind someone else controlling the ads on your site, it's a good option.

- **Homestead:** (www.homestead.com): Another free hosting provider, Homestead offers templates that make creating your Web site fast and easy.

- **Free WebSites:** (www.freewebsites.com): This service hosts your site for free, but requires that you allow them to advertise on your site. The ads are small, but you don't control them.

Most of these services provide a Web page creator tool that lets you design your pages in minutes. You can literally sign up for an account and have a Web site online in less than an hour, and that's if you're being very creative about putting your site together.

The problem with pages like these — pages that are part of a community — is that you don't have a direct URL. The URL for the site — which, if you remember my advice, should reflect the actual topic of your site — is usually something quite generic, like www.yoursite.community.com.

Nothing's wrong with being generic — if you don't mind ending up buried in search results — and nothing's wrong with being buried in the search results if you don't want to generate income with AdSense.

Oh, and one more thing. These pages are usually free because they're preloaded with advertisements from which you make no money. However, that would make it even harder for you to generate an AdSense income with these pages.

If you *do* want to generate income with AdSense, your Web site address should reflect your site name and it should be a direct address. A *direct address* states *www.yoursite.com* loud and clear and nothing else. I don't know about you, but I'm much more likely to type that than to type http://www.example1.com/ Search-Engine-Optimization /dp/0470175001/ ref=sr_1_10?ie=UTF8&s=books&qid=1208363273&sr=8-10 if I'm looking for a particular type of Web site.

What's in a name?

The exception that proves the Name a Site in Accordance with the Site's Content rule is when a personal name is also the name of the domain. For example, my personal Web site, JerriLedford.com, has a variety of information on it, all different types of articles and personal interests that I have. Over the past decade or so, the site has changed dramatically in design, but the variety of the content remains largely the same. This is because that's the site I use to showcase (to editors) what type of work I can do. The goal of that site isn't to sell a product but rather to sell a package — me.

JerriLedford.com does its job well, but it's not the only dog I have in the World Wide Web race. Another site that I have is Google-Geek.com, which I built for a very different purpose — to help people understand the different products and services that Google makes available. The site's focal point is the Google Geek blog, but the site also has other pages that showcase different Google-related topics. Some are more in-depth articles about Google products and services, and a few are tutorials that guide users through using those products and services. The content of the entire site is focused on helping users use Google better. As you might expect, Google-Geek.com consistently lands much better targeted AdSense ads than the content on the JerriLedford.com site.

Getting set up with a premium Web site that provides you with a direct address is a little more involved. You first have to purchase a domain name, which you can do from the following companies:

- ✔ **GoDaddy** (www.godaddy.com): Offers regular sales on domain names. You can also purchase your domain name, hosting, and other Web site services through GoDaddy.

- ✔ **Register.com** (www.register.com): Also offers domain names as well as hosting packages and other services. You can order domain names online through Register.com or by phone.

- ✔ **NameSeek** (www.nameseek.com): This company strictly sells domain names. It might even be more accurate to say this company negotiates the sale of domain names between current owner and purchaser.

After you have a domain name in hand, build the site and upload it to the Web. Many of the companies that sell you a domain name (or URL) will also offer to host your Web site for a monthly or yearly fee. (*Hosting* is like having land on which to put a house. You host your Web site on a server somewhere or on your own server.) You don't have to host with the company you purchased the domain name from, however. Any hosting company that you're comfortable with will do.

I use GoDaddy.com because their pricing for domain names is good and they offer the convenience of Web site hosting as well. However, you have plenty of options out there. Prices vary from one company to another, and what's included with the domain name also varies. With some companies, you're purchasing the name only. With others, you might be purchasing the name and security, the hosting, or any of a hundred or so other services.

Review each company to find the one that suits you and ask others what company they use. Find one that you like and then stay with it. That way, if you purchase multiple domain names, you can manage them all from one location. (For more on Web site hosting, check out the "Selecting the right Web host" section, later in this chapter.)

Getting with the plan

Before you register your site, put some thought into what you want the content of the site to be. In fact, it doesn't hurt to write a short plan for the site. It doesn't have to be a formal document, but getting your ideas on paper will help flesh them out and will also help you stay on track while you're working through the site design and implementation. Some of the details to include in your plan are

- **Site name:** Remember, don't get too cute, here. Make the name fit the site.
- **Topic:** You do know what your site will be about, right?
- **Subtopics:** Each of these will be a separate page or section of your site.
- **Hosting:** On what real estate will your site sit? You can use your own server or pay someone to host the site for you.
- **Design:** This includes the look of the site, the navigational structure, and even the kinds of images you want to include.
- **Types of content:** Will your site have only text, or will you also have video, audio, or downloads on the site?
- **Special considerations:** Do you plan to offer products for purchase? If so, include e-commerce capabilities.

You may think of other aspects of your site that you want to address in your site plan. If so, by all means, add them. Write it all down in as cohesive a format as you can and then put it away for a day or two. Come back to it after it's had time to season a little and re-read your plan to see if it's still as good an idea as you thought to start with.

Selecting the right Web host

Web sites need a place to park. Like the land your house or apartment sits on, a Web host is the physical place on a network where the files that make up your Web site are stored. This physical place has an address (the URL) that makes it possible for people to find the Web site, like a street address.

When you're looking at Web hosting, the whole idea of parking your Web site somewhere can get a little complicated. How much space and bandwidth do you need? What about things like managing the domain, security, and having an e-mail address to go along with the domain? These are all aspects you should consider when examining your Web site hosting options.

In most cases, a domain hosting company has several tiers of hosting packages. The basic package usually gets you enough space on the server to house a few dozen pages of text and light graphics. You may even be able to slide a video or two into the mix.

From there, packages get progressively more involved until you have every service imaginable for your Web site, from e-commerce and content management to download capabilities and streaming audio and video. What's right for you is determined by your needs, and you can always start with a smaller package and increase hosting capabilities if you find you need them at some later date.

One thing to keep in mind when you're selecting your Web host is the way in which your Web site will be designed, technically speaking. If you're writing your site from scratch with HyperText Markup Language (HTML) or some other programming language, you have less to worry about. But if you're using an HTML editing program (like FrontPage or DreamWeaver) to design your Web site, you may need to have special extensions installed on your site to allow file transfers from your computer to the server. These additional extensions usually add a few dollars extra to the cost of the hosting package. Knowing what you need before you get started could save you a few headaches and maybe even a little money.

Smart site design

After you come up with a name for your site and figure out where it'll be hosted, it's time to begin actually designing your Web site. You can deploy a few strategies that will make it easier to optimize your Web site for AdSense purposes.

First and foremost, keep in mind that the layout of your site will dramatically affect how your AdSense ads perform. This ain't rocket science, by the way. All you really have to do is picture what most people do when they surf the Web. In general, a user nearly always uses a Web site in the same fashion. When a user clicks into your site, his eyes first take in the heading of the page, travel down the right side of the page, and finally move to the middle. The exception to the normal state of affairs is when there's something flashy in the middle of the page that catches the visitor's eye first. The left side of the page is where most Web sites include the navigational structure, so users are less inclined to look there until they're ready to move on to another page on the site.

In Web site design, flashy isn't usually a good thing. Neither is Flash-y. *Flash* is a Web design protocol that animates objects and allows designers to embed video into a Web page. The problem with Flash is that it tends to hog a lot of resources, so it slows users' computer performance down, which users hate. The fastest way to lose visitors is to bog their systems down with your Flash (or flash). Make your pages attractive, but also make it possible for those pages to load quickly even with (gasp) dialup service.

Because visitors nearly always approach a Web site in the same way, many designers have discovered that the most important information on a Web site should go in certain places. That's why you often see that Web sites have a navigation bar on the left side of the page. Some sites include text links at the top of the page, and the most important content on the page is nearly always above the fold.

Above the fold is a newspaper term used to designate the placement of the most important story in the day's news. Newspapers are folded about halfway down the page. When a reader picks up the paper, she always turns it so the title of the paper is on top. (This is human nature; we don't like things displayed upside down.) So, the most important story of the day gets in the top half of the page, above the fold.

The same term can be used to relate to Web sites as well, though the orientation is a bit different. Because no fold is on a Web page, you have to think in terms of a browser window. Essentially, the *fold* on a Web page lines up with the bottom edge of your browser before the page has been scrolled. (*Scrolling* a page involves using the page's scroll bars to move the page up and down so you can view content that's not visible when the page appears in your browser window.)

Figure 3-1 illustrates where the fold is on the page. The figure also includes labeling for other important elements of the page.

A site visitor clicks your page and, in many cases, makes a determination about the value of the page before he ever scrolls down or moves the page in any way. Essentially, you have only one shot to make a good first impression: Whatever a visitor sees when that browser window loads is, for all intents and purposes, what he gets. So, the most important elements of your site should be loaded into that area above the fold. Information that's not quite as important should be placed below the fold.

For your AdSense strategy, this means placing ads smack dab in those sections of your site where a visitor's eye is most likely to land, which are

   ✔ **At or near the top of the page** (either immediately above or immediately below the title of the site, depending on how well the ads integrate in that spot)

✔ **Above the content**, or at the least, imbedded in the content above the fold

✔ **On the right side of the page,** blended with the other content that usually appears in the sidebar

✔ **On the left side and the bottom of a page** (only effective when the ads blend well with the other elements of those sections)

Figure 3-2 shows one of the most popular (and most effective) ad layouts.

While you're designing your pages, keep in mind that the areas shown in Figure 3-2 are most desirable for ad placement. That doesn't mean that ads should dominate those sections or that ads can't be effective anywhere else. It only means those sections are optimal for ads. Also, ads should be integrated into the content in those sections without being overpowering, and they should logically fit with your Web site design.

The click-friendly top spot.

Figure 3-1:
The fold of a Web site might not even be halfway down a page; it technically falls where the browser window ends.

Readers look left for navigation.

Keep important info above the fold.

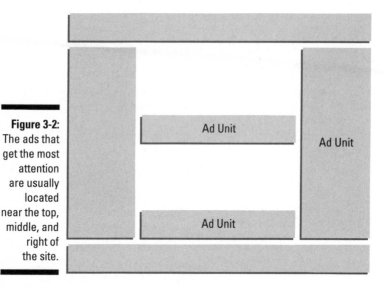

AdSense optimized content

I spend a lot of time in this chapter talking about ad placement for a simple reason — it's important. If nobody sees your AdSense ad, it'd be like the proverbial tree falling in the middle of the forest — no moneymaking proposition, in other words.

With the ad placement basics out of the way, it's time to figure out how to convince the good folks at Google AdSense to place ads on your Web site that have meaning to your site visitors. Your ultimate goal by implementing AdSense is to entice visitors to click or view the ads that appear on your page. That only happens, though, if the ads are appealing to visitors. Having the right content is the key to having the right ads.

The technology behind Google AdSense — Web crawlers, spiders, and bots diligently scouring the World Wide Web for info — tries its best to determine the content of your site, but it ain't perfect. If all the articles on one page refer to grading diamonds and other gemstones, the ads that are pushed to your page for display will (more likely than not) feature loose diamonds and gemstones or diamond and gemstone jewelry. (Duh!) If you have a thing for free association so that articles on any given page jump from one topic to another with no cohesion, AdSense will have a much harder time placing relevant ads on your page. You could end up with ads for frog food when your site is related to planning a wedding at the lake. Try to keep your page as cohesive as possible and don't combine topics on a page if you can help it.

Wanted: Good writers for Web site startup

You don't need a degree or any other fancy identifier to ensure that you have good content. You don't even have to be a writer, although it helps. There are all kinds of ways to find the right content for your Web site. If you don't want to write the content, try using a content provider, such as EzineArticles.com, FreeSticky.com, or ArticleGeek.com. Dozens of other services are also available. A quick Web search will turn up more places that offer free articles than there are cars in Detroit. One problem with these sites though is that the content is often overused and stale. Remember that original content means better ads.

Another great option for having the right content on your site is to hire a writer. Online services, such as Elance.com, allow you to create a project listing that available writers bid on. You then determine the winning bid. It doesn't have to be the lowest bid, either. You determine what looks like the best bid with your own factors.

With a service like Elance.com, you or the writer pays a fee for the ability to list a project that is then bid on. Someone has to pay Elance's bills. The fee isn't unreasonable, and in fact, it's more than worth it to many Web site owners that need original content.

If the whole bidding scene doesn't paint your wagon red, you can also place advertisements for writers on Web sites, such as WritersWeekly.com, Craigslist.com, or JournalismJobs.com. Some of these Web sites charge a fee for listing your call for writers.

One thing to remember when you're looking for a writer is that you often get exactly what you pay for. A writer willing to work for pennies is probably new and untested, which isn't to say he's not a great writer, just that you're taking a gamble. Be willing to pay a little more to get a professional to write your articles, and always check references and provide a written contract before you enter into any business relationship with writers or any other vendors.

Google uses the same technology to index your pages for search results that it uses to examine your pages to determine the most relevant ads. To improve ad targeting for your site, you can do some things that are designed to pique the interest of the Google indexers, like using keywords in your content and in the design of your site.

Piquing the interest of Google indexers has become a science in its own right — the science of search engine optimization. *SEO,* as it is referred to by those in the know, has tried to come up with a set of Web design principles that deal with everything from choosing content to actual structure to help search engines more easily analyze your site to determine where in the search results it fits best.

One of the most basic elements of SEO is how the content on your site is formatted. Assuming your content is mostly text, the titles and headings of your text are important. Including *keywords* — words that indicate the topic of your site — in titles and headings as well as a few times in the text of the articles you're using, is one way to ensure that a search engine crawler will properly classify your site.

The most important principle behind SEO involves making sure that you design your Web site so that it's both useful and relevant to visitors. Site visitors will come to your site either by conducting a search for a specific topic or by directly typing your Web address into the address bar of their browser. If you design your Web site with the intent of providing something the visitor needs, search crawlers are more likely to classify your site properly. As an added bonus, you'll probably also end up ranking higher in the search results.

I have lots more on SEO in Chapter 4, but for now, the most you need to know is that if you apply the same techniques that you would to optimizing your Web site for search engines, your AdSense ads will be spot on.

In Figure 3-3, you can see how content can be placed around AdSense ad units to provide users with what they need and to feed the Google crawler so that ads are properly targeted.

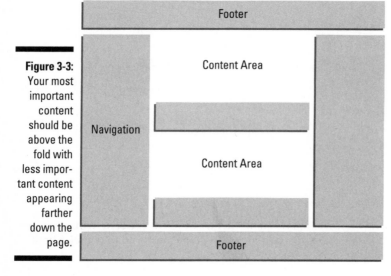

Figure 3-3: Your most important content should be above the fold with less important content appearing farther down the page.

You may say it's just not enough to be told that the Google crawler knows its stuff when it comes to pushing content-specific ads to your site. It may not even be the content that you're worried about. The big questions for you might be "Where will the ad lead?" or "How will it look after you put it on your site?" Sometimes you just want to see for yourself, and that's fine. Just don't make the mistake of clicking your own ads. Instead, use the AdSense preview tool to see what kind of ads will be returned for your site. (You can download the preview tool at `https://www.google.com/adsense/support/bin/answer.py?answer=10005&topic=160`.) When you find the file, follow these steps to download and install it:

1. **Right-click the AdSense preview tool filename.**

2. **In the menu that appears, select Save and then save the file to your desktop.**

3. **When the download is complete, double-click the file to open it.**

4. **In the confirmation dialog box that appears (see Figure 3-4), click Yes.**

   The program does its installation thing, usually quite quickly.

Registry Editor

Are you sure you want to add the information in C:\Documents and Settings\Jerri Lynn.JERRI-806E95BFC\Desktop\preview.reg to the registry?

Yes   No

5. **When the Successful Install confirmation message appears, click OK.**

6. **Open Internet Explorer and navigate to the site whose ads you want to preview.**

   Sorry, this doesn't work with Firefox or other browsers.

7. **Right-click inside the page but not inside the ad unit.**

8. **In the menu that appears, select Google AdSense Preview Tool, as shown in Figure 3-5.**

   A list of the ads showing on your site appears.

9. **Click the link for each ad to be taken to the advertisers' Web sites, or place a check mark in the check box beside each ad and click Show Selected URLs to see the Web addresses the ads lead to.**

Section targeting

In AdSense terminology, *section targeting* is a method of ad placement that allows advertisers to decide where on a page they want their ads displayed. If it turns out that you have ad space available in that place on the page, and if your page is related to the topic of the ad, the ad can be placed on your site. (I use *can be* because you probably won't be the only publisher that meets the requirements the advertiser sets forth, and the ad can be placed on any site that meets said requirements.)

Ads rotate, so an ad may appear on your site one day and not the next. Advertisers' budgets also vary, and that's another determining factor on where and how often you may see the ad.

```
Back
Forward

Save Background As...
Set as Background
Copy Background

Select All
Paste

Create Shortcut
Add to Favorites...
View Source

Encoding                          ▶

Print...
Print Preview...
Refresh

Convert to Adobe PDF
Convert to existing PDF
Export to Microsoft Excel
Google AdSense Preview Tool

Properties
```

Figure 3-5:
Select
Google
AdSense
Preview
Tool
from the
menu that
appears.

You'll encounter two types of section targeting:

✔ **Contextual:** Uses such factors as keyword analysis, word frequency, font size, and the overall link structure of the Web site to determine what a Web page is about and to precisely match ads to each page.

✔ **Placement:** Advertisers choose specific ad *placements* — sections of specific Web sites they've take a shine to — on which to run their ads. Ads that are placement-targeted may not exactly jive with the content of your page, but they're hand-picked by advertisers who believe there's a match between what your users are interested in and what the advertiser is advertising. For the privilege of making these specific choices, the advertiser pays a slightly higher fee. As a publisher, you benefit because you'll be paid every time someone comes to your site and sees the ad rather than by the number of times the ad is clicked.

Using RSS feeds for content

Really Simple Syndication (RSS) is a way of delivering news stories, articles, blog entries, and other types of content to subscribers by way of an e-mail or a *content aggregator* — a program that collects RSS feeds and delivers them all to a single location.

Think of RSS like a newspaper delivered to your home. You don't have to go out to get every single story in a newspaper. You subscribe to the paper, the reporters do all the legwork, the publisher puts all their stories together in one package, and a delivery guy brings it right to your front door. An RSS feed is an electronic version of a newspaper.

The most important aspect of RSS feeds is that they deliver fresh content as often as it's available. If you're trying to put fresh content on your Web site to improve your AdSense revenues, that's huge. It's more content, less work, and Google loves it.

Wait. I can hear your objection. It's *not* plagiarism or copyright infringement. Content owners who put their content out via RSS feeds want that content to be distributed to as many readers as possible. You still need to ensure that the content is attributed properly, but as long as you do, you should have no problem using RSS feeds to add content to your Web site.

You do have to consider a couple logistical problems when using RSS, though. One problem is that RSS feeds don't always deliver full articles. The *content owner* — the person or company that publishes the article, news story, blog, or other type of content — can set how much of his content he wants delivered through the RSS feed. That means you may only get about 250 characters delivered (which is usually about a paragraph). Some RSS feeds (the Google Reader, for example) link the titles of feeds to a pop-up window. When you click the title, the window pops up for you to read the feed. Because the bots and spyders Google uses won't be doing that clicking, they probably can't associate the RSS content with your Web site.

The way feeds are displayed varies from reader to reader. What's more, the feed display (or a feed reader) isn't likely to be customizable, adding yet another wrinkle to your plan to let someone else do all the hard work.

If you've embedded an RSS feed on your Web site to help generate fresh, new content, having only 250 words of an article can be a real problem because it's hard to place relevant AdSense ads around that content. Even when the full article is available, feed readers often interfere with AdSense displays, making it difficult, if not impossible, to use RSS for content for your Web site. Back to the drawing board, right? Nope, not yet.

One way to get around those display issues is to use an RSS script that allows you to add the feed to your site and to change the way it's displayed. RSS scripts, such as the RSS Equalizer (`http://milleniumb.rssalizer.hop.clickbank.net`), CaRP (`www.geckotribe.com/rss/carp`), and FeedForAll.com's PHP script (`www.feedforall.com/free-php-script.htm`), make it possible for you to grab RSS content and display it more effectively on your Web site. For example, if the script converts your RSS feeds to HTML, you can add articles to your site without ever even logging on. And best of all, you can also place AdSense ads around and within those articles. So now you not only have automatically updated content, but you also have content with AdSense ads. Life's good!

A word about "baiting"

If you've read a bit about Web marketing here and there, you may have come across link baiting. *Link baiting* is the creation of an article that's so unique or interesting that people, because of its content, want to link to it. Link baiting can be a good tactic for driving content to your site, which of course, will drive up your AdSense revenues. But to be successful, you have to make your link bait fun, informative, or creative — and it still has to be quality content.

The link bait has a dark side, too. When content is gimmicky, misleading, and unrelated to the content of your Web site, it can get you into trouble with Google. For example, if you place a gadget on a page of your site with the specific intent of drawing users to your site, and that gadget isn't directly related to the site's content, you're skirting on the dark side of link baiting. Users may come to download that gadget, but they'll be disgusted that your site isn't relevant to their real interests, so they'll go somewhere else.

After a while, even Google's crawlers will realize that the increase in traffic to your site is only superficial. After they do, your ranking in search results will be penalized and your site traffic will drop dramatically. Misleading link baiting is expressly forbidden by Google, and because it's become such a popular way to drive Web site traffic, Google has developed some new ways to judge whether you're using link baiting tactics.

Nothing's wrong with adding a bit of fun or creative content to your site, just make sure you create it within the guidelines that Google has established. (Need a refresher on Google's guidelines? You're in luck. That section is coming up right . . . now!)

Understanding Google's Webmaster Guidelines

Google seems to have guidelines for everything, and Web site design is no exception. Google's Webmaster Guidelines (which I cover in some detail in Chapter 2) are the de facto guidelines for how any Web site associated with Google should be designed.

Google is certainly one of the most visible companies in the world. The number of people who watch Google in hopes that it will one day screw up is shadowed only by the number of people who are watching Microsoft hoping for the same. And because Google is such a target, the company needs to ensure that anyone who's even very remotely associated with it meets certain guidelines to help avoid the ire of an offended public.

The Google Webmaster Guidelines are only one step in the requirements that Google has for people, but the guidelines are an important step — and it'll benefit you to understand them completely. Here's a quick overview, but take the time to read the complete guidelines at `www.google.com/webmasters` as the ideas underpinning them are valuable for Web design even if you're not planning to use AdSense or any of Google's other applications:

- ✔ **Make your site easy to navigate by creating a consistent navigational structure across your site and by making that navigational structure obvious to visitors.** Nothing's worse than getting stuck on a Web page without a link to the home page or another way off the page without using your back button or closing your browser completely.

- ✔ **Include relevant links to other Web sites.**

- ✔ **Use a *site map* (a text document that links to every page on the site) and submit it to Google.** To submit your site map, you have to be a member of Google's Webmaster Central, but signing up for that is as easy as signing up for any other Google account. After you sign up, submit your site map by using the form. (You can find links to the forms as well as other pertinent info at `www.google.com/webmasters/start`.)

- ✔ **Include clear, relevant content.**

- ✔ **Make sure the HTML that makes up your site is written correctly.**

- ✔ **Repair broken links as soon as they're noticed.**

- ✔ **Allow crawlers access to your Web site by including a robots.txt file in the design of your site.** The `robots.txt` file has two lines:

```
User agent: *
Disallow: /
```

- ✔ **Create the file with a text editor, such as Notepad, save it using robots. txt, and then when you upload your Web site to a server, be sure to also upload this file.** The file tells Web site crawlers that they're welcome to look at all the pages on your Web site.

- ✔ **Design your pages for users, not for search engines.** Users come to your site because they need something. Design your site so that the visitors you're targeting get exactly what they need — information and products that they're searching for. By designing your site with your visitors in mind, you'll automatically hit most of the requirements that search engines have for ranking you in search results. A good rule of thumb is the more useful your site is to real people, the better crawlers will rank the site.

- ✔ **Avoid any kind of underhanded Web site design, such as using hidden pages or hidden text that's only meant to be seen by Web crawlers.** Believe it or not, crawlers recognize this kind of sneaky design, and you'll be penalized in search rankings for it.

✔ **Use only relevant keywords in the titles, headings, and text of your Web site.** (You'll also be using them in your HTML code, but more about that is in Chapter 4.)

Many more guidelines are in the document, but these basics are a good place to start. And one in particular really sums up the whole concept of Google's Webmaster Guidelines: Build your site for people, not for search engines. If you do that, the chances that you'll end up in trouble with Google (or AdSense) are very slim.

A word (or two) about extreme content Web sites

When you hear *extreme content,* visions of something less than moral — or worse, less than legal — may come into your head. I understand the associations such a term may call up, but in the AdSense context, extreme content isn't adult content, graphic violence, or even anything terribly controversial. Extreme content refers to large Web sites with thousands of pages of content — as many as 300,000 pages!

Web site owners build extreme content sites specifically to increase the real estate on which they can place AdSense ads. The content is gathered from all over the Web; wherever the owner can find free content, she'll grab it and sometimes she'll even grab content that's not free and, by extension, not for use by whomever wants it.

The problem with extreme content sites is that they're built only for the ads, not for the users. And that makes it taboo if you're really looking to create a decent recurring income with AdSense.

AdSense doesn't look kindly on Web sites that are built specifically to maximize AdSense

income without any thought of the user in mind — and that's exactly what extreme content sites are. Still, if you spend any time at all building your AdSense business, you'll find someone online that tells you extreme content Web sites are the golden ticket. Don't believe them.

Navigating through such a large site is nearly impossible, and the organization for and management of such a site is a nightmare. It's time-consuming and costly to create and maintain such a site, and when the Google crawler realizes what you're up to, your site will be penalized. You can even be banned from the AdSense program for using this kind of scheme to generate income.

Ultimately, it's much better to design a Web site that users will want to use. Include the information that visitors are looking for, and not only will your Web site rank better in search results but your AdSense income will be higher because your ads will be much more relevant to the people who are visiting your site. You also won't run the risk of being banned from AdSense, which would mean no income at all. It's really not worth the risk for the short term jump in revenues, so don't bother.

Chapter 4

AdSense and Search Engine Optimization

*Y*our AdSense income is affected by many different factors, including how much advertisers are willing to pay for ads and how much Google decides to take for its trouble. As for factors that you, as an AdSense user, can actually affect, site design, of all things, is probably the most important because the design of your site affects the way that search engines rank the site in search results. The higher your site ranks, the more traffic that hits your Web site, which means (potentially) more AdSense income.

Traffic translates into page views, and page views translate into clicks of your AdSense ads. The more clicks you get, the better your income. Naturally, you want to do everything you can to increase traffic to your site. Search engine optimization is your first step. Ensure that your site is optimized for search engines, and the traffic on your Web site will increase dramatically as your search engine rankings rise.

People search for stuff all the time — that's just what people do. We want information, and in the 21st century, the fastest way to find information is to go to a search engine. Now, if you have a Web site, you want those folks looking for pertinent info to be directed straight to *your* Web site rather than that other guy's Web site one domain block over. You want your site to *rank* well in search engines — in other words, search engines like Google. In fact, ranking well in search engines is so important that Web site owners are willing to pay thousands of dollars each year to ensure their sites rank as high as possible. *Search marketing* — the practice of creating marketing targeted at getting your Web site listed high enough in search engine rankings that it's noticed by people — is a $12 billion a year industry and is one of the fastest growing marketing segments out there.

The way you optimize your Web site so that it's easier to find online is *search engine optimization (SEO)*. Go figure. It's kinda obvious, isn't it? Where it begins to look a little muddy is in defining what, exactly, is the best strategy to adopt when optimizing a Web site. I'm here to tell you, though, that even if the topic is a bit muddy, you can still follow a few guidelines — guidelines that make a big difference in where your site ranks in search results. The rest of this chapter lays out a few of these SEO truths in all their glory.

Optimizing Your Site for Search Engines

Search engine optimization is a lot like trying to catch the steam that you breathe on a cold winter day. You can see it. You know it exists, but there's no way to actually contain and quantify the steam. You can see the results of SEO and you can figure out how best to achieve it, but it's still possible to do everything right and not achieve the ultimate goal — landing the very first listing on a *search engine results page, or SERP.*

Good news though, you don't necessarily want to be the very top listing on a SERP. Think about this — how often do you click the first search result and not go any farther? Even if you find exactly what you're looking for on the first page you jump to, you still click through some of the other results just to make sure the first page isn't lying to you.

As a general rule, I go through the listings of about ten results pages, just to make sure I'm getting the best info. Admittedly, I may be a little more patient than your average searcher. Most people don't go much deeper than the second page of results. Because you should probably be targeting your Web site to normal folks rather than obsessive-compulsive types like me, you want your Web site to fall somewhere on the first or second page of results. If it does, you're fine — you can count your search marketing efforts a success, even if your site isn't at the very tippy-top of the first SERP.

Achieving that first- or second-page placement isn't a sure thing — it requires a little effort on your part. You can take a number of steps to ensure a better search engine ranking — steps I get to in a bit — but the most important piece in your SEO puzzle involves the keywords on which your Web site is based. You do have keywords, right? If not, you need them. However, not just any keyword will do, which the next section makes clear.

A Keyword By Any Other Name

It doesn't matter what you call it, a keyword will always be . . . well, a key word or phrase around which your Web site content is centralized. A single word is sometimes not enough to narrow the possibilities for a Web site, which is why some keywords are actually *keyword phrases* or *keyphrases*. It's the same concept — a centralized theme — just using more than one word. I use the term keyword generically to mean both keywords and keyphrases.

Web crawlers are programs that travel around the Internet examining and categorizing Web pages by keyword. That's how search engines, like Google, know to return your Web site when someone searches for a specific keyword or phrase. The crawler has already had a look-see and has placed your Web page into a category along with all the other sites on the Web that fit into that category.

Keyword marketing, then, is using that keyword or phrase to market your Web site. Advertisements for a Web site, product, or service are designed using the keyword or keyphrase as the "foundation" for the ads. Then, when Internet users search for that keyword, the ads are displayed in the search results. Google then takes this process one step further by placing ads on Web pages that are built around — or optimized for — that keyword. So, whoever said a picture is worth a thousand words didn't realize the Internet would come along and reduce that value to just one or two — three at the most.

Understanding Keyword Marketing

Before finding out how keywords work, you first need a quick overview of how Web sites are cataloged and then returned as search results. The way things go, you first put up a Web site. It doesn't have to be anything fancy — maybe it's your personal blog about your busybody Aunt Louise and how crazy she makes you, or it could be a serious site about how frogs hibernate in the muck at the bottom of ponds during winter. The topic of your Web site doesn't matter, but you have to get it on the Internet.

After you put up a Web site, a *search crawler* — a specialized software program that examines Web sites and categorizes them by keyword — finds your Web site. Search crawlers are designed to crawl every Web site within parameters that are outlined by the search crawler's designer. A designer could order a search crawler to, say, examine Web sites contained on a list drawn by the designer.

The crawler's first stop is the first Web page of the first Web site on the designer's list. The crawler *reads* through the pages of the Web site, looking at each word on the site.

Crawlers also look at what words are used together. For example, *cosmetic makeup* is different from *exam makeup,* but the crawler knows that makeup is used in two completely different ways because it looks at the words surrounding it.

While the crawler makes its way through a site, it records the number of times a keyword, a keyphrase, or a set of keywords is used on the site. If *exam makeup* is used in the title and then three times in a 300-word section of text, it's probably a good bet that the Web site being crawled is about makeup exams. Of course, the search engine crawler isn't betting on anything. The crawler's like the skeptic who doesn't count on anything that's not immediately visible and physically touchable. *Exam makeup* may be there, but it needs proof!

The crawler uses a very lengthy and complicated algorithm as its search formula. The algorithm compares the number of times a keyword is used to indicators that tell it if that keyword is important on the Web site. Like color coding, that algorithm makes it possible to define a Web site in terms of how it relates to a specific topic.

Algorithms in general are computer programs that systematically solve problems such as determining how many times a keyword is used on a Web site. They're complicated creatures, highly technical in nature, and they are a search engine's lifeblood — which is why they're so jealously guarded. Just try to pry Google's secret algorithm from their tightly clenched fist and see where that gets you.

The crawler takes a stab at what your Web site's all about by registering the site's keywords. The crawler then takes another look at the site, this time considering those keywords in the context of the Web site — not just the keywords but also things like *keyword placement* (where on the site the words appear), the *alternative text* you put in for graphics (the stuff that shows up if the graphic won't load), and the links into and out of the Web site.

After looking at all these elements and many others (some search engines use over 100 different considerations), the crawler makes a determination about where in the great scheme of things a particular Web site belongs. That information is then stored in a database the size of Manhattan.

Okay, it's not really the size of Manhattan, but it's huge. Way larger than any database you've ever encountered before.

After the Web site's cataloged, it can be pushed to visitors that do a search based on keywords related to the main keyword of the Web page. That's another algorithm altogether. That algorithm cross-references the search that a user makes with the data stored in the database to determine which sites — of the billions of cataloged sites — are the best fit for the keyword or phrase that the searcher used.

In other words, your Web site basically boils down to the keywords on which it's built. To rank successfully in any search engine, you not only need the right keywords but you also need keywords that are closely associated with the topic of your Web site. Those keywords also need to be at the right places on your Web site. If they're not, the search crawler won't feel completely confident about which particular section of the database is the proper home for your site — so the site might be put lower in the rankings behind many other (perhaps far less relevant) sites.

Choosing the right keywords

Choosing the right keywords is a bit of a science — but it's also a bit of old-fashioned luck. No keyword guide is out there for the perplexed that can tell you whether the keyword is perfect for this or that subject. Instead, the words that apply to your subject are what they are. So, the best place to start looking for the right keywords for your topic is to brainstorm all the words that are most prevalent when the topic is in discussion.

Use search engine optimization (SEO) as an example. In any conversation you ever have about SEO, you'll hear the term *keyword* come up time and again. *Keyword* is clearly one of the top keywords for SEO — come on, SEO is built around keyword marketing!

Okay, that was the easy part. Getting the number-one keyword down is like shooting fish in a barrel, but you can't stop there. You need a larger pool of keywords to get you started. If you keep brainstorming additional words, you'll probably come up with the following keywords:

> *Search engine*
>
> *Search*
>
> *Marketing*
>
> *List*
>
> *Link*
>
> *Linking strategy*
>
> *Alt tags*
>
> *Metatags*
>
> *Metadata*
>
> *Media*
>
> *Content*
>
> *Social media*

That's just the short list. If you really put some time into brainstorming the SEO topic, you could come up with a couple hundred words. And don't forget phrases, too — up to three words. They're more useful and help you target better than just single words.

You'll find hundreds of words for your own Web site topic, too. Sit down with a pen and a piece of paper and think through your topic. Write down all the words that come to mind as you consider each aspect of your business. Don't worry about compartmentalizing the words, just get them on paper. When you're done, cover up the page and walk away for half a day or so.

Walking away gives the list time to rest. Take the time away from the list to do something completely unassociated with determining keywords. During that time, try to keep your mind off the list so that when you come back to it, you can look at it with fresh eyes.

When you do return to the list, read through it slowly and take the time to consider each word while you read it. Ask if a particular word is really a term that a searcher would use to find your Web site or a page on your site. If the answer is a resounding "No," cross the word off the list. When you're done, you should have a reasonably sized list from which to choose that magic number of words.

So, what's the magic number? Who knows? Just use exactly the number of words you need (to market your site properly) and not one more. Here are some general rules you should follow:

✔ **Start with a list of 50–100 keywords.** You won't use all the keywords, but the list gives you a good point from which to narrow the words that are most likely used to find your Web site.

✔ **Don't use more than three words on a single page.** Also, only use three words if they're all contained within a phrase. It's better to use one word or phrase per page on your Web site, but each page can have a different word or phrase.

✔ **Avoid words that are overused.** Overused words are obvious search terms, but they're also the most competitive terms and can cost a fortune if you're targeting them for advertisements. No kidding. It's not unheard of for some words to cost as much as $50 per click to advertisers who want their ads prominently displayed if someone searches for that keyword. Advertisers would have to have an endless budget to market with these words. On the other side of that equation is AdSense — which arranges to display those superexpensive ads on Web sites like your own — and yes, those words pay really well, but the competition for sites to place those ads on is also very tough. Best to stick with something that will get you a regular listing of some great ads that will truly interest your visitors.

✔ **Try to think like site visitors think.** What keywords represent your visitors' interests? One way to keep up with this information is to use a Web site analytics program, such as Google Analytics (www.google.com/analytics). An *analytics program* tracks visitors to your site, such as where they came to your site from and what keywords they used to find your site on search engines, along with many other statistics. If you don't have a Web site analytics program, get one. Right now.

After you narrow down your keyword list, put in the hard work — research the words on the list. Researching keywords isn't difficult, but it can be time-consuming. That's one of the reasons you don't want to start the process with a list of 500 potential keywords. You'd never have enough time to research them all. It's also unwise to use too many keywords on your Web site because it makes it hard for crawlers to properly classify your site — a problem that could leave you without well-targeted AdSense ads.

The first step in researching keywords is to select the top 20 or so words or phrases that most accurately reflect your Web site. Then, with that list, start searching for each word or phrase on the list.

Look through the first couple results pages for matches to your site. Do the pages returned by your search engine reflect the content of your site in any way? If not, how do the sites that do get returned differ from yours? Are they structured differently, for example? If you examine your results critically, you can find clues that help you decide how well the word or phrase you selected will actually result in traffic to your site.

The next step is to look at statistics, such as the amount of competition and the cost of advertisements for the keyword or phrase. Keyword research tools like the Google AdWords Keyword Tool (`https://adwords.google.com/select/KeywordToolExternal`) and the Yahoo! Search Marketing Keyword Tool (`http://pixelfast.com/overture` can help here). You must have a Yahoo! Search Marketing account to use the Yahoo! tool, and while I write this, Yahoo! Search Marketing is still under construction, but should be up and running soon.

The Google AdWords Keyword Tool performs two functions: It allows you to see what other keywords you might be missing when putting together your keyword list and it also lets you see which of those keywords are most valuable to you as a publisher. The Keyword Tool is easy enough to get the hang of. At first glance, it may look like it's just a generator for keyword ideas, but as you dig deeper into using it, you can learn valuable facts about keywords, such as how much competition there is for a keyword, what kind of placement an advertiser can expect for ads targeting that keyword, and what the search volume is for the keyword. Here's how a typical keyword search using the Keyword Tool works:

1. **Point your browser to** `https://adwords.google.com/select/KeywordToolExternal`.

2. **Under the How Would You Like to Generate Keyword Ideas? heading, select the Descriptive Words or Phrases radio button.**

3. **Enter a few keywords from your list into the center text box, as shown in Figure 4-1, and then click Get Keyword Ideas.**

   After a few seconds (the exact time depends on the number of words you enter), the suggested keywords appear beneath the search box, as shown in Figure 4-2.

   The default information shown includes the Advertiser Competition (how many advertisers are bidding on that keyword), the previous month's Search Volume (how often that keyword was searched for in the past month), and the Avg Search Volume. (The average is figured monthly, based on the number of searches each month for the past year.) Each statistic is represented by a colored bar, representative of what you see in a bar graph. The more color in the bar, the greater the competition or volume.

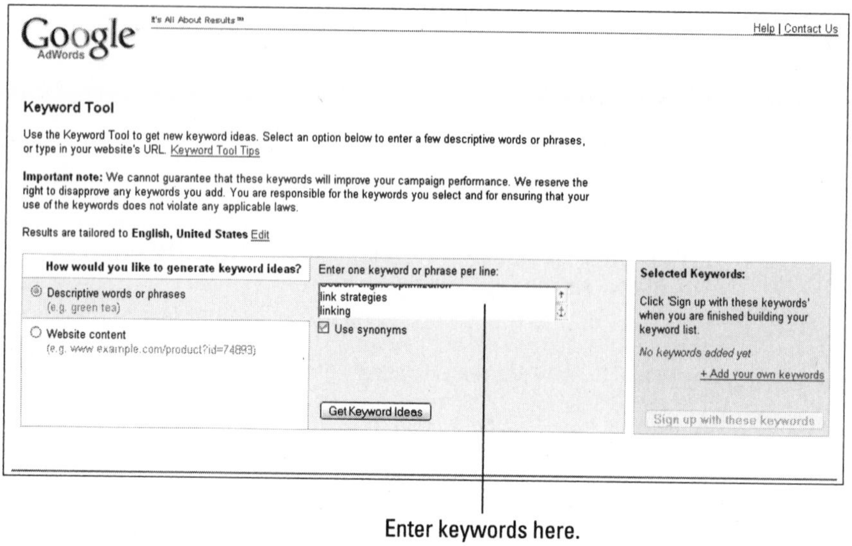

Figure 4-1:
The Google
AdWords
Keyword
Tool
suggests
available
keywords
for a topic.

Google AdWords — It's All About Results™   Help | Contact Us

Keyword Tool

Use the Keyword Tool to get new keyword ideas. Select an option below to enter a few descriptive words or phrases, or type in your website's URL. Keyword Tool Tips

Important note: We cannot guarantee that these keywords will improve your campaign performance. We reserve the right to disapprove any keywords you add. You are responsible for the keywords you select and for ensuring that your use of the keywords does not violate any applicable laws.

Results are tailored to **English, United States** Edit

How would you like to generate keyword ideas?	Enter one keyword or phrase per line:	Selected Keywords:
⦿ Descriptive words or phrases (e.g. green tea)	link strategies linking	Click 'Sign up with these keywords' when you are finished building your keyword list.
○ Website content (e.g. www.example.com/product?id=74893)	☑ Use synonyms	No keywords added yet + Add your own keywords
	Get Keyword Ideas	Sign up with these keywords

Enter keywords here.

The average cost of a keyword to the advertiser doesn't appear automatically, but you can change the way the keywords are filtered (see Figure 4-2) with the Filter drop-down menu.

4. To determine the average cost of a keyword, choose Show Estimated Avg. CPC from the Filter drop-down menu.

The *CPC,* or *cost-per-click,* is the amount that it costs an advertiser every time one of their ads based on that keyword is clicked. That amount is paid to Google, which then distributes portions of the money to AdSense publishers that allow those ads to be shown on their Web sites. Of course, Google keeps a fair chunk of it to line its own pockets, too.

After you make your selection from the Filter drop-down menu, another small section appears immediately below the Filter drop-down menu (as shown in Figure 4-3).

5. Choose your currency from the menu provided; and then in the text box beside it, enter the maximum CPC and click Recalculate.

The keyword list changes slightly, and a new column appears with the estimated average cost-per-click (CPC) for each keyword suggested, as shown in Figure 4-4. Now you not only see the competition for the keyword or phrase, but you also see what it costs advertisers who use those words. Only a percentage of that is paid to *publishers* (you) who show the ads, but this gives you an idea of how valuable your available ad space is, based on the keywords you use on your Web site.

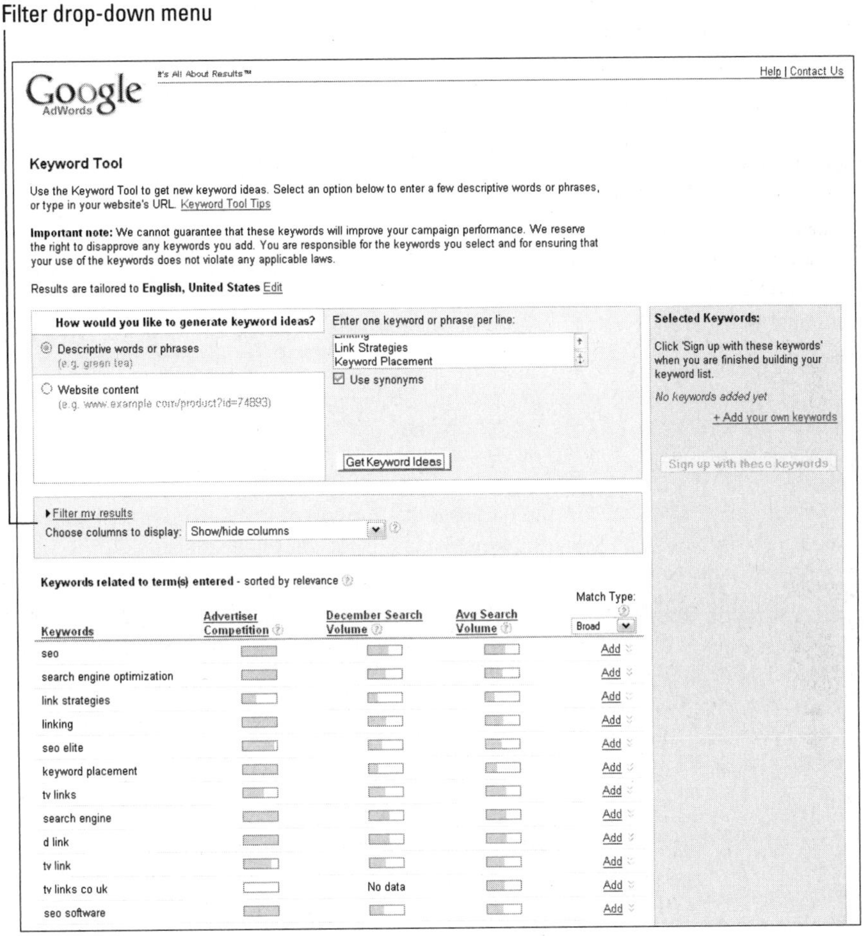

Filter drop-down menu

Figure 4-2:
A list of suggested keywords appears under the search box.

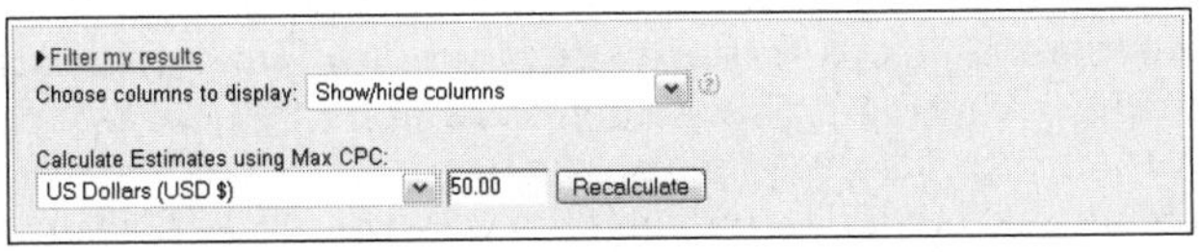

Figure 4-3:
Use the Show Estimated Avg. CPC filter to find the approximate value of the suggested keywords.

Understanding and optimizing click-through-rates

The more traffic you have on your Web site, the higher your *click-through-rate (CTR)* will be. Click-through-rate is exactly what it sounds like — the rate at which your site visitors click through the ads that you display. This rate is based on the number of visitors to your site versus the number of visitors who click your AdSense ads.

What's considered a good CTR is a hard figure to nail down. It's against Google's policies for publishers to publicly discuss the results they have with the AdSense program. So, despite the fact that you may have seen discussions about it on the Internet, you should avoid following suit. Still, it helps to have a general idea of what you can expect.

The rates I've heard all hover around the 2–4 percent range. That's 2–4 percent of your total traffic who actually click through the ads on your Web site. If you get 100 visitors per day, with these percentages, two to four of those visitors will click through your AdSense ads, generating money for you.

The thing to remember is that those numbers are in no way official or accurate. They're whispers heard and accurate only to the specific cases (and circumstances) in which they actually happened. A wide variety of factors can affect your CTR, from placement of the ads and the amount of traffic on your Web site to the mood of site visitors in a given day and the colors of the ads themselves.

All these factors are variables that change often. To further cloud the picture, fluctuations in the popularity of certain keywords, changes in the budgets of advertisers, and the ways in which those advertisers choose to write their ads have to be considered.

To some extent, your click-through-rate is dependent upon the advertiser. If the advertiser isn't doing his homework and properly targeting his ads, your click-through-rates could be affected because the ads won't appeal to your site visitors.

Advertisers pay this amount per click on their advertisments.

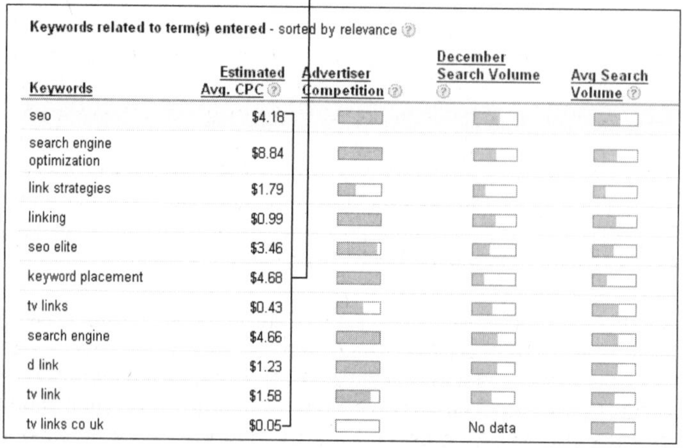

Figure 4-4: The Estimated Avg. CPC column provides an idea of the value of suggested keywords.

Keywords	Estimated Avg. CPC	Advertiser Competition	December Search Volume	Avg Search Volume
seo	$4.18			
search engine optimization	$8.84			
link strategies	$1.79			
linking	$0.99			
seo elite	$3.46			
keyword placement	$4.68			
tv links	$0.43			
search engine	$4.66			
d link	$1.23			
tv link	$1.58			
tv links co uk	$0.05		No data	

Because you're researching keywords for your Web site with AdSense income in mind, use a high figure for your maximum CPC, like $50 per click. This really doesn't determine how much you make per click on advertisements that appear on your site, but it gives you an idea of which keywords you'll be paid the most for. In keyword marketing, the advertiser pays a fee to display ads. How much they pay for that privilege directly affects how much you make. So, the more a keyword costs the advertiser, the more you'll make as a publisher of those ads.

Keep in mind that whatever keywords you choose should be used intelligently on your Web page. If you include the keywords but don't use them properly, you'll do yourself more harm than good by causing inappropriate ads to appear or by causing Google to disqualify your site from the AdSense program for not following proper Web design practices. More information about Web design practices can be found in Chapter 3, and I address how to properly use keywords on your Web pages in the next few sections, so keep reading.

The importance of keyword placement

After you finish researching your keywords and then selecting the most valuable — those worth most to your pocketbook — and the most appropriate words for your Web site, you have to actually integrate them into your Web site. Using those valuable and appropriate keywords in your site's content is good practice, and more information about how to use those words in your content is in the section "It's all about placement," later in this chapter, or you can flip back to Chapter 3 for even more Web design help. But there's more to keyword placement than just putting the words into the content on the page, as the next few sections make clear.

Placing keywords in site design

Face it: You don't need much of the old gray matter to place keywords in prominent places in the content of your Web site. Stick them in a title, a few headings, or the opening paragraph and *voilà* — you've placed your keywords. The thing is, if any idiot can do it, many will; which means that all those Web sites with keywords prominently placed in the text start looking alike — at least to Web crawlers sent out by search engines. To make your site stand out, feature your keywords in the less-obvious corners of your Web site, such as places that may never be seen by Web site visitors but *are* visited by Web crawlers. "Where are these dark corners?" you ask. Read on to discover the hidden mysteries of Web site design.

When you're designing your Web site, there are places under the *hood* — in the actual *HTML (HyperText Markup Language)* structure of the site, in other words — that you can use as hidden storage areas for placing informational tidbits about your site. Because all this stuff is information about your Web site content — information about your information, in other words — such tidbits are referred to as *metadata,* or data about your data. Metadata is placed within special HTML tags (dubbed, curiously enough, *metatags*) within the code for a Web site that search engine crawlers then *read* when cataloging your site for inclusion in search results. As such, you'd be smart to stuff your metatags with as many keywords as your HTML structure will bear.

Metatags where keywords should appear include the following:

- ✔ Title metatags
- ✔ Description metatags
- ✔ Keyword metatags
- ✔ Heading metatags
- ✔ Alt text

Now, for those of you out there who are faint-of-heart when it comes to HTML coding, be aware that you need to physically place these metatags (with the exception of the alt text) in the top section of the HTML code of your Web page, between the tags that indicate the head of your page. Figure 4-5 shows part of the *raw* HTML code for the Google Geek Web site, including the head tag, metatags, and body tag.

As I mention earlier, metadata are usually indicated within the HTML of your Web site as metatags. The code here shows how the metadata might appear on your site:

```
<Head>
<Title>Your Web Site Title Goes Here</Title>
<Meta name="description" content="Include a quick keyword-
        rich blurb about your site here.">
<Meta name="keywords" content="enter keywords here,
        separated by commas">
</Head>
```

Metadata tags

Figure 4-5:
Metatags
should be
placed in
the HTML
header of a
Web site.

```
<!DOCTYPE html PUBLIC "-//W3C//DTD XHTML 1.0 Strict//EN" "http://www.w3.org/TR/xhtml1/DTD/xhtml1-strict.dtd">
<html dir='ltr' xmlns='http://www.w3.org/1999/xhtml' xmlns:b='http://www.google.com/2005/gml/b' xmlns:data='http://www.google
<head>
<meta content='text/html; charset=UTF-8' http-equiv='Content-Type'/>
<meta content='true' name='MSSmartTagsPreventParsing'/>
<meta content='blogger' name='generator'/>
<link rel="alternate" type="application/atom+xml" title="Google-Geek - Atom" href="http://www.google-geek.com/feeds/posts/def
<link rel="alternate" type="application/rss+xml" title="Google-Geek - RSS" href="http://www.google-geek.com/feeds/posts/defau
<link rel="service.post" type="application/atom+xml" title="Google-Geek - Atom" href="http://www.blogger.com/feeds/7662296931
<link rel="EditURI" type="application/rsd+xml" title="RSD" href="http://www.blogger.com/rsd.g?blogID=7662296931546595910" />
<link rel="openid.server" href="http://draft.blogger.com/openid-server.g" />
<title>Google-Geek</title>
<style id='page-skin-1' type='text/css'><!-- body {background:#ffffff;margin:0;color:#333333;font:x-small Georgia Serif;font-
<!-- --><style type="text/css">@import url('http://www.blogger.com/css/blog_controls.css');
@import url('http://www.blogger.com/dyn-css/authorization.css?targetBlogID=7662296931546595910');
#navbar-iframe { display:block }
</style>

<link rel='stylesheet' type='text/css' href='http://www.blogger.com/widgets/3936352919-blog.css'/><link rel='stylesheet' type
<body>
```

The head tags usually have far more information between them because this is where the heading of your Web site is set up. Information about the colors, images , and styles of the page are also included here, but those don't really concern you when you're thinking about keywords. Those elements are all associated with site design, not keyword placement.

Working with alt text

Another area in which you can place your keywords is the alt text on your page. *Alt text* is the alternative text that's used to describe images on your page to search engines and to site visitors who can't view the images. This alt text is usually included in the image tag in your page's HTML and looks something like this:

```
<img src="imagefilename.jpg" alt="keyword descriptor">
```

Alt text should be limited to as few effective words as possible. So, if the image on your Web site is a magnifying glass, the alt text might simply be search if that's one of your keywords.

Adding keywords to the HTML descriptors on your Web site is far from a difficult task. When you know where to put the keywords, it takes little time to do it. If you're writing your Web site code from scratch, you can insert your keywords in the appropriate places while you write it. If you're using an HTML editor or a WYSIWYG — what you see is what you get — Web site design program, you can switch to the HTML view for the HTML editor and add the tags that way.

The extra effort improves the search engine rankings for your site and ultimately makes it easier for Google to find the right AdSense ads to appear on your site. The tags also help to ensure that ads appearing on your site are targeted to the correct audience — assuming that the keywords you're using are well targeted.

The secret of keyword density

If you've been following along in this chapter so far, you've already found out that your chosen keywords need to appear somewhere in your content. *(D'oh!)* Clearly, your Web site articles and other elements (stuff like video content) should be targeting the topics your potential visitors are searching for — which means your articles and other elements will have your keywords embedded in them somewhere.

That's pretty much a no-brainer. But if you take this a little bit further, it gets a bit more interesting. Some folks might be tempted to adopt what I call an *in for a penny, in for a pound* strategy — if a little bit of something is a good thing, a lot of something is a very good thing. Why settle for a sprinkling of keywords on your Web site when, with a little bit of effort, you can saturate your Web site with a veritable blizzard of keywords?

Why indeed? Because if you yield to temptation, you're guilty of committing *keyword spam,* the act of deploying your keywords merely to increase search engine results placement (bad!) rather than using them to provide site visitors with desired information (good!). No one likes spam. You don't like spam, your potential Web visitors don't like spam, and even spammers don't like spam. Keyword spam doesn't even help you increase your search engine results placement. In fact, Web crawlers that recognize keyword spam can get your number and list your site deeper in search results, or worse, completely de-list your site from those results.

The secret to having the right balance of keywords in your site content is *keyword density* — the ratio of keyword occurrences to the overall number of words used on your site. Search engines vary on what's acceptable for a keyword density. Google, for example, looks for a keyword density of around 2 percent, whereas Yahoo! and MSN look for a keyword density closer to 5 percent. Remember, these are guidelines. So, if your keyword density is less than 5 percent, your page will still appear in Yahoo! and MSN search results. But over 2 percent and you might be penalized by Google.

Most folks who do search engine optimization for a living tend to stay around the 2 percent keyword density mark to stay in Google's good graces.

Time to picture what a 2 percent keyword density might actually look like. Think of it this way: If the page contains an article that's 1,000 words in length, your selected keyword or phrase should appear no more than 20 times in the article. Twenty seems like a small number until you start adding keywords to articles and then you find that it takes some serious work to spin 1,000 words around one word or phrase and still have everything make sense and not sound repetitive.

The key here is to build an article around a specific topic, like "credit monitoring," but then not to go overboard using the keyword or term — which in this case is "credit monitoring." The article should be a coherent information piece, and the use of the keyword or phrase will automatically grow out of that. You just have to be careful not to stuff that keyword or phrase into the article out of context in a misguided attempt to use your selected keyword as often as possible.

One trick that might help, though, involves thinking outside your body text box. It turns out that putting keywords into the body text of your article is only half the work when you're dealing with keywords. Keywords should also appear in the title and the headings of articles you place on your Web site. Titles and headings are also given additional weight in search engine rankings because those are the elements on a page that catch a visitor's eye.

Think of it as being like reading a newspaper. Most people scan a page of the newspaper before committing to reading any of it. They look at headlines, paragraph headings, and bold or italicized text before they decide which stories to read. Reading behavior is the same online — someone clicks onto your page, scans the titles, headings, and specially formatted sections of the articles there, and then decides to read deeper or click away.

Keywords in your titles and headings help pull readers into the content of the article and help search crawlers classify your site by those keywords. See, search crawlers are designed to weigh the appearance of keywords in certain places — like titles and headings — just like people do. It's written into their programming, so you might think of a search crawler as the ultimate reader.

The Magic of Linking Well

Search engine optimization plays a key role in generating AdSense income because how well your Web site places in search results determines how much traffic your site sees. If you plan to have AdSense ads on your site and you hope to generate a decent revenue stream with them, having a well-optimized site is essential. And part of site optimization is having a *linking structure* — the links that connect the pages of your site together as well as the links that connect your page to other pages on the Web — that leads to other, complementary sites as well as having other sites link to you. Like keyword placement, link management is almost as much of an art form as it is a strategy.

Linking schemes

Linking schemes are nothing more than the structure of how your Web site is linked to other sites, how other sites are linked to you, and where internal links lead. Good Web design principles include all three types of linking schemes, and all are important to search engines because what a search crawler is looking for is site usability first — how easy it is for visitors to go from one place to the next on your Web site — and then site relevancy, or how appropriate your site is to the topic for which a site visitor is searching. Crawlers literally follow all the links on a Web page to make sure that what's connected together makes sense and is useful in the context of where the links appear both in text and in navigational menus.

When you're creating your linking schemes, remember that the ultimate goal is to make your site as usable and as valuable as possible to your site visitors. Assume that your visitors have landed on your page because it contains information for which they're searching; the idea here is to make your site as valuable to those visitors as possible by providing your visitors with the info they're looking for and then some. (It's the *and then some* that keeps them coming back for more.)

Creating value for your user encompasses one concept — provide the user the information he seeks. It's that simple. That doesn't mean that you need to have every detail or product related to a specific topic on your site. But if you don't have it and you don't plan to put it there, at least be prepared to point visitors to another site that does have the information or products sought.

All of that is accomplished through linking. You're either linking to another page on your site where the information being sought is available or you're linking to another site entirely. In return, you should also have other sites linking to your own, for the same reasons. (I have some tips on how to get other sites to link back to you later in the chapter.)

Internal linking

Internal linking is the process by which the pages on your site are actually linked together. The type of links isn't nearly as important as the way in which the pages are linked, but even the structure can have some benefits. For example, text links — called *hotlinks* — *can* be more valuable than graphic links because they allow you to use your keywords within the link. But it's also important to have a consistent navigational structure — the links that usually grace the side or top of a page that lead to different sections of your Web site. Both hotlinks and navigational links can be used in your internal linking process.

Using keywords in your navigational structure gives you freebie opportunities to use them — the keywords within links don't count toward the keyword density of a page because the percentage of times a keyword is used is based solely on the content on the page. This means you can use your keywords more often. But using hotlinks does count toward keyword density, so be careful about how you place those links.

It's also important that no matter how your links are formatted, you always need to leave an escape hatch — every page on the site has to have a clearly defined navigation area with easily recognizable links that make it a snap to return to whatever page the visitor wants. Users who click from one page to another in your Web site may not appreciate having to click the Back button to get them back to the page they were previously on. Even more importantly, if there's no way for users to go back from whence they came, they'll leave. Typical surfer behavior when they can't escape a page is to close the window or browser that's pointing to the site on which you have them trapped. They may also just type a new address in the browser bar and navigate away from your page that way.

Internal links all qualify as navigational links, even when they include hotlinks. Use these links wisely, and always provide a way for users to navigate back the way they came. I don't care whose fault it is; if you lock a visitor in Web page hell, she'll leave and probably won't come back.

It's far better to have all your pages (even those that are unrelated) connected in a loose kind of way. Every page should have a way to go back to the main page as well as a way for visitors to get back at least to the previous page if not to the beginning of a section. It may be that your navigational structure expands to show previous pages or sections of your Web site, based on where the visitor is on the site at any given moment. Whatever you choose to do, make sure visitors have plenty of ways out.

When you're creating the way that your internal pages are linked, also remember to keep like pages grouped together. When you think of the structure of your Web site, think of it as a tree. The trunk of the tree is your main page, and each of the branches is a major topic. Subtopics are the smaller branches off the main branches, and the leaves are individual pages of information.

If you were to draw your Web site structure, it should resemble (in an abstract kind of way) a tree lying on its side, as shown in Figure 4-6.

Each different topic of content on your Web site should be related to the overall theme of the site — nobody would argue with that — but each topic should also be further broken down into smaller categories so that site visitors can quickly find what they're looking for. For example, if your site is about healthy cooking, every page on your site should be related to healthy cooking. However, individual sections of your site can be broken down into the different types of dishes that you cook or the techniques that you use to create healthy dishes. Keep like content together and keep it all related to the main theme of the Web site.

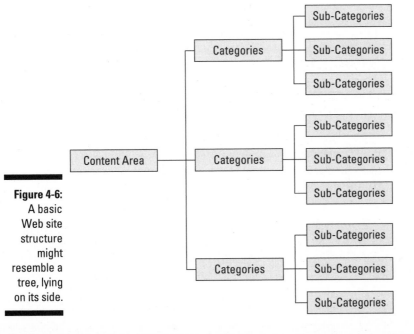

Figure 4-6:
A basic
Web site
structure
might
resemble a
tree, lying
on its side.

External linking

External linking — the links you use to connect your Web sites to other relevant sites on the Web — is also going to play a major role in the way that your Web site is categorized by search engine crawlers. *External links* lead away from your page, and for this reason, many Web site designers think it's best to avoid external links on a page. Not true. In fact, if you don't have some element of external linking on your page, it becomes an obstacle in both search rankings and in helping potential visitors find the information they're searching for.

Search crawlers look for external linking on a page as a sign of how well connected the page is to the industry or category that it's included in. For example, if your site is about mental health issues, users will expect to find links to other sites on the same topic. Crawlers will too. And if a crawler examines your site and finds you're not linked to other related sites, it devalues the site, assuming that the site will be less useful to site visitors (because no single site can have every piece of information about a topic or category).

What you don't want to do is create a Web page that's an *island* — surrounded by cyberspace, but cut off from everything. Even the most beautiful islands can become useless if nothing connects them to the rest of the world. And if your Web site isn't connected to other Web sites, (especially where search crawlers are concerned), the usability rating of the site falls considerably.

It's necessary to have outgoing and incoming external links to your site. But there's a catch (isn't there always?): The external links on your site should lead to or from other sites that are relevant to the content on your site. If you're linking to other sites in some disorderly, couldn't-figure-it-out-with-a-clear-explanation kind of way, you might as well not have any links at all. Search crawlers follow every link leading out from your site and will evaluate the content on the linked site for relevancy. If the content doesn't compute, your search rankings will plummet.

Having one or two links to unrelated sites isn't a big worry. It's not at all unusual for your best friend, who sells handmade soaps, to link to your Web site about money management. But if you want search engines to take notice of your Web site, I recommend that you have far more links to other sites related to money-management vehicles, tools, and information.

Reciprocal linking

One way to gather links to your site and to share your site with other relevant Web sites is to use *reciprocal linking*. Reciprocal linking is the new-age version of *you scratch my back, I'll scratch yours*. You find sites that would be of interest to your site visitors and then approach the Web site owner with the offer of putting a link to her site on your own if she'll do the same for you in exchange.

It's a good strategy to get some inbound links built into your site if it's a new site, but don't rely on this type of linking to gain you much favor with search crawlers. A limited amount of reciprocal linking is acceptable, but when a search engine is examining the links to your site, it ranks them by determining if the keywords used on your Web site are similar to the keywords on the sites that are linking to you. That's why links always need to be generated out of true interest in the content on your site. If your link to another page is matched by a link back to your own page on too many pages, the value of those links is lessened because the pattern of "I'll link to you if you link to me" becomes obvious.

Think about the wildly popular Web sites in your business (or personal) scope. Even better than just thinking about it, surf on over there and have a look. Click through a few of the external links on the page and look at where they lead. Are there links back to the page you just left? In most cases, the answer to that will likely be "No" because the most popular pages on the Web don't need reciprocal linking schemes. People link to them all the time because the site offers information that's of interest to everyone concerned with that topic.

It's all about placement

One last strategy to extend your linking mileage: Where you place your links matters. When a crawler is navigating through your site, it's looking at the usability of your site. So, if you're hiding links in places that users can't find them simply to improve your Web site ranking, you'll find your Web site in search results' nether regions. And yes, that's a trick some Web site designers really use. The idea behind hidden links is to have them there because you must have that linking structure, but to have the links hidden in places users don't think to click so they won't navigate away from your Web site. Wrong move. That kind of linking strategy will turn the curious search crawler into a snotty search crawler that doesn't score your Web site well for ranking purposes.

Keep in mind that hidden links are very different from strategies like using metadata keywords, as I talk about earlier in this chapter. Metadata keywords and tags are built into the structure of your site and are designed to provide additional information to crawlers. Hidden links and keywords are actually built into the visitor-facing structure or user interface. Hidden links and keywords, however, are intentionally blended into the site so that visitors can't see them. This is a deceptive way to include elements of Web design that crawlers look for but that a Web site owner might not want the site visitor to see.

Creating a well-designed site that uses a more traditional link placement structure is much better. Not only are Web surfers accustomed to seeing a navigation structure, or links, in a few places (the top of the page, the left side of the page, or within the text), but a well-designed site meets a need —

the visitor's need for information. By meeting that need, you give visitors a reason to return to your site again and again.

Most often on a well-designed site, some combination of those navigation structures is going on. Most Web sites have their main navigation bar on the left side of the page, and users know that that's where they can usually go to find the link to the next page within the site. Links to *other* sites can be included in the text or in combination with the navigational structure on the sides of the page.

Once in a while, a page will have the main navigational structure on the right. In fact, that's a common structure in blogs, and there's nothing wrong with setting up your page that way. Web crawlers don't give a hoot if your navigational structure and other links are located on one side of the page or the other. But it's important that however you decide to do it on the main page of your Web site, you maintain that structure across every other page on the site. Users get frustrated if the navigation scheme changes on every single page, and Web crawlers will notice the inconsistency and lower the usability ranking of your site.

Keyword marketing is like watching the news. A big story could hit today, and it might hang around for a few days until journalists have wrung all the interest out of the story. Then something else happens, and those same journalists toss that story aside in favor of the newer, more interesting piece of news.

With keyword marketing, marketers might be willing to fight hard to win the bids on one keyword today, only to find that another keyword is much more popular and worth more to them in advertisements tomorrow. These changes affect the income that you make from each click through, as well as affecting the click throughs themselves. When the higher-paying marketer moves on, it opens a keyword for lower-paying advertisers. Sometimes, though, those lower-paying advertisers aren't writing ads that are as appealing to your users.

Users' moods change, too. What they're interested in today will certainly not be the same tomorrow or next week. So, to keep your CTR optimized, you have to stay on top of your keywords. Watch the effectiveness of the keywords around which your Web site is built. And don't be afraid to test new and different keywords, especially if your traffic statistics begin to fall. Your AdSense income depends on you staying at the razor's edge of the marketing curve. And that requires attention from you.

Chapter 5

Installing the AdSense Code

. . . .

. . . .

*O*ne reason many people shy away from using AdSense on their Web sites is because they think that the whole AdSense thing is just too hard to manage. Surely there has to be some trick to adding AdSense to your Web site — a trick that only some uber-geek could figure out.

Nope. If I can figure it out, just about anyone can. I'm a consumer technologist — I can tell you all about why you should use a program and how that program works. If you want me to program the program though, you're looking at the wrong gal. Programmer, I am not, and that includes HTML.

That didn't make a bit of difference when it came time to put the AdSense code on my site. I did it, and it wasn't that hard and didn't leave me wondering what in the world I was doing wrong. You won't have any problems either because it's a cut-and-paste job. The catch is that you have to know where to paste the code that Google provides for you.

Choosing AdSense for Content or AdSense for Search

I make putting the code on your Web site sound really easy because it is. Before you get to the whole cut-and-paste part, you'd best understand a few things about AdSense ads, and it's these facets of the ads that can be confusing.

First of all, you have to decide whether you'll use AdSense for Content or AdSense for Search. (I don't talk too much about AdSense Referrals, Video Units, or AdSense for Mobile, just yet. Those capabilities are discussed in Part III.) To make the decision, you need to know how the two differ, so here goes: *The difference between AdSense for Content and AdSense for Search lies in how your ads are displayed.*

- **AdSense for Content** displays *linked* ads — ads that contain links that lead to the advertisers' Web sites — in text or graphical formats on your pages.

- **AdSense for Search** displays a search box on your Web site that site visitors can use to search for additional information if they don't find what they need on your pages.

  Figure 5-1 shows an AdSense for Content ad and an AdSense for Search ad side by side.

AdSense for Search is a tough sell. Not because it's not useful. Many people like having the option of searching for what they need right from the page they're on. However, the fact that it takes two clicks before you get paid turns a lot of folks off.

Figure 5-1:
AdSense for Search is completely different from AdSense for Content.

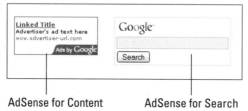

AdSense for Content   AdSense for Search

Link Units: The Other AdSense for Content Ad

AdSense for Search ads are not the only AdSense ad type that requires two clicks. Link units, which are a subset of AdSense for Content, also require two clicks. Figure 5-2 shows you what I mean. Users click once on the link on your page, which takes them to a list of targeted advertisements that looks like a search results page (as shown in Figure 5-3). Users must then click one of those advertisements for you to get paid. The neat thing about this (when they're used properly and work for you) is that often you can get paid for multiple ad clicks from one display because users will follow the initial link and then check out several of the ads on the results page.

Figure 5-2:
A link unit
displays
links only, no
advertise-
ment text.

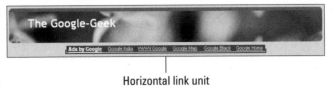

Horizontal link unit

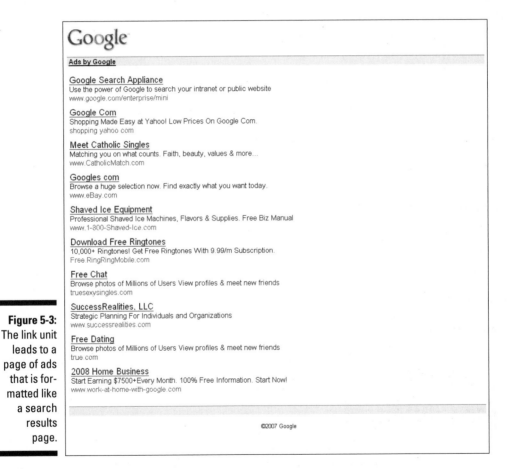

Figure 5-3:
The link unit
leads to a
page of ads
that is for-
matted like
a search
results
page.

Generating Search Box Code

Life doesn't always demand stark choices. It's not as if you can get only
chocolate or vanilla ice cream. In fact, throw in strawberry, and you have
Neapolitan, the ice cream for indecisive folks everywhere.

The same principle applies to AdSense for Search versus AdSense for Content on your site — there's no reason you can't have both. AdSense for Content works well in and around your articles and other printed content, and an AdSense for Search box at the beginning of the page (or end of the page or in a blank space on the page) works pretty well, too. The results from the search box can add to your AdSense income; although if I were you, I wouldn't rely on the search box alone to generate income for your site.

My advice to you: Go with a combination of both content ads and the search box.

With that out of the way, it's time to do some code slinging. I start out with the AdSense for Search code, just because today is Tuesday. (I cover the AdSense for Content code later in this chapter.) Keep in mind, though, that all the AdSense ad formats are created in about the same way. You work through the wizard, copy the text, and paste it into the HTML on your Web site. Pretty simple, in other words. You'll probably spend more time debating *where* to put your search box than you'll spend actually dealing with the code.

You can install the search box wherever you have some blank real estate that you don't plan to put higher paying ads or other content on. Some designers place their search box at the top of the page, others at the bottom. Very few actually use a search box in the center of the page or off to either the right or the left because the box looks awkward and out of place in those locations. Site visitors usually look to the top or bottom of the page if they want to search.

To create a search box for your Web site:

1. **Point your browser to** www.adsense.com, **log on to your AdSense account, and click the AdSense Setup tab.**

2. **In the Setup tab, select the AdSense for Search option.**

   Doing so calls up the AdSense for Search Wizard.

3. **On the top of the first wizard page, as shown in Figure 5-4, select either the Google WebSearch option or the Google WebSearch + SiteSearch option.**

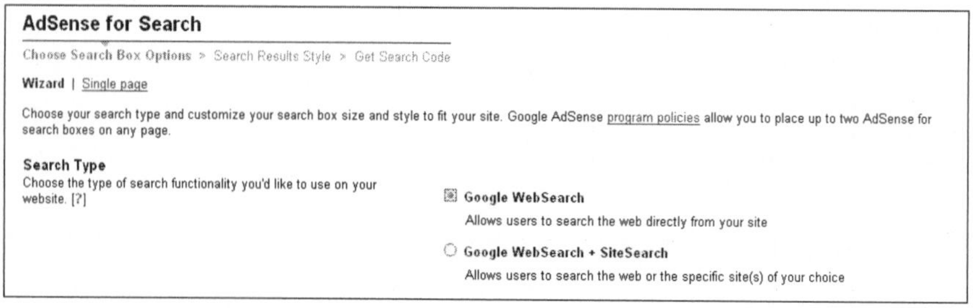

Figure 5-4:
Choose the type of search box you want to create at the top of the wizard page.

AdSense for Search

Choose Search Box Options > Search Results Style > Get Search Code

Wizard | Single page

Choose your search type and customize your search box size and style to fit your site. Google AdSense program policies allow you to place up to two AdSense for search boxes on any page.

Search Type
Choose the type of search functionality you'd like to use on your website. [?]

☒ **Google WebSearch**
  Allows users to search the web directly from your site

○ **Google WebSearch + SiteSearch**
  Allows users to search the web or the specific site(s) of your choice

WebSearch allows visitors to search the Web for additional information whereas WebSearch + SiteSearch allows users to search up to three Web sites that you specify in addition to the whole Web.

4. **If you select WebSearch + SiteSearch, a new form appears in the wizard, as shown in Figure 5-5. Fill in the Web addresses of the sites you wish to allow visitors to search in the appropriate text boxes.**

   If you select WebSearch, you can skip to Step 5.

   In most cases, those sites will be your own sites, but you can select any sites you like. You also don't have to enter three sites — one or two are fine if that's your preference.

5. **Scroll down to the middle of the page, as shown in Figure 5-6, and then choose your search box style.**

   Each of the options has a preview that appears when you select that option. You can choose to move the Google logo above the search box, or to remove it completely and place it on the search button. Another available option is to move the search button down below the text field of the search box.

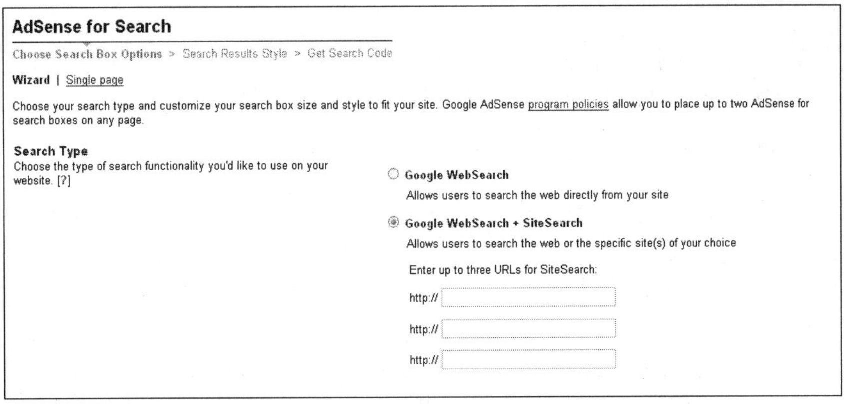

Figure 5-5:
If you choose the SiteSearch option, enter the Web sites to be searched.

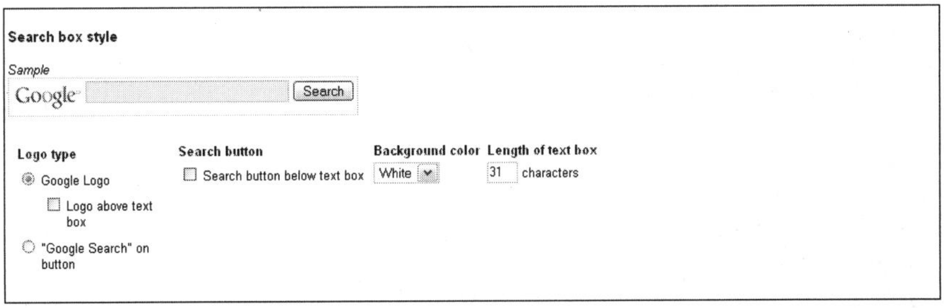

AdSense for Search

Choose Search Box Options > Search Results Style > Get Search Code

Wizard | Single page

Choose your search type and customize your search box size and style to fit your site. Google AdSense program policies allow you to place up to two AdSense for search boxes on any page.

Search Type
Choose the type of search functionality you'd like to use on your website. [?]

○ **Google WebSearch**
   Allows users to search the web directly from your site

◉ **Google WebSearch + SiteSearch**
   Allows users to search the web or the specific site(s) of your choice

   Enter up to three URLs for SiteSearch:

   http://
   http://
   http://

Figure 5-6:
Choose the style you want to use for your search box.

Search box style

Sample

Google [   ] Search

Logo type	Search button	Background color	Length of text box
◉ Google Logo	☐ Search button below text box	White	31 characters
☐ Logo above text box			
○ "Google Search" on button			

Next to the search box style you'll find options to change the background color, text color, and allowable text length of the box. Feel free to select the options that work best with your Web site.

6. **From the drop-down menus at the bottom of the wizard page, select the default language for search results. (See Figure 5-7.)**

   There are 30 — count 'em, 30 — options besides English.

7. **Choose the type of page encoding that your Web site uses from the options in the drop-down menu provided. (Refer to Figure 5-7.)**

   The type of encoding that your site uses depends on how it's designed. If you don't know what type of encoding your site uses, check with your Web site designer. The most common encoding used for Web sites is UTF-8, but Western (Windows 1252) is another common encoding format.

8. **In the final drop-down menu on the wizard page, select the country you're in so Google knows which domain to search from. After you make your selection, click the Continue button.**

   The second page of the wizard appears where you have a chance to customize your search results page.

9. **Use the Palettes drop-down menu (see Figure 5-8) to select a different palette for your various color needs, or click the small, colored box next to each element of the search box — Text, Background, Border, and so on — to create a custom palette.**

   If that's still not good enough for you, you can always enter the six-digit, hexadecimal number in the text box provided for each element. By the way, don't let the term *hexadecimal* scare you; it's just a number that represents the color you want to use. A nifty sidebar in Chapter 7 explains colors and hexadecimal numbers in more depth.

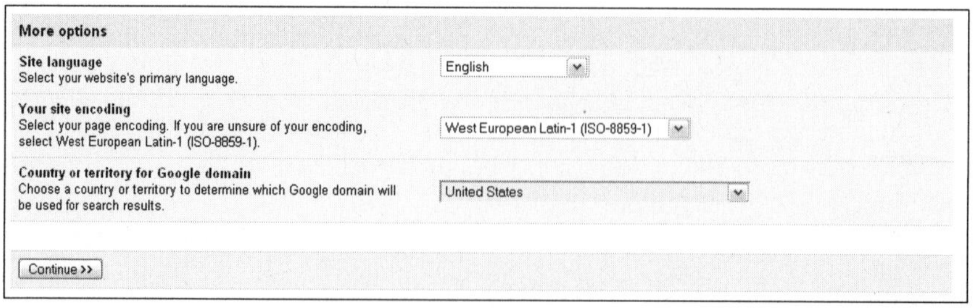

Figure 5-7:
Use the drop-down menus to choose the default language for search results.

More options	
Site language Select your website's primary language.	English
Your site encoding Select your page encoding. If you are unsure of your encoding, select West European Latin-1 (ISO-8859-1).	West European Latin-1 (ISO-8859-1)
Country or territory for Google domain Choose a country or territory to determine which Google domain will be used for search results.	United States

Continue >>

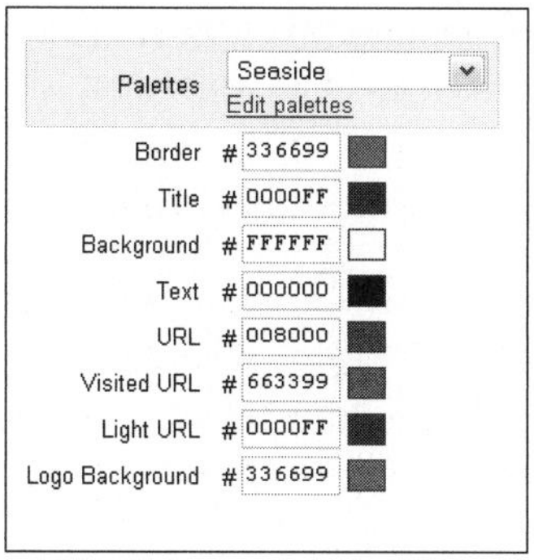

Figure 5-8:
Customizing
the colors of
your search
results page
using the
palettes,
Color Picker,
or hexa-
decimal
numbers.

Palettes	Seaside ▼
	Edit palettes
Border	# 336699
Title	# 0000FF
Background	# FFFFFF
Text	# 000000
URL	# 008000
Visited URL	# 663399
Light URL	# 0000FF
Logo Background	# 336699

10. **If desired, use the logo customization tools shown in Figure 5-9 to upload a personalized logo to your search results page.**

It's easy to do, enter the URL showing where your logo is located on your Web site. If you're not certain of that URL, right-click the logo in your browser and select Copy Link Location. Then, paste that link location into the Logo Image URL box, and AdSense pulls your URL whenever a search results page is shown. After you enter the location of the logo, the preview display changes to reflect the logo you want to use.

The second text box, Logo Destination URL, is there so that you can make the logo on your search results page a link back to your Web site if you like. To do that, enter the URL of your Web site — or whatever page you would like to send visitors to — in the provided text box.

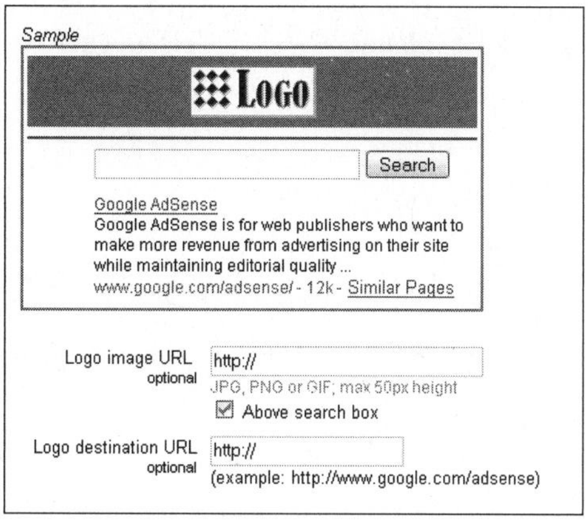

Sample

Logo

[Search]

Google AdSense
Google AdSense is for web publishers who want to
make more revenue from advertising on their site
while maintaining editorial quality ...
www.google.com/adsense/ - 12k - Similar Pages

Figure 5-9:
Add a cus-
tom logo to
your search
results page
to make it
blend better
with your
Web site.

Logo image URL	http://
optional	JPG, PNG or GIF; max 50px height
	☑ Above search box
Logo destination URL	http://
optional	(example: http://www.google.com/adsense)

11. **In the More Options section, as shown in Figure 5-10, select whether you want the search results page to open in a different page or window, or to open in the same page by selecting the desired option.**

Opening the search results page in another window or page is best. That leaves your Web site open for visitors to return when they're finished looking through search results. After all, the idea here is to give them additional tools to help them make better decisions about using your site, not to direct them away from your site (potentially) for good.

12. **Decide whether you want to customize the type of search results with the help of the Site-Flavored Search option.**

Site-flavored search customizes search results over time to your topic and to your Web site visitors. It takes some time for the search results to become highly targeted because Google tracks which results are most clicked by site visitors that use the search box. Site-flavored search can add an additional element of functionality to your search capabilities, however, because it discovers how to provide the best possible results to your visitors. If this is an option that you want to use, select the Customize the Type of Search Results I Get to My Site Content check box.

If you do choose this option, the site-flavored search options expand, as shown in Figure 5-11, so that you can select a profile to use to track the search results.

13. **Use the drop-down menu provided to select the desired profile.**

There may be no profiles available to choose from if this is the first time you've selected this option. To create a profile, select the Add New Profile link. A text box appears where you can enter the name of the desired profile. When you're finished, click OK and the profile is created.

14. **If you want to protect visitors from being exposed to adult-themed search results, select the Use SafeSearch check box. (See Figure 5-10.)**

The SafeSearch option blocks adult content.

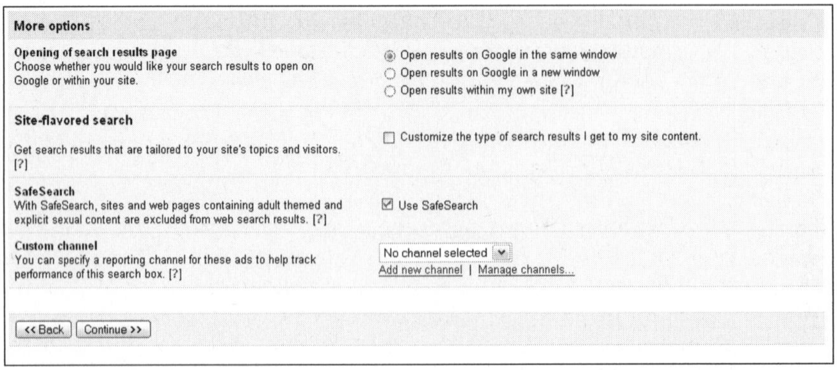

Figure 5-10:
Additional customiza-tion options are near the bottom of the second wizard page.

More options	
Opening of search results page Choose whether you would like your search results to open on Google or within your site.	⦿ Open results on Google in the same window ○ Open results on Google in a new window ○ Open results within my own site [?]
Site-flavored search Get search results that are tailored to your site's topics and visitors. [?]	☐ Customize the type of search results I get to my site content.
SafeSearch With SafeSearch, sites and web pages containing adult themed and explicit sexual content are excluded from web search results. [?]	☑ Use SafeSearch
Custom channel You can specify a reporting channel for these ads to help track performance of this search box. [?]	No channel selected ▼ Add new channel | Manage channels...

[<< Back] [Continue >>]

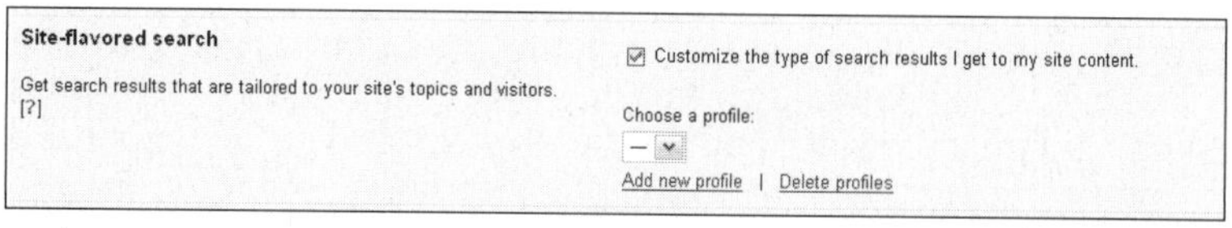

Figure 5-11:
Selecting
site-flavored
search
enables cus-
tomization
options for
the special-
ized search.

Site-flavored search

Get search results that are tailored to your site's topics and visitors. [?]

☑ Customize the type of search results I get to my site content.

Choose a profile:
— ▾

Add new profile | Delete profiles

15. **For the last option on this page, decide whether you want to use a custom channel to track your results.**

    Custom channels are like Web counters. Each time a visitor uses a search box that you've assigned to a custom channel, the *count* for that visit is credited to that specific channel. Custom channels provide a way for you to keep track of which ads are successful and which ads get low amounts of traffic.

    You can choose to add a custom channel that separates this traffic from other AdSense traffic. To create a custom channel, click the Add New Channel link. This opens a dialog box where you type the name of the channel you want to use and then click OK. The channel is then auto-matically set for you. If you already have an existing channel you want to add, select it from the drop-down menu.

16. **When you finish customizing your search box and search attributes, click the Continue button.**

    The final page of the wizard appears, containing the code for your search box in all its glory.

17. **Copy and paste this code into the HTML of your Web site and you're done.**

    If you're not sure where to paste it, keep reading. You can read more about code placement a little further along in this chapter in the section, "Code Placement for Optimum Traffic."

Now you have a search box for your Web site. Go ahead and try it, just to see if it works. Ain't technology grand?

If you're not generating any income from the search box, you can always remove the code after a few weeks of testing. With AdSense, testing is the key to finding what works for *your* Web site. Keep in mind that what works for you might not be the same thing that works for others. That doesn't mean you should ignore what others have figured out; only that you shouldn't be limited by others' experiences.

Understanding Ad Formats

If you're not using search boxes on your site, you're probably using AdSense for Content, and with content, creating the right ads gets a little trickier. Trickier, as in negotiating a strange house blindfolded — it's pretty certain you'll bump into things and your path won't always be the most direct to your destination, but you'll eventually end up in the right place through trial and error.

But that's the worst-case scenario. Why go through all that trouble when you have someone who can take the blindfold off, let you see exactly where you are, and show you the path to exactly where you want to go? (Me, in other words.) When I get you to understand the ad formats in AdSense and understand what works best where, it's like taking off that blindfold.

The infinite variety of AdSense ads

AdSense gives you dozens of different types of ads and ad formats to choose from. Options include

- Text ads
- Image ads
- Video ads
- Link units
- Referral buttons
- Themed ads

Each of these categories includes 8 to 12 different sizes of ads, and then you can further customize ads by choosing the *referral partners* — the folks whose products or services you want to recommend to your Web site visitors — or the colors of the ads. There are enough choices to keep you busy testing different types of ads for a couple years, at least!

Text ads

Text ads are the most popular type of AdSense ad. If you've seen a Web site using AdSense, you've seen text ads. It gets a little confusing, though, when you step back and try to determine exactly what kind of text ad would be best for what space on your Web site. Should you use a leaderboard ad or a medium rectangle? What's the best placement for a vertical banner? When considering options on your Web page, you could probably come up with dozens of potential places for placing ads, but really *knowing* what works best — rather than just guessing — can be a little tricky.

Here's where I come in. Table 5-1 shows you at a glance what types of text ads are available and what the best placements for those ads are. ***Note:*** The size of each ad format is noted in *pixels* (or the tiny little squares that make up online images). It's not essential to know this, but I thought I'd mention it in case you were curious.

Table 5-1	Text Ad Formats	
Format	*Size*	*Placement*
Leaderboard	728x90	Top of the page or between blog entries
Banner	468x60	Not great anywhere but can be used at the top of the page
Half banner	234x60	Top of the page, end of articles, between blog entries
Button	125x125	Sidebars
Vertical banner	120x240	Either side of the page
Skyscraper	120x600	On either side of the page
Wide skyscraper	160x600	Right side of the page
Small rectangle	180x150	Beginning of an article
Small square	200x200	Beginning of an article
Square	250x250	Beginning of an article
Medium rectangle	300x250	Beginning of an article
Large rectangle	336x280	Beginning of an article

Obviously, you won't use every single one of those ad types on your page. Instead, you should select two or three of the ads that seem to work best in the natural flow of your pages. For example, if you have a Web site that regularly features articles about products or just provides information for site visitors, it might be best for you to consider using a *skyscraper ad* — an ad that's tall and narrow, just like a skyscraper — on the right side of the page and a rectangle ad — a shorter and wider fellow — at the beginning of an article.

The size of the ad and the size of the space that you have available for an ad determine which ones fit best where on your page. The first four ads in the table (leaderboard, banner, half banner, and button) are horizontally oriented, as shown in Figure 5-12. Okay, so the button ad is squarer, but it fits really well in the screen shot.

The best places to put horizontally oriented ads are at the top of a page, between articles or blog entries, and sometimes at the bottom of the page. Don't expect much by way of performance out of ads that you place on the bottom of the page. On rare occasions they do well, but for the most part, you want to remember the rule about keeping your ads above the fold of your page.

Remember, the fold is considered the bottom of the Web browser window. The idea is that you don't want your visitors to have to scroll to see your ads because they'll often only look at the top of the page without scrolling further down. If you need a refresher about the importance and function of the fold of the page, flip to Chapter 3. The exception to that fold rule is with a blog, where you can (somewhat successfully) place ads between blog posts.

Here's my take on five of the most popular ad formats:

- **Leaderboard:** Probably the most successful format — so much so that you're sure to have seen them everywhere. *Publishers* — that means you or anyone who signs up with AdSense and publishes ads to a Web site — usually put leaderboard ads at the top of the page because they fit nicely there. They're designed to be about the same width as a Web page, and they can blend underneath the header of a page very well.

- **Banner:** I'd say banner ads are the least successful of the top five. That's not to say banner ads won't work at all. Your circumstances might make them work beautifully for you. However, site visitors tend to hate advertisements, and the banner ads of old are the reason. When Internet advertising first started to take off, banner ads were one of the first types of ads to appear — and they were a pain in the rear. Too often, early banner ads were graphically challenging to Web browsers, slowing users down when they went from one Web site to another. Back when dialup was the main way to access the internet, downloading anything with large graphics was a pain.

Most Internet users today use broadband (you know, cable and DSL), but the bad taste left by those early banner ads still remains. Users can spot a banner ad, and out of sheer habit will usually avoid them like that smelly compost heap in the back corner of the yard.

Another problem with banners is that they're not the full width of your Web site, which leaves lots of open space on one side or the other of those ads. That's another factor that makes them look like ads. People will click your ads, but only if they don't glaringly look like ads.

✔ **Half banners:** Half as bad as banners, but that still doesn't make them good — and they leave even more open space around them than banner ads.

✔ **Vertical banners:** Standing a banner upright doesn't make it any less banner-ish, it just changes the orientation, but vertical banners still work on some Web sites in the right column. They're more graphic than skyscraper ads, and are somewhat more acceptable than their horizontal counterparts.

✔ **Button:** Useful little buggers for any small space that you have available. Usually, that small space falls in the sidebars of your pages, on the left and right sides, which is the best placement for those ads. If you have a small spot on your sidebar where your links don't reach or there's open, empty space, a small button ad fills that space nicely without being overbearing.

Okay, so that's the top five. On to the next type of text ads from Table 5-1: the two vertical ads — the skyscraper and the wide skyscraper, as shown in Figure 5-13. (I treat them both at once.)

I think its okay to place vertical ads on either side of your Web page, right there in the sidebar area; but in my opinion, the wide skyscraper seems to do best on the right side of the page. Some experts suggest that could be because most visitors tend to be right-handed, and the right side of the page is technically closer to their hand, making it easier to click the ad. I'm not sure I buy that line of reasoning.

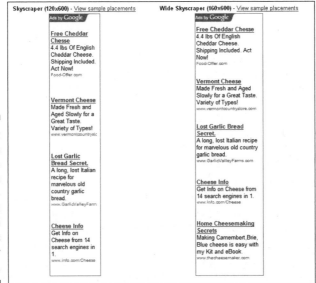

Figure 5-13: Skyscrapers and wide skyscrapers are vertical ads you should use on the sides of your pages.

I think it's more accurate to say that the wide skyscraper on the right side of the page *feels* right. Flip back to where I talk about the way that users tend to view a Web site (Chapter 3, I believe). Users look first at the top of the page, and then at the right, and finally at the left side of the page. Only after glancing at those three areas do they look to the content in the middle of the page.

On the right side, the wide skyscraper just *fits* well. It looks like it belongs there, and that's where users expect to see it. One key to success with any online endeavor, including with AdSense, is to meet the visitor in her comfort zone. It's one reason that so many business people in the real world no longer do business in the office — business types go where their clients are most comfortable: the beach, a restaurant, Starbucks, or into the client's home. Potential customers (which are what your Web site visitors are) are more likely to be agreeable to your terms or to purchase your product if they're comfortable, so make them comfortable. Put the skyscrapers on the outer edges of the pages and use the wide skyscraper on the right.

Going down the list in Table 5-1, you see a set of square and rectangular ads, represented in living black and white in Figure 5-14.

The square and rectangle ads are the most versatile of the AdSense offerings. These ads do well when placed in text, as long as the text is wrapped around the ad, making it look like part of the article or blog post. Of the six ads shown in Figure 5-14, the large rectangle is usually the most successful when placed in text, with the medium rectangle being the next most successful.

The thing to remember about these ads, though, is that just because others find that one type of ad performs better over another in their case, the same might not hold true for you. Testing is the key to determining what your best choices are. Look at the space in which you plan to use the ads and then, based on the space that you have available, try a few different configurations.

If the traffic flow to your site is already established, testing each ad will probably only take about a week. Put up an ad, watch the numbers for a week, and then try something different for another week. After you test several different configurations, you can tell what works well, what works great, and what doesn't work at all. Remember though, the effectiveness of your ads could change over time and with changes to your site, so testing will likely be a constant process.

To make it easier to keep up with your results over time, write down everything. Keep track of the dates, the ads and placements used, the format of the ads (colors and styles, in other words), and anything else that might be pertinent to the results that you see. After a while, you'll instinctively know what will work on your site and what won't. Until then, you have a written record to help you keep track.

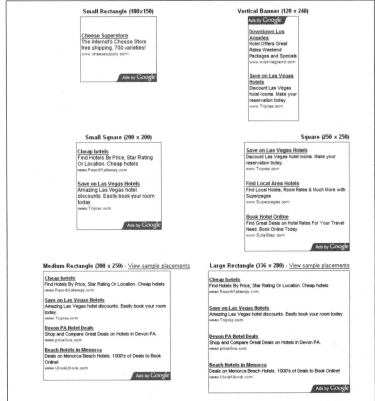

Figure 5-14:
The square and rectangular ads are the most versatile text ads that AdSense provides.

Image ads

I have this feeling that image ads are what you probably think of when you think "Ah, yes, Web advertisements!" You have your nice image and your pithy text, just like the banner ads I mention earlier in the chapter. And, as is the case with banner ads, everyone has them and everyone ignores them. Does that mean you shouldn't use image ads? Not necessarily. Just don't expect them to generate as much income as text ads do.

Image ads include pictures or other images that can be very eye-catching, like the ad shown in Figure 5-15. No mistaking it for anything else; you know at a glance that it's an ad.

Now, there's nothing inherently wrong with visitors knowing that your ads are in fact, ads. Most users will recognize all kinds of AdSense ads for what they are. However, visitors really do tend to hold a grudge against image ads of all kinds, so the better you can blend them into the content of your site, the less likely they'll be ignored.

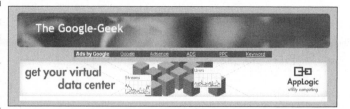

Fortunately, there are several different sizes of image ads that you can add to your page. Table 5-2 gives you a quick overview of those sizes and how they're best used. (If you notice some similarities with Table 5-1, your eyes aren't playing a trick with you. The formats are pretty much the same.)

Table 5-2	AdSense Image Ad Formats	
Format	*Ad Size*	*Placement*
Leaderboard	728x90	Top of the page
Banner	468x60	Top or bottom of the page, in between articles or blog posts
Skyscraper	120x600	Right or left side of the page
Wide skyscraper	160x600	Right side of the page
Small square	200x200	In sidebars, on the right or left of the page
Square	250x250	In sidebars, on the right or left of the page
Medium rectangle	300x250	In the text of an article or a blog post
Large rectangle	336x280	In the text of an article or a blog post

Image ads, like text ads, need to blend into the surrounding elements of your page as much as possible. You don't want to make them invisible — if that's your goal, you might as well not put any ads on your site. If you can make them appear as if they belong on your page, your site visitors will be less likely to shun them completely.

For horizontal placement, the leaderboard and banner ads are your best options. These ads, as shown in Figure 5-16, work well at the top of pages, usually directly below your page header, or between articles or blog posts.

The thing to remember with these horizontally oriented ads is that they have to be really great ads that work really well on your pages, or users will ignore them for the most part. It might take some tweaking to get the ad just right for your page. If you have a choice, text ads are probably the better option. Save the image ads for other areas on your Web site.

Figure 5-16:
Leader-
board and
banner
ads are the
horizontal
offerings for
images.

The next set of image ads — the skyscrapers — are also likely to be ignored if not integrated well into your site. Such ads, as shown in Figure 5-17, are best suited to the edges (the right and left sidebars) of your pages. And much like the text ads, the wide skyscraper is always better suited to the right side of the page.

As for square and rectangular ads, they work best embedded in (or surrounded by) the text on your page. These ads, when placed in the text and matched to the color palette of your Web site, can actually look like they belong with the article or blog post. When they look like they belong, that's when visitors' old aversions to image ads are less likely to rear their ugly heads.

Figure 5-17:
The image
skyscraper
ads are best
placed just
like text ads,
on either
side of the
page.

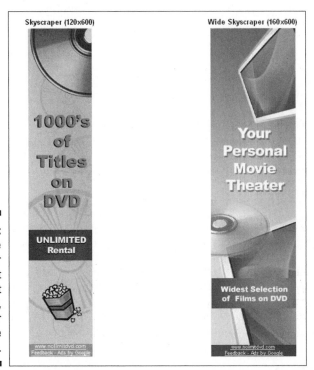

The square and rectangle ads you see in Figure 5-18 are the least evil of the image ads. Test a few of them in your text and see how they work for you. If they don't do well, you can always switch back to text ads.

Video ads

Video ads are one of the newest additions to the AdSense family. Technically, though, the ad is *not* the video. Yes, videos are streamed for advertising partners that have YouTube accounts, but the actual ads are displayed in the video player that's embedded in your content, not in the video itself. To see what I mean, check out Figure 5-19.

The formats available for video units include

✔ Leaderboard

✔ Skyscraper

✔ Wide skyscraper

✔ Small square

✔ Square

✔ Rectangle

✔ Large rectangle

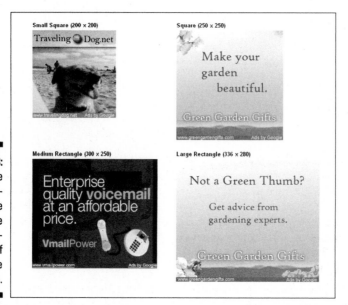

Figure 5-18: The square and rectangle image ads are the most visitor-friendly of the image ad group.

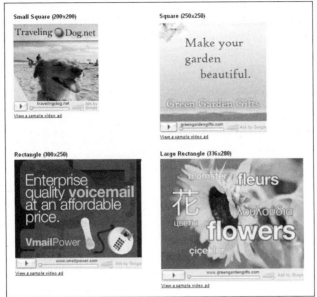

Figure 5-19:
Video ads
stream
videos from
sponsors'
YouTube
accounts
and include
links to the
sponsor.

I won't subject you to another table because the size and placement of these ads are the same as the size and placement of the image and text ads shown in the earlier tables in this chapter.

When a site visitor clicks the video player, the content from the advertiser's YouTube account is shown, along with a link to his site. The video player also becomes a large graphical link when the video is finished playing.

For you to get paid, your site visitors must click through the video player to the advertiser's site. It'd be nice if these types of ads were shown on an *impression only basis* — you'd get paid each time someone viewed the video — but that's not the case. The click actually has to happen.

That doesn't mean video ads aren't good for your site. Today's Internet users love video content. If the content of the video units on your site isn't too *advertise-y,* you may find that these units are good for your AdSense income. Of course, that also depends on how well they work with your Web site content. Test them to see how they perform. If you don't like the results, you can always go back to image or text ads.

Link units

Probably the second most used ad type in the AdSense program (after text ads) is the link unit. Link units are very cool because — when used properly — you can make them look like they belong on your page, so users are more likely to click them.

Making a link unit look like it belongs on your page is pretty simple. You adjust the template colors of the ad to match the template colors of your page. Then, when the link units are displayed on your page, they look like links that are related to the content of the page.

Link units come in several sizes, as detailed in Table 5-3. (In the table, you see some ad sizes followed by the number 4. This indicates there are four links in that ad display. All others have five links displayed within the ad.)

Table 5-3	Link Units Ad Formats	
Size	*Number of Links*	*Best Placements*
120x90	Up to five links	Sidebars
120x90_4	Up to four links	Sidebars
160x90	Up to five links	Sidebars
160x90_4	Up to four links	Sidebars
180x90	Up to five links	Sidebars
180x90_4	Up to four links	Sidebars
200x90	Up to five links	Sidebars
200x90_4	Up to four links	Sidebars
468x15	Up to five links	Top and bottom of the page, between articles and blog posts
468x15_4	Up to four links	Top and bottom of the page, between articles and blog posts
728x15	Up to five links	Top and bottom of the page, between articles and blog posts
728x15_4	Up to four links	Top and bottom of the page, between articles and blog posts

Although there are several sizes of link units, there really are only two types — vertical and horizontal.

Vertical link units are best used in the sidebars of your page. Use them at the top or bottom, before or after any set of links that you might have in your sidebar. The ads, as shown in Figure 5-20, work well when matched or blended with your template colors. In essence, users think those links belong with the links surrounding them, and they're more likely to click those ads than most other ads.

Several different sizes of vertical link units make it easier to integrate them into the sidebars on your Web site. When you tweak colors with the color pallets provided by Google, you can make them appear as if they're an intentional part of your site design.

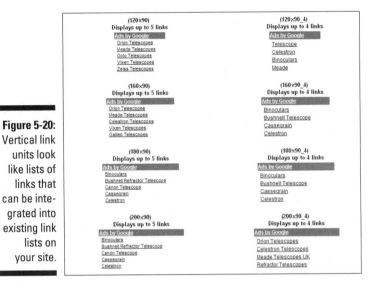

Figure 5-20:
Vertical link units look like lists of links that can be integrated into existing link lists on your site.

The horizontally oriented link units, as shown in Figure 5-21, work essentially the same way — they just work better on the top and bottom of your pages, and between articles and blog posts. Like the vertically oriented link units, tweak the colors of these, and they'll blend well on your Web site. The key is to make them look like they belong.

As with everything good, there has to be a catch. Link units are great to blend in with your Web site, and they look less like advertisements than anything that's available in the AdSense program. But here's the rub — with link units, site visitors have to click *twice* before you get paid. They must first click a link within the link unit, which takes them to a page that looks very much like a search results page. The real difference is that the results shown on the page that the link unit leads to are all advertisements. For you to get paid, users must click through one of the links on the results page.

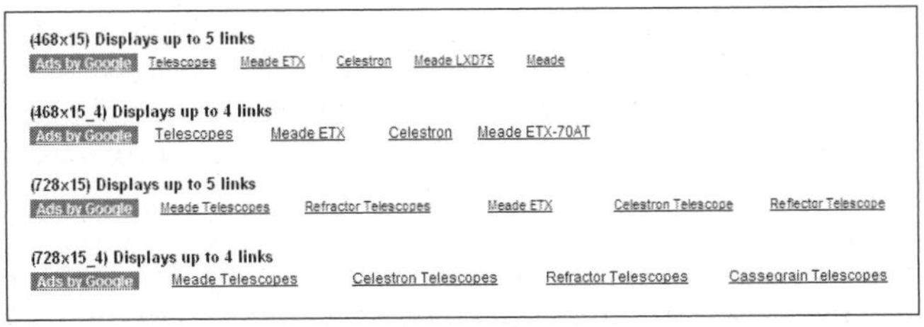

Figure 5-21:
Horizontal link units work well on the top and bottom of pages, and between articles or blog posts.

Here's the trade-off, though. If users are inclined to click through the links on the results page, it's also likely that they'll click through more than one of those results, meaning you *could* get paid for more than one click.

With link units, they either work really well or they bomb completely. The only way to know is to test link units on your site and see how they perform for you. Try different configurations and locations. If they're going to work, you'll find your sweet spot. All you have to do is watch the change adding up.

Referral buttons

One last type of AdSense ad that you should consider is the referral button. These ads, shown in Figure 5-22, are small buttons that refer site visitors to a sponsored program.

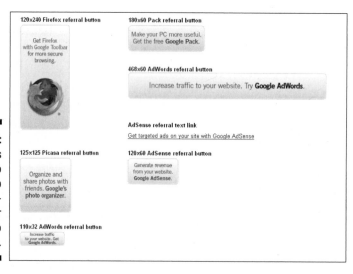

Figure 5-22:
Referral ads allow you to choose up to 15 companies or products to endorse.

The ads shown in Figure 5-22 show specific types of programs, such as Google Pack, AdSense, and AdWords, but Google has referral buttons from hundreds of different advertisers that want you to endorse their products.

All the referral ads are basically the same, with the exception of the text link variety. The text link referral ad is literally a line of text that displays a referral. You can place this text link anywhere in your content. The remaining ads are all buttons of various sizes:

- 120x240
- 180x60
- 468x60
- 120x60
- 125x125
- 110x32

When you're setting up your referral button ads, you can select up to 15 different ads to rotate through the referral button. So, if you choose to use a 125x125 square referral button, you can have referrals from up to 15 different advertisers. That doesn't mean you have to choose 15 companies to refer visitors to. You can select just 1, 5, or 12 if you like — whatever works best for your site.

As an added bonus, with referral button ads, you get to choose exactly the companies that you want to show referrals for. You're not surprised by an ad from a competitor or a company you're not willing to endorse.

When you're making the selections for your referral ads, you can browse the different categories of vendors and even look at the products and URLs that you'll be supporting. Referral values are also listed next to each product, so you'll have a ballpark figure of how much you're paid for each referral.

Themed ads

Themed units are basically text ads that have a specific theme. Google offers these around holiday times, and they just appear in your ad structure. You don't have to do anything special to use themed units — they're automatically enabled in your ads when you set up your AdSense account.

You'll find themes that surround the various major holidays on your calendar. How themed ads work varies from the way that text ads work, however. The theme makes it obvious that an ad is an ad, unless you've changed your whole site to reflect the holiday theme.

If you're into decorating for the holidays, you might consider using themed ad units. If your site stays the same (appearance-wise) day in and day out, it's probably best if you just avoid the themed unit altogether.

If you decide you'd rather not have the themed advertisements showing on your Web site, you can disable themed ads (they're enabled by default) using these steps:

1. **Point your browser to** www.adsense.com **and log on to your AdSense account.**

2. **Click the My Account tab.**

   You should be automatically taken to your Account Settings page. If not, click Account Settings in the link strip below the tabs.

3. **Scroll down the page to the Ad Type Preference section, as shown in Figure 5-23, and then click the Edit link, next to the Ad Type Preference heading.**

   You're taken to the Ad Type Preference page.

4. **On the Ad Type Preference page, as shown in Figure 5-24, select the Display Text Ads Only in All Ad Units option.**

5. **Click the Save Changes button.**

That's it. Themed ad units are disabled and won't show during holiday periods. Of course, neither will any other kind of picture ad, so you have to decide whether you want text only or if you're okay with themed units on occasion.

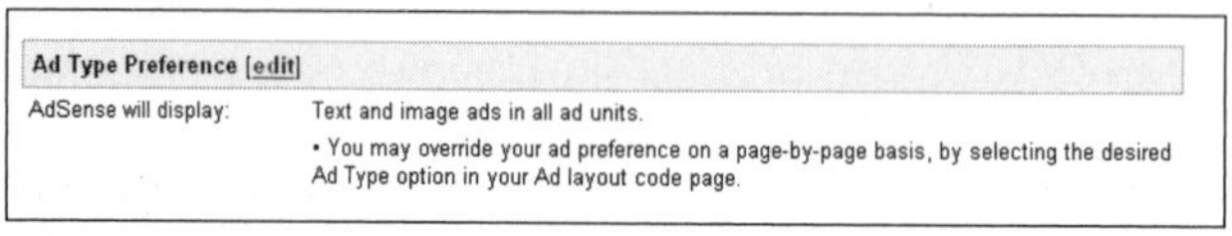

Figure 5-23:
Click the
Edit link
next to the
Ad Type
Preference
heading.

Ad Type Preference [edit]

AdSense will display: Text and image ads in all ad units.
                            • You may override your ad preference on a page-by-page basis, by selecting the desired
                            Ad Type option in your Ad layout code page.

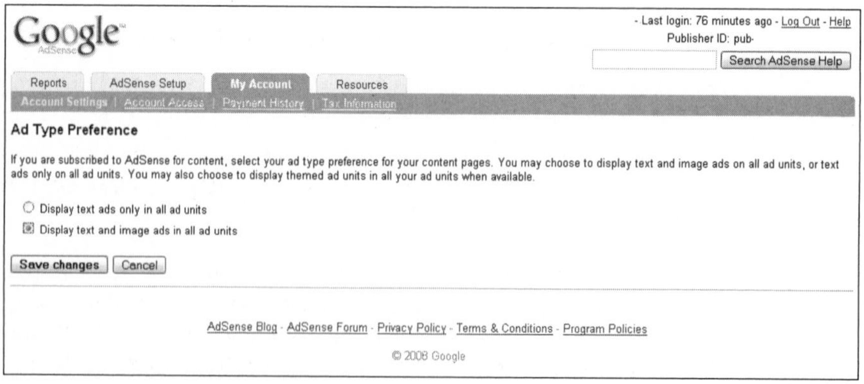

Figure 5-24:
To disable
themed ads,
change your
Ad Type
Preference
to text only.

Google
AdSense

- Last login: 76 minutes ago - Log Out - Help
Publisher ID: pub-

Search AdSense Help

Reports | AdSense Setup | My Account | Resources
Account Settings | Account Access | Payment History | Tax Information

Ad Type Preference

If you are subscribed to AdSense for content, select your ad type preference for your content pages. You may choose to display text and image ads on all ad units, or text ads only on all ad units. You may also choose to display themed ad units in all your ad units when available.

○ Display text ads only in all ad units
☒ Display text and image ads in all ad units

Save changes   Cancel

AdSense Blog · AdSense Forum · Privacy Policy · Terms & Conditions · Program Policies

© 2008 Google

With any of the AdSense formats, only half the art is knowing what ad to place where. The other half is knowing how to format your ads to make them more appealing to site visitors. Because the name of the game is garnering clicks on your ads, you want them to appeal to site visitors — the color, style, *and* placement should all entice the visitor to click the ad. So, there's way more to it than just placement. The fine details make all the difference, and those details are covered in Chapter 7.

Generating Other Types of Ad Code

Okay, if you've followed along in this chapter, you now have a better grasp of the kinds of ad formats AdSense makes available to you. And, if you were really good and read the opening section in this chapter, you know all about generating the code for search boxes on your Web site. Generating the code for other types of AdSense ads works pretty much the same:

1. **Point your browser to** www.adsense.com **and log on to your AdSense account.**

2. **Select the AdSense Setup tab.**

3. **Choose the type of ad that you want to have on your site — content ads for text, search boxes to allow visitors to search, or video ads if you use video on your site.**

4. **Select the ad size you want to have displayed.**

5. **Customize the ad to work on your Web site, using the color and display customization options I show you in Chapters 3 and 4, as well as earlier in this chapter.**

6. **Select the *channel* — the tracking information — you want to use for the ad.**

7. **Click Submit and Get Code to generate the code for the ad.**

8. **After your code has been generated, copy and paste the ad code into the HTML on your Web site.**

   Don't worry if you're not quite sure where to put the code. The next section, "Code Placement for Optimum Traffic," contains all the details you need.

That's it. The AdSense wizard walks you through making all the selections that you need to generate the code. Then all you have to do is copy and paste it into the HTML of your Web site. Of course, copying and pasting the code isn't as easy as it sounds. If it were, there wouldn't be a dozen or more books about improving your AdSense income.

Code Placement for Optimum Traffic

You're now in a position where you understand ad formats and you can generate the ad code. Does that mean you're all set? Far from it. You still need to figure out precisely where to put all that nice HTML code you've just generated on your page and watch the dollars ad up.

In Chapter 2, I point you to the AdSense help pages for information on code placement. If you made your way through those pages, you may already know where to put your code, but if you're like me, you haven't made it over there yet, so you're still clueless. No worries. I help you get up to speed right now.

Getting code where you want it

How you place the AdSense code on your site depends on how you're accessing the HTML for your Web site. There are two basic ways to do it:

- ✔ **Using a WYSIWIG (what you see is what you get) HTML editor:** If that's your weapon of choice, be sure to switch from Design view to HTML view.

- ✔ **Using an HTML Insert capability:** If your Web site design software application offers an HTML Insert feature, all you have to do is paste the HTML into the window provided and click OK.

In both cases, when you view your Web site (or preview your Web site), the ad should appear. Of course, it's a little more complicated than that because you need to know exactly where to paste the code.

If you're using the HTML editor, you'll have to navigate your way through your HTML code. One major landmark to look for involves the <body> tags on your Web site. You may remember from Chapter 4 that a very scaled down version of your HTML might look something like this:

```
<Head>
<Title>Your Web Site Title Goes Here</Title>
<Meta name="description" content="Include a quick keyword-
        rich blurb about your site here.">
<Meta name="keywords" content="enter keywords here,
        separated by commas">
</Head>
```

After the heading of your Web site comes the body. That looks like this:

```
<HTML>
<Head>
<Title>Your Web Site Title Goes Here</Title>
</Head>
<Body>
The body of your Web site goes here.>
</Body>
```

It's between those body tags that the code for your AdSense ads should be placed. If the code doesn't appear between those body tags, the ads won't show up on your Web site.

Now, if you go back and look at the source code for any given Web site (remember, you do this by choosing View➪Source or View➪View Source Web from your browser's main menu), you see that there's a whole lot of gobble-dygook between the body tags. Basically everything that you see on your site below the header and above the footer will appear in there somewhere.

Knowing where in that jumble of code to paste your AdSense code makes all the difference in the world. It takes a little bit of trial and error to get the code in the right place if you're not an HTML guru.

If you read through the HTML (don't panic, after you focus on it for a few minutes, you begin to see the patterns that translate into a Web site), you'll start to see common tags, like `<div>` (which means *division*) and `<table>` (which indicates the beginning of a table).

As you begin to see the patterns in your code, you also begin to recognize where you want to paste the code. For example, if you're pasting the code for a leaderboard-sized link unit into your page, you want to paste it immediately following the opening body tag (`<body>`). This ensures that the ad gets placed at the top of the page.

To paste a rectangle text ad into the beginning of an article, paste it immediately before the first word of the article. And if you want to place an ad in a sidebar, place it after the `division` tag for the sidebar.

It's only slightly different if you're using a Web design program that allows you to insert snippets of HTML into your site design. If that's the kind of program you're using, place your cursor or pointer at the place on the page where you want the HTML snippet to appear, and then select the HTML Insert command from the main menu. In the window that appears, paste in the code and then click OK. You can then drag or resize the section that contains the HTML code until it's in the exact location where you want it displayed.

When installing the HTML code onto your site, remember that location is everything. Review the placements that I share with you earlier in the chapter and try them to see how they work for you. Of course, don't let those guidelines become your prison, either. Test different sizes, colors, and locations until you find the combination that suits your site the best and draws the most clicks.

Resisting the urge to change the code

When you're installing your AdSense code, one of the most important things to remember is that you can't change the AdSense code in any way. You can't add to it, take away from it, or otherwise change it. Period. It's not only against the AdSense policies, but it could also render the code useless.

When Google generates code for you to use as a display on your site, there are some very important elements in that code. Among those elements is your user ID as well as information that tells Google what ads to display on your site.

If you start messing with the code, Google might not recognize it and ads won't be pushed out to it. Or worse, ads that are completely irrelevant to your site might be pushed out. At least until Google figures out you monkeyed with the code — and then you could be banned from the AdSense program altogether.

So don't *ever* mess with the AdSense code. Copy it; paste it; forget it.

Blocking Ads from Your Competitors

One last tidbit before I wash my hands of this chapter completely: competition. Everyone hates it, but it's what makes it possible for you to have that AdSense revenue stream. Still, you may decide that you don't like the idea of having your competitors' ads show up on your site. You can stop that, you know.

The Competitive Ad filter allows you to specify the URLs of sites for which you don't want ads shown. You have a couple options, too. You can filter broad URLs, like an entire site, or you can filter specific pages within a site.

To filter broad URLs, follow these steps:

1. **Point your browser to** `www.adsense.com` **and log on to your AdSense account.**

2. **Click the AdSense Setup tab and select Competitive Ad Filter from the row of links below the tab.**

   A new page loads (as shown in Figure 5-25) that contains a form you can use to block your competitors' ads.

3. **In the space provided, enter the URL of the Web site that you want to block.**

   For example, you could use the broad URL `http://www.competitor.com`. Enter one URL per line.

4. **When you finish listing the URLs of the competition you want blocked, click Save Changes.**

   You're done — although it could take up to a couple of hours for ads from the URLs you've blocked to stop showing on your site.

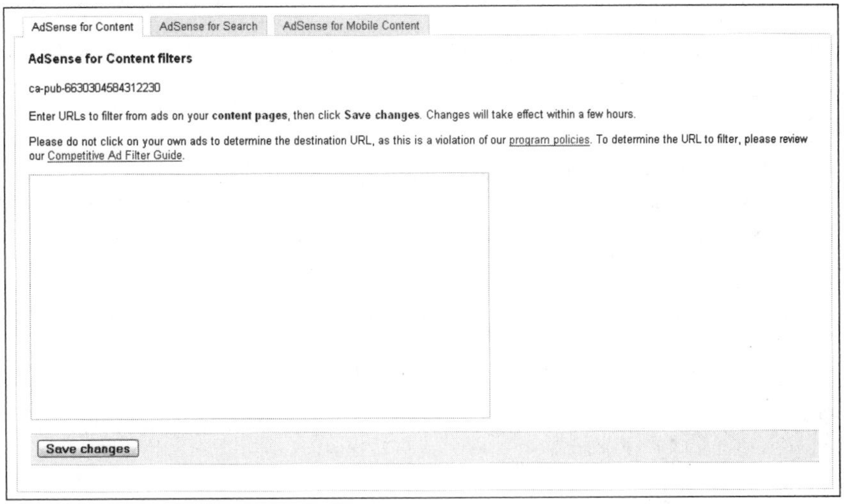

Figure 5-25:
Enter competitors' URLs into the form to block their ads from displaying on your Web site.

AdSense for Content	AdSense for Search	AdSense for Mobile Content

AdSense for Content filters

ca-pub-6630304584312230

Enter URLs to filter from ads on your **content pages**, then click **Save changes**. Changes will take effect within a few hours.

Please do not click on your own ads to determine the destination URL, as this is a violation of our program policies. To determine the URL to filter, please review our Competitive Ad Filter Guide.

[Save changes]

If you use a broad URL, like the one in the steps above, every page with that base URL will be blocked. If there are only certain pages that you want to have blocked, you can enter a more specific URL for that site. So, for example, if there's a single product page on your competitor's site that you want blocked, you could enter the URL for that product page only. It might look something like this: `http://www.competitor.com/product/product1.htm`.

The more specific the URL, the less you're blocking.

If you want to target a specific ad to be blocked from your site, wait until the ad shows up, right click it, and then select Copy Shortcut or Copy Link Location from the contextual menu that appears. Then paste that URL into a text editor and look for the link within the link.

Here's what I mean: When you right-click the ad and copy the link, you're copying both Google's location and the link that the ad leads to. It might look something like this when you paste it:

```
http://www.googleadservices.com/pagead/
         adclick?adurl=http://www.blogger.com/
         signup.g&sa=
```

If you look closely at that URL, you see that there are actually two sets of http://. The first, at the beginning of the URL, points to Google Ad Services. That's the URL that's serving up the ad. The second one (after the equal sign) points to http://www.blogger.com/signup.g&sa. *That* is the URL that you want to paste into your competitive filter because it's the actual URL for your competitor.

Many Web site owners who end up publishing AdSense ads use the Competitive Ad filter to ensure that their visitors aren't sent to their competitors' sites by mistake. It's easy to use, so if you have any doubts about losing your visitors to your competition, take advantage of it.

Part II
The Major Players: AdSense for Content, AdSense for Search

The 5th Wave By Rich Tennant

"Honey – remember that pool party last summer where you showed everyone how to do the limbo in just a sombrero and a dish towel? Well, look at what the MSN Daily Video Download is."

In this part . . .

As you can tell from the title, this part of the book focuses on AdSense for Content and AdSense for Search. To help you take advantage of AdSense for Content, this part gives you all the details you need to create great content and design the perfect content ads, as well as help you build the perfect AdSense for Search box.

This part shares how to create content that visitors are looking for as well as how to design your ad to appeal to those visitors. After content is out of the way, I provide an overview of AdSense for Search and the differences between the two.

Chapter 6

Building the Right Content

I promise not to grind the content horse completely into ground meat, but content is important, so you have to put up with me as I dive into a few more content issues. I know you know that content is the cornerstone of your Web site — actually, it's great content but that's such an overused term — and you also know that there are quite a few different avenues for collecting the content that you can use to populate your site. (You know that because you're smart, and I know you're smart because you bought a *For Dummies* book.)

What I think still needs to be covered is the actual writing process, the option of hiring someone *else* to do it, and using content other than written articles and blog posts. Don't get me wrong. Written articles and blog posts are important, and you'll probably have far more written content on your site than anything else, but using video is a great option, too — especially because the occasional video helps acclimate your visitors to seeing video on your site. Then you can use AdSense video ads once in a while, too.

One more thing. What do you do with all that content after you find it, write it, or purchase it? Keeping content fresh can be a full-time job if you have a site that's more than a few dozen pages in size. Think of those sites that have hundreds or even thousands of pages. Keeping that content interesting and new is a nightmare endeavor!

Well, it is unless you have some method to tame that monster, and taming methods do exist. It's just a matter of finding the one that works best with the plans that you have in mind.

So, yeah, I've already talked about content, but there's still plenty to cover, so bear with me just a little longer, okay?

Foundations for Great Content

Great content — what a terrible, horrible phrase. What, exactly, constitutes great content? Isn't "great" content kind of like a college (or a high school) literature course? Remember those? You go to this class, and the instructor thrusts a book at you and says, "You must read this and tell me what it means."

Great. I would read those books, but the meaning I found was never the same as the meaning the instructor found in them. I always got so-so grades in literature because of it, and I still don't understand. Who is that instructor to tell me what that writer was thinking when he or she wrote that piece of literature? Was the instructor sitting on the writer's shoulder during the writing process? Or maybe the writer dialed up the future and asked the instructor for direction on what should be written? Not likely.

Literature is subjective — as is content. What I think is great content might absolutely drive the next visitor to your site completely insane. He could find the article boring or lively, instructing or condescending. Every person interprets what's put before them differently.

That doesn't mean that great content can't be achieved, though. It's more accurate to call it appealing content — your content should *appeal* to the majority of visitors that land on that page. The truth is you can't purchase, steal, borrow, or copy anything that will appeal to everyone. What you have to shoot for is content that appeals to the majority, and there are some guidelines for writing to the majority of people that will land on any one of your pages.

Knowing your audience

Before you can put anything on paper (or on-screen as is the case here), you have to know who you're addressing. If you've done any targeting research on your Web site, you already have some of this information. If you haven't, you'd better get to it. The only way you'll ever reach your audience in the first place is to have a Web site that's well targeted to them.

Here's an example: Say you own the Web site Greenparenting.com (in real life, the site actually forwards to GreenForGood.com, but we're talking hypothetical here). Just looking at the name for that site, you automatically know that the site should be targeted to parents who are environmentally responsible. Now, what you need to know is who those people are.

If you know your industry, you can do a little research and find out that the people who would be interested in green parenting are probably upper-middle class adults in their late 20s to early 50s. These are people who fall into the parenting age. Being environmentally friendly isn't cheap, so a decent income is required to be truly dedicated.

Now you have a profile. Your site visitors have these characteristics:

- ✔ They're parents.
- ✔ They're in their late 20s to early 50s.
- ✔ They have a household income of $75,000 or more.
- ✔ They're concerned about the environment.

As you're reading through those few facts, you should already have a picture of these Web site visitors in your mind. If you haven't done the spadework necessary to come up with a picture of a typical visitor to your own Web site, do it now. You can't accurately target anything on your Web site until you know who you're serving. That includes creating content that your visitors are looking for and that they want to read.

Language considerations

The language that you use in your content can be addressed on a couple different levels. First, is the *what language do most of your readers speak* level. Obviously, this level is completely out of your control. It makes no sense at all to create content for your site in English if most of your visitors are Japanese.

If you have any doubts at all about the native language of your visitors, look at your analytics software. Most analytics packages have some element of tracking visitors based on their language. In Google Analytics (which I highly recommend because it's very user-friendly and FREE!), the actual report is in with a group of reports that segment users according to differing characteristics, such as language location.

A language report tells you the native language of each of your site visitors based on what's set as the default language in their Web browser.

A different aspect of language is the words that you actually use to communicate with your visitors. I can quote you all kinds of facts about how the average person reads at an 8th-grade level or how readers perceive words on a screen differently than how they perceive words on a page — all that is true. What's more important to understand about the language that you use to communicate with your visitors is that it should be *familiar* to them.

Jargon (those words that are inevitably coined for every topic on the planet; really, every topic can be explained with jargon) isn't familiar. For example, *analytics* is actually jargon. It's used to mean Web site traffic statistics. Analytics is actually a derivative of the word *analyze,* which means to examine critically. So, by definition then, analytics would be the science of analyzing. Yet, I use it most frequently when associated to Web site traffic statistics.

Understanding visitors with Google Analytics

Google Analytics is Google's free Web site traffic analytics program. It's easy to use and provides a wealth of information about the visitors to your site, so don't let its dry-as-dust name scare you away from using it. Detailed coverage of Google Analytics is in Chapter 14, including where to get the application and how to make it work with your Web site, but I thought you might like to know a little more about it right now.

Google Analytics, which started life as *Urchin Analytics* — a program that wasn't free — offers nearly 50 standardized analytics reports as well as reports that you can customize, all of which tell you about the visitors to your site. As a free program, it's one way for you to find out more about your site visitors without having to spend a tidy sum on the insight that an audience research firm will cost you.

Broadly speaking, Google Analytics offers you reports in four different areas: Visitors, Traffic Sources, Content, and Goals. The neat thing about Analytics from an AdSense perspective is

that it features reports that are AdWords-specific (very handy, that) and reports that apply very specifically to any SiteSearch capabilities enabled on your site (including those capabilities that you may have enabled through AdSense).

Installing and using Google Analytics is simple and doesn't require a technology degree. It takes about an hour to set up an account and paste the provided code into the HTML on your Web site. After you place the code on your site, it should take a couple days to start seeing statistics. And after you collect statistics for about a month, you can begin seeing patterns in how your site visitors use your site.

Google Analytics may well be the secret weapon that you never knew you needed. At worst, it tells you more about your site visitors than you could ever gather with your AdSense reports alone. At best, you'll find out enough about your users to begin understanding what they're looking for and how you can provide it for them.

The problem with jargon is that if you stay immersed in a subject long enough, it becomes part of your normal speech and thought patterns. Unfortunately, that might not be true for your Web site visitors.

If you place an article or blog post on your Web site that's full of jargon and your site visitors don't view that jargon from the same perspective as you, they'll get frustrated very quickly. Visitors don't want to struggle through articles and blog posts filled with terms that seem to be used as part of some coded language. (BBC World War II Upper Class Twit Announcer Voice: "The geese are carrying the potatoes over the vicar's pond. I repeat: The geese are carrying the potatoes over the vicar's pond.") They want to skim your stuff, pluck out the information they need like the ripest and sweetest grapes, and move on. Jargon slows them down, so don't use it.

If you do find that jargon is necessary in your content, be sure to explain what it means the first time it appears in any article or blog post. The idea is to make your content as easy to read as possible without being overly simplistic. This is where it gets a little tricky.

If you're too simplistic in the language that you use in your content, most readers are turned off. I find it's usually best to choose one person that represents your audience and write your content so that person can understand it. For me, it's my best friend, who happens to be a serious technophobe while at the same time being one of the most intelligent people I know. I write with her in mind, phrasing things in such a way that I don't insult her intelligence and yet get the fundamentals of (an at times rather complicated) technology across.

If I can write about technology at a level that she understands but that doesn't grate on her nerves, I count myself successful. Use the same trick with your site visitors. Think of someone you know who represents your readers, assume his or her knowledge of your topic isn't as deep as your own, and then write to that person. If necessary, you can even ask that person to read what you've written the first few times. If he has questions, he'll ask. If he understands it and the language doesn't annoy him, you know you're on the right track.

Getting Fresh with Content

Here's a simple exercise for you. Do a quick search on Google for whatever topic interests you. It doesn't matter what the topic is, just pick something. When the search results come in, click through 20 or so of the results and make note of what you see. How many times does the same article or group of articles appear in those search results?

I bet it's more than once. I research a lot of topics on the Web, and the one thing that I've noticed in nearly every topic is that the same articles appear over and over again. It's a phenomenon that happens both in print and on the Internet, but it's far more noticeable on the Internet because information is just a Web search away. In print, you actually have to collect the books and newspapers together in one place to notice the patterns.

Everyone uses the same articles. Well, okay. Maybe not everyone, but a lot of people do. It's *content syndication* (or *article syndication*), and sometimes it happens on purpose — writers work hard to get their articles and stories syndicated and books published because that's how they reach wider audiences. Sometimes it happens accidentally though — an article is placed online (it's less likely to happen accidentally in print), and other Web site owners find it, like it, and either with permission or without, copy it and use it on their own Web sites.

Another reason you see the same article everywhere is because companies exist that sell packages of pre-made Web pages or even just packages of articles that you can place on your Web site that are targeted around a specific keyword or topic. These packages are sold both on Web sites and on auction sites like eBay, and they're available to everyone — and I *do* mean everyone.

The problem with that kind of content is that although it's easy to find and for the most part inexpensive to purchase, it's old. It's so old it's bleu-cheese moldy — which is precisely why you find it everywhere. Nothing's more frustrating to someone than clicking through a bunch of links looking for information just to find that one-third of those links all lead to the same article on a different Web site.

If you truly want to generate traffic volume for your Web site (and you do, because the more traffic you have, the more AdSense revenue you generate), fresh content is what you need. Fresh content is new, different, and doesn't show up on 5,000 different Web sites. It's your own content that you've written or had written for your specific audience to meet their exact needs.

Your Web site visitors will love you for it. Potential Web site visitors are more likely to stay on your site, reading your articles, viewing your other types of content, and eventually clicking your AdSense ads if you're offering them content they can't find elsewhere. The only place to get that kind of content is to either write it yourself or hire someone to write it for you.

Article Wrangling

Folks who want to take the easy way out when populating their Web sites with content snatch up as many reprint articles as they can. (*Reprint articles* refer to that small pool of articles that gets replicated out onto a gazillion Web sites, kind of like that Agent Smith guy in *The Matrix.*) You can get reprint articles anywhere. A ton of content syndicates are online where you can purchase articles for a few dollars, but so can everyone else.

You can even use *public domain works* — those written articles and books for which copyright has expired and thus have slipped back into the public domain. You can publish them without the permission of the author, but again, so can everyone else.

If you want truly original content, you have to do it the hard way — you have to write it or hire someone else to write it.

Creating original content

Writing your own articles and blog posts isn't as hard as it sounds unless you have hundreds of Web pages to populate, which could become a very time-consuming effort. If that's the case, you'll have to use *some* reprints, but it's still best if you try to keep the most important pages on your site filled with original content.

Selecting the best fonts

The whole issue of fonts can be a little confusing, especially when you begin to listen to the *experts* on the topic. It seems that every expert has a different opinion on what's best to use on the Internet.

Fonts come in two flavors: serif fonts and sans serif fonts. *Serif fonts* have small strokes that lead into a letter; *sans serif fonts* don't. There's a lot of debate as to which is easier to read both online and in print. The fact is, though, that there's really no easy answer to that question because other factors — spacing, font size, and screen resolution — also make a difference in what works and what doesn't.

The most common serif fonts that you find online are Times New Roman and Georgia. The most common sans serif fonts online are Arial and Verdana. Which ones are best? Consensus is that Verdana is one of the best fonts to use for Web pages because of the spacing of the font and the design of the letters. However, you'll find that many Web sites also use Times New Roman and Arial.

Personally, I use Arial in a lot of the work I do online, simply because it's a more appealing font to me. Verdana is my second choice. When you get below a 10-point font (the size of the font), Arial becomes very difficult to read because the letters are so closely spaced.

Choose the font you use on your site based on the layout of the site and the needs of your visitors. Obviously, you want to appeal to the largest audience possible, so common wisdom is that you should use the font best suited to as many people as possible — Verdana.

One thing is certain, however. Whatever you do, don't use a crazy font like Vladimir Script or Curlz MT just because you think it looks neat. Those fonts are very difficult to read. Because reading on-screen is already harder on their eyes than reading from a printed page, you want to make it as easy as possible for your visitors to get through an entire article (or even several articles) on your Web site.

Coming up with ideas for your original content isn't too difficult. If you don't already have a list of ideas based on what you know your visitors are looking for, spend about an hour brainstorming some ideas. You won't use them all, and some of them will be just plain silly, but you'll come up with some good ideas. Here's a secret every writer knows: The more you write, the more ideas you have.

When it's time to actually write the articles for your Web site, a few basic principles should be applied. These principles help make it easy for your site visitors to read your articles. The short list looks like this:

✔ **Article layout:** The experience of reading on-screen is very different from reading on paper. On-screen, it's much easier to get lost. Eye strain is also much more common when you focus on a computer screen for too long. Computer screens have an invisible bar that scrolls across the screen refreshing the image constantly. If you've ever seen a computer on TV that has a black line scrolling through it, that's what I'm talking about.

You don't *see* this line because of the rate that it rolls across your screen, but it causes slight vision anomalies that your eyes pick up on, even though it doesn't register in your brain. These anomalies are what cause eye strain.

One way to combat eye strain is to keep your articles as sparse as possible. That doesn't mean skimping on the content but does means you need to use lots of *white space* — open space without words — and use a type font that's screen-reading friendly.

It works best when you're laying out your articles if you single space (or even use a space and a half) between each paragraph of type. Also try to keep your paragraphs short and resist the urge to pack everything, kitchen-sink style, into a single sentence. Long sentences are easy to get lost in.

Between paragraphs, use a double space. The extra white space between paragraphs gives the eyes a second to rest before moving into the new text.

✔ **Reading-friendly colors:** Color can be your best friend or your worst enemy online. The first thing to remember when dealing with Web site colors is that colors display differently on-screen than they do on paper — and colors display slightly differently on different screens. So test your colors in the *real world* — online rather than on paper. It wouldn't hurt to take a peek at your Web masterpiece from a few different computers.

The second thing to keep in mind when dealing with colors is that computers are already prone to causing eyestrain, so if you use wild colors on your Web site, that exacerbates the problem. Believe me: Nothing's worse than clicking through a link to find a Web site with a black or dark blue background and yellow type. It's hard to read and will send your readers clicking back to where they came from.

It's always better to stick with muted colors, and white or black text. Some of the most successful Web sites online have white backgrounds with black text. These combinations are not only natural, they're also eye friendly. Even a black background with white text can get tiring very quickly. So, if you absolutely insist that your Web site have broad swaths of color, try to make it something that you don't mind staring at for five to ten minutes. If you can't read a whole article in the color scheme that you choose for your site, find a different color scheme. If you don't, your visitors will go elsewhere.

✔ **Titles and headings:** Because reading is much more of a chore online, many people don't completely read everything. Those who do read everything skim a page first just to make sure it'll be worth their time to read through it. That means you need to catch your visitors' attention as quickly as possible.

The best way to do that is with your article or blog post titles and headers. Titles are the first impression you get to make with your article. They should be catchy and in a larger font than the rest of the article. It's also a good idea to make them bold to stand out.

Headings are the mini-titles that signal new sections of your article or blog post. Like titles, they should be larger than the text surrounding them (but not as large as the title size) and should be in bold type-face. This makes them both easy to skim and easier to read.

You want your headings to be catchy, but they need to be descriptive as well. It does no good at all to use a header like, "Lost in Space," when your article is about pruning your prize roses. Readers won't get it, so they won't connect the dots. A better heading might be something like "A Snip in Time."

There's an added bonus to using apt titles and headings in your articles — titles and headers are often closely examined by search engine crawlers in their ongoing attempts to correctly categorize your site. The crawler pounces on titles and headings to determine the content on your site, so be sure to fill such elements with appropriate keywords and phrases whenever possible.

✔ **Links within articles:** One last element that you should include in your articles and blog posts is links to other, related articles and blog posts, both on your Web site and on others' Web sites. Linking to other resources provides additional information for your site visitors. Usually, those visitors will click through those links and then click back to the page from which they came. If you worry about visitors clicking away from your site, never to return, set your links up so that they open in a new window. Opening links in a new window keeps your Web site open and in front of the visitors. When they're finished examining the site you've linked to, they can close the window and be right back on your Web site.

Another advantage to using links to other resources is that when you create links within your content, you're adding to your *link structure,* a facet of your Web site that search engine crawlers consider when ranking your Web site.

Think of a link structure as the framework of links that you create on your Web site. The framework includes *internal links* — those links that connect your pages within your site — and *external links,* which lead visitors away from your site. It also includes links that lead *to* your site from other pages. Although it's true that you have a little less control over how many other sites link to your site, don't underestimate the power of a little *you scratch my back and I'll scratch yours* negotiating. You can offer free articles to other Web sites that include a link back to your site, for example, or you can just exchange links with other Web sites.

The key is to keep a good balance of the links to other pages on your site and the links to other pages off your site, and work diligently to bring other links into your site from relevant sources. Links from Web pages that are unrelated are much less useful than links from relevant pages. Just remember that having too many internal links or too many external links could be more detrimental than helpful. Try to keep an even mix of internal and external links.

Creating your own content isn't difficult. It can take a little time, but when you get the hang of formatting your articles and blog posts for the Web, it goes faster, making it almost as easy as writing down your thoughts.

You'll be rewarded for putting out the effort to come up with original content. Web surfers are looking for new, original, and helpful information online. Surfers who log on to the Internet do so for many reasons, but the number-one reason stated by surfers is to find information. If the information you provide is fresh and new, you'll have more (and higher quality) visitors than would ever be possible if you were using recycled content.

Hiring someone

Some Web site owners just don't have the time to write their own content. If that's you, you don't have to lose out on the value of original content. Instead of doing it yourself, you can hire someone to do it for you.

Hiring someone, of course, means paying them. You *can* put ads on the Web for writers to produce content for your site for free, but you get what you pay for. In every case, the writer who's willing to work for free has no (or very little) experience, and many of them have no talent.

That said, exceptions to the rule do exist. Once in a while, you can find a great writer, with experience, who's willing to work for free because she loves to see her name in print. This might work out for you one-tenth of a percent of the time. The rest of the time, it's just more headache than it's worth.

You can, however, hire a writer without breaking the bank. Good writers are often willing to work for small amounts of money (say $10 to $50 per article) if the exposure is right, and if the person or company requesting the work pays quickly and consistently. It also helps when articles aren't too involved. If what you're looking for is a 1,000 word piece with three interviews, however, you're not likely to find a good writer to do it for $50. However, if you're willing to pay $200–$400, you won't have a problem finding writers.

If you *do* decide that hiring a writer is the way to go, you need to get (and give) contractual specifications in writing. Even if it's nothing more than an e-mail that states the guidelines for the article, the size of the article, the due date, and the pay, you have to have something that both you and the writer agree on. Then stick to your side of the bargain.

You may encounter writers who say they'll provide what you're looking for, but then don't. It happens, and the only way to be sure you're getting someone who won't leave you high and dry is to check references. Treat writers just as you would employees. Make sure they are who they say they are. Then, be flexible about how the writer goes about writing the article you request. As long as the article is turned in on time and meets the specifications that you set forth in the beginning, don't bug them about how they get to that point. (Unless plagiarism's involved — then you must get involved, but there's more about that near the end of this chapter.)

One other option that you have — one which could potentially cost you a lot less than hiring a writer — involves inviting guest writers to put together articles for your site. You have to use caution with this method, too, though. Guest writers sometimes write a few articles that they pass around to everyone on the Internet, which makes their contribution to your site not nearly as valuable as if they wrote the article specifically for your site.

You can ask for that specificity, though. When you approach a guest writer, nothing's wrong with asking him to write an article specifically for your site. Make sure you lay out exactly what you're looking for, though. Usually it's okay to ask for the right to publish the article first for a specified amount of time (like six months) before the writer allows others to publish it. You also want to make sure you have the right to archive the article on your Web site so that it remains available to users even after that six-month period (or however long you choose) is over.

In exchange for writing for you, most guest writers want a small blurb or link pointing back to their products and services. It's usually worth it. In fact, it's so worth it that many companies have a stable of writers that write these types of articles for them all the time. They offer these articles to all publications that target their own audiences. It saves the company marketing dollars and provides great content for your site.

One caveat when it comes to guest writers: If you plan to use a guest writer, make sure the article that's provided isn't too *sales-y*. When someone comes to your site to read an article, he doesn't come because he wants to be sold to. He comes because he's looking for information. Nothing's wrong with making a recommendation for products or services, and nothing's wrong with allowing guest writers to include a small paragraph about themselves or their products and services at the end of the article, but it still needs to be as objective as possible.

A guest writer's purpose is always to sell something. Whether that something is a product or service, there's an ulterior motive. It's your job, as the site owner, to keep that motive in check so you're not running a big advertising service. Always remember to give your visitors the information that they're looking for first and foremost. If you do, everything else is gravy.

Tapping multimedia

Content can be so much more interesting these days than it was in the past. Back in the early days of the Internet, content was stuff you wrote down. Period. There were few pictures and almost no audio or video. The adoption of broadband Internet access has changed that.

Today, in addition to your written content, you can also feature audio and video content. *Podcasting* — recording spoken messages that your site visitors can download — and streaming videos are some of the hottest technologies on the Web right now.

You do have to have some specialized equipment to create podcasts and videos, though, and it's a little more involved when it comes to placing them on your Web site so that others can download them. I don't go into the details of how to do that here. If you want additional information about creating those kinds of content, there are dozens of really good books (including *For Dummies* books like *Podcasting For Dummies,* by Tee Morris and Evo Terra) on those topics.

You don't have to create videos to have them as content on your site, though. YouTube — Google's video service — is a great way to include video content on your site. All you have to do is find videos that relate to your Web site and then you can add them to the page or to your blog by copying and pasting a snippet of code into the HTML on your site.

Multimedia content offers a little variety for your Web site. Because multimedia is the Internet darling of the moment, there's no reason not to tap into this alternative to fill out your content offerings. Anything that draws visitors to your site is a useful tool for improving your AdSense revenues.

Automating Content Management

Hundreds of Web pages on your site mean hundreds of pages of content that you have to deal with. That's a massive undertaking for even the most industrious of Web site owners. Fortunately, tools are available — known as *content management systems* — to help you manage your content without driving yourself completely into a coma, and some of them won't even make you crazy.

A content management system is a piece of software that's used for organizing and facilitating what's referred to as *the collaborative creation of documents and other content.* In other words, content management systems help you to create and manage the content on your Web site. For example, if you have a set of articles that you want to first feature on your Web site and then have moved to an archival section when a new article is featured, a content management system helps you do that without having to build a new Web page every time you change the feature articles.

The problem with content management systems is that if you get a *proprietary* system — a system built specifically to meet your content management needs — you'll pay upward of $100,000. If you fork over that amount of dough, you can rotate articles from features to archives to your heart's content and even set it up so that several people can seamlessly contribute to blogs on your site. This might all sound dandy, but just keep in mine that if you're having the system designed specifically for you, you'll shell out some serious coin to have it done.

You don't have to use a proprietary system, though. Several open source software applications for content management exist.

Open source software is software that's created by an individual or company and then shared freely with others. Others can use the software and even change it to specifically meet their needs, without having any expenses to worry about.

The only real drawback to open source content management systems is that you either have to be very knowledgeable in certain types of programming or you have to hire someone who *is* knowledgeable to take care of it for you. True, you *could* pick up some good books on the topic, but if you're not a code jockey, you'll find that the books probably leave you a little lost.

Still, if you think you can handle the challenge, Drupal is a good open source content management system, and believe it or not, so is the blogger's friend, WordPress. Okay, I know WordPress is usually thought of as being a blogging system, but it can also be used as a content management system. If you're intrigued, check out the next sections.

WordPress as a content management system

Although WordPress is primarily known as a blogging tool, it really is much more. With a few modifications — a couple plugins and custom templates — it's possible to use WordPress as a content management system. In one sense, WordPress is already a content management system because it's a blog application. All blog applications are essentially content management systems because they allow you to create, share, and store content from a single location. By modifying WordPress just a little, you can also use it for other content management functions, such as managing

- ✔ Portfolio sites
- ✔ News and magazine sites
- ✔ Article libraries
- ✔ Gallery sites
- ✔ Photologs
- ✔ E-commerce sites

WordPress site designs are based on the idea of themes. *Themes* are basically design templates that can be uploaded to your server and then assigned from within the WordPress Control Panel. The beautiful thing about templates or themes is the ability to alter them. WordPress and other blog platforms tend to use a lot of proprietary code that can be difficult to get just right when you're putting together a design template. By relying on a pre-designed template, you can focus on editing the graphics and moving snippets of code around to get the design that you want.

WordPress also has a handy little feature — *Page Management* — that allows you to create static Web pages — pages that always remain the same. You can create top-level pages that show in the navigation bar of your Web site or you can create lower-level pages that live underneath your main navigation topics. These secondary pages appear as drop-down navigation under the main links in your navigation bar.

Other features of WordPress include a built-in blog roll, which makes creating a list of related links as simple as filling out a small form to add a new listing. The best part? No HTML is required to do this. The WordPress panel also allows site owners to quickly change the appearance of their sites by switching from one theme to another as simply as selecting a new theme. WordPress does the rest.

WordPress also has plugin capabilities, meaning you can 'plug in' small additional bits of code that someone else creates to add functionality to your WordPress site. Examples of plugins are the capability to use WordPress as a content management system, or even features you can add to your WordPress blog, like a picture viewer or video player.

Plugin management is mostly seamless in WordPress, and that's where you find the real benefit of using WordPress as a content management system. Plenty of plugins are available, and there are usually detailed instructions for installing and using those plugins.

Going forward with WordPress

You don't have to be a certified geek to use WordPress as a content management system, but there is a learning curve, and it can take a while to traverse. If you want to find out more about installing and customizing WordPress to be your content management system — no matter what type of Web site you've created — check out *WordPress For Dummies,* by Lisa Sabin-Wilson and Matt Mullenweg. If you prefer getting your info right from the source, grab the WordPress Codex at http://codex.wordpress.org. The *Codex* is nothing more than a fancy name for the user manual. (If you don't know where to find it, you could spend days searching for it.)

If you're trying to populate hundreds of pages and keep the content on those pages fresh, a content management system helps you automate the process. If you don't have such a system in place, you might as well go ahead and shine up your coffin now because you'll run yourself into the grave trying to keep up.

Understanding (And Respecting) Copyright

With all these content issues floating around, it's only right to address copyright. As I mention earlier in the chapter, one of the reasons you see so many articles on the Web in dozens of different places is because those articles are placed on Web sites without the owners' permissions.

This is the epitome of copyright infringement, and it's illegal. It's the same as using a program like Napster to download music that you don't want to pay for. It's out there, but it's not ethical to use it, and it's likely that you'll eventually wind up in some serious hot water if you don't go through the proper channels to get permission to use the article.

If you write articles for your own Web site and then find them on other people's sites without your permission, you'll understand completely why copyright is such a big deal. You worked hard to put that article together, and whenever someone else puts it on their site without your permission, that person is just being a lazy so-and-so. What's more, having your article pop up on every corner of the Internet devalues your content.

So, if you're thinking about snagging someone else's articles for your Web site without her permission, forget it. It may look appealing now, but when you get hit with a lawsuit for damages, it won't be such a small deal. Writers are usually fiercely protective of the articles and stories that they right. If you're stealing it, they'll find out.

Determining copyright

Copyright infringement is a big deal, but copyright can be one of those tricky determinations that leave you wondering whether you're okay to use an article or other piece of content. The following are basic guidelines for dealing with copyright issues:

✔ For any work published prior to 1978, and marked with the proper copyright (©) notice, copyright lasted for an initial term of 28 years, renewable in the 28th year for an additional 28 years.

- ✔ With the introduction of the 1976 Copyright Act, copyright could be renewed for an additional 47 years.

- ✔ The Sonny Bono Copyright Term Extension Act of 1998 added another 67 years to that renewal period.

- ✔ If a work published prior to 1964 wasn't formally renewed, it entered the public domain when the initial 28-year term expired.

- ✔ In 1992, copyright renewal became automatic for any works published after 1963. Copyright owners after that period no longer had to apply for copyright renewal.

- ✔ When all these considerations are taken into account, if the copyright was renewed, the term of renewal was actually 75 years from the year of publication — expiring on December 31 of the 75th year following the initial publication — until the Sonny Bono act extended this to 95 years. This all means that if a work was published in 1922 or earlier, it is probably now in the public domain.

- ✔ Works that were published between 1923 and 1963 have a 95-year term, provided the copyright was formally renewed in the 28th year.

- ✔ Works published between 1964 and 1977 have a flat 95-year term.

- ✔ Works by individual authors created (meaning they just had to be written, they don't have to actually be published) after 1977 have a term of the author's life + 70 years.

- ✔ Works by corporate authors, which are usually billed as *works made for hire,* that were created after 1977 have a term of 95 years.

Determining when a work was first published can be a little tricky. If a copy is available with a copyright notice, the notice should contain the year of first publication. New editions, which are sometimes called *derivative works,* meaning they have been derived from the original, often contain notices with the year of the publication of the derivative work and not the original year of publication; but if the date is prior to 1923, you can be confident that the work in question and all its predecessors are in the public domain. Anything published after 1923 is likely still under copyright protection, so you'll have to be granted permission before using that work or part of the work.

The guidelines I lay out earlier apply both to print and electronic works. If someone's created an original piece of work that appears on the Internet, he owns the copyright on it, whether it was *officially* registered with the copyright office or not. So, when you snag articles that are floating around the Internet, you're stealing copyrighted materials. Writers can be a fiercely protective bunch. If you're stealing their work and they find out about it, expect to have some legal issues to deal with.

If the work you want to use falls into that borderline territory (originally published before 1964), you may have to do a little more research. Every year, the Copyright Office publishes a *Catalog of Copyright Entries*. This is in hard copy form for the years up to 1982 and solely in electronic form since then. The *Catalog* is online for entries since 1978. Some collegiate libraries have a copy of the *Catalog*. If yours doesn't or you don't have access to a collegiate library, you can visit the nearest Copyright Office to find a copy that you can browse to find the work in which you're interested.

The thing to remember is that even if a work was first published between 1923 and 1963, it's in the public domain unless a timely renewal application was filed with the copyright office. However, works first published between 1964 and 1977 must be assumed to be under copyright for the full 95-year period.

Requesting usage permissions

Unless you're populating your Web site with material that's turn-of-the-century old, it's a pretty good bet that you need to request permission to use a piece that's been published elsewhere. To do that, you must first determine who holds the copyright.

Most materials contain the copyright symbol (©) and then a *by* line. It usually looks something like this: © *by The Author or Owner's name and a date*. The name that follows the copyright symbol is who you need to contact to ask permission to reuse the material or portions of the material. Under the Fair Use doctrine of U.S. copyright law (specifically the Copyright Act of 1976), you're permitted to use a small portion of a work, without having to request permission *under certain circumstances*. Those circumstances, however, aren't always clearly defined. In most cases, it's up to a judge to determine if the circumstances in which you use copyrighted material are permissible.

The size of a small portion is determined by the work that you're planning to use:

- ✔ **Motion media (such as movies):** You can use up to 3 minutes, or 10 percent of the original production, whichever is less.

- ✔ **Text:** With text you're allowed to use up to 10 percent, or 1,000 words without permission, whichever is less.

- ✔ **Poetry:** Poetry is a little different. You can use entire poems, up to 250 words, no more than three poems per poet, or no more than five poems from a single anthology. If a poem is longer than 250 words, use is limited to 250 words from the selection, no more than three excerpts by a poet, or no more than five excerpts by different poets.

✔ **Music, lyrics, and music videos:** Like other forms of content, with music, lyrics, and music videos, you can use up to 10 percent of the original work — not to exceed 30 seconds in the case of video. Also note that you may not alter a work to change the basic melody or character of the work.

✔ **Illustrations and photographs:** Usage for illustrations and photographs is limited to not more than 10 percent of the total number of images on your site, or 15 images, whichever is less. No more than five images may be used from a single artist or photographer.

✔ **Numerical data sets:** You can use up to 10 percent, or 2,500 field or cell entries, whichever is less, from a copyrighted database or data table.

Even though these guidelines are provided, it's still possible to use only a small amount of a copyrighted work and to be sued for *copyright infringement* (which is using copyrighted material without proper permissions). That's because there's also a spirit of intent taken into consideration. Any judge can rule that the intent of your use of a piece of copyrighted material is unlawful, meaning you can be liable for damages if this is the case.

For that reason, you should always seek to attain permission if you plan to use any materials on your Web site that are copyrighted by another person or entity. To obtain permission to use copyrighted materials, usually all you need to do is request that permission be granted in writing. A sample letter like the one below is usually enough to legally gain permission. When you send the letter, ask that the copyright holder sign and return the letter to you, and then keep it on file in the event that any question arises in the future about whether you were granted permission.

Here's the sample letter. Customize it to include your specific information:

Date

Material Permissions Department

Copyright Owner/Company Name

Street Address

City, State Zip Code

Dear Sir/Madam:

I would like permission to use the following for *<brief description of project>*.

Title: Enter the title of the book here.

Copyright: Copyright information, including copyright date, goes on this line.

Author: Enter the author's first and last names here.

Material to be duplicated: List the exact material to be used and enclose a photocopy of the selection.

Number of Copies: List the number of copies you expect to make. If this is for inclusion in a book, list that intent and include the title, publisher, and publishing date of the book on the next line.

Distribution: List the title of the work in which the copyrighted material will be included. If it will be included in a book, include the book title, publisher, and publishing date. If the material will appear in a periodical, include the periodical details and publishing date.

Type of Reprint: List the type of reprint. This can be a complete reprint or a quoted section of the original work.

Use: Finish up with a brief description of how you intend to use the requested materials.

Please select the correct option below and then sign and return this letter in the enclosed self-addressed, stamped envelope.

Thank you for your time and consideration.

Sincerely,

You Name

__You have permission to use the copyrighted material detailed above.

__You **do not** have permission to use the copyrighted material detailed above.

Signed_____Date_____

Chapter 7

Designing the Perfect Content Ad

· ·

· ·

*J*ust in case you haven't gotten this by now — AdSense success is all about the ads. Ad design and ad placement are crucial when it comes to AdSense, but the most important thing is that your ads don't appear to be ads — as counterintuitive as that may sound.

I know; it's nearly impossible to completely remove the advertising element from AdSense ads. No matter how well you integrate the ads into your content, the Ads by Google label is still there. Even so, the more your ads look like ads, the less likely it is that site visitors will bother to click them.

That means you should integrate your ads into your site content as well as you possibly can. That's accomplished by changing the style of the ad — the text styles, colors, shapes, and borders — until the ads and your content flow together as one.

"Easier said than done," you might say, but here's where this chapter comes into play. Success with AdSense is all about knowing what works and what doesn't. By the end of this chapter, you'll have a whole slew of tips and techniques under your belt that you can use to make your AdSense strategy work for you.

Ad Appeal

You're smart, you know the score: For site visitors to even consider clicking your ads, the ads have to be appealing. The way to make those ads appealing is to integrate them into the content that's situated around them. Fortunately,

AdSense gives you some good tools for matching your ads with the surrounding content. Remember, though, that what you're creating here is just the *container* for the ad — its outside appearance. The actual ad text — or if the ad includes pictures, the images — are designed by the advertiser.

Customizing ads to work on your Web site begins when you create your ads. To create a new ad, simply log in to your AdSense account and then click AdSense Setup. From that page, select the type of ad you want to create. (If you need a refresher, the process of creating ads is covered in greater detail in Chapter 5.) In this chapter, I walk you through setting up AdSense for Content (in other words, a content ad) because it's the type of ad that you'll use most often. The principles that follow, however, work when you're designing other types of ads, as well.

Text matching

Text ads need to be just as appealing as any other kind of ad. So, the natural inclination might be to *dress up* your text ad by making the text all kinds of pretty colors. Big mistake: Dressing up your text ads only makes them look more like ads.

One of the reasons that text ads are so appealing — and certainly the main reason they perform so well when compared to the other types of ads that AdSense makes available — is because text ads can be made to blend well into your Web page. Notice my use of *can be* here — they really only blend well if they look like their surroundings.

 Keep in mind that you can't change the font styles for the ads that you build with AdSense. You can, however, change the fonts on your Web site to help blend your ads better. If there's a significant difference between the fonts of your ads and your Web site, that's just what you'll want to do.

Did I mention that making your ads appear to be part of your Web site is essential? Well, it bears repeating over and over again because this one little factor can completely change the success of your ads. Try to keep font styles similar between your ads and the text on your Web site. They don't have to be an exact match. As great as that would be, it's not always possible, especially because Google has decided not to make the font it uses in their ads available to normal mortals like us. (Okay, it kind of looks like several common fonts out there, but any *typographer* — someone who designs typefaces or fonts — will tell you that even subtle differences like spacing are very noticeable.)

Back to text design. What you *do* have control over with AdSense is the color of the text that you use for your ads. When you're creating an ad, you have several preset options for color designs as well as the ability to create your own palette of colors for your ads. The next section shows you how you can put these options to good use.

Color or camouflage?

Google provides its AdSense users with a set of preset palettes offering what Google considers your best design options for your ads. You call up these palettes using the drop-down menu in the Style area as you're creating your ads. Be aware though, that the preset palettes may or may not work on your pages — it really depends on the design of the page.

Here are the palettes that are available:

- ✔ **Default Google:** This palette includes a white background, white border, black text, blue title, and green URL.

- ✔ **Open Air:** This palette is exactly the same as the Google default. I'm not even sure why it's included in the list, but it is. It's a clone of the default — absolutely nothing's changed.

- ✔ **Seaside:** In the Seaside palette, the only change involves the border. Instead of having a white border, this palette includes a seafoam-colored (yes, seafoam is actually a color) border.

- ✔ **Shadow:** With this palette, the colors begin to get progressively more noticeable. The title (which, by the way is also a link) is still blue, the text of the ad is black, and the URL is green, but the border is black and the background is pale blue. Drop this ad onto a white background, and it screams *advertisement.*

- ✔ **Blue Mix:** This ad style is significantly different from all the other styles. A light blue border, white title, light blue text and URL, and dark blue background make this one stand out. The only page that might be able to pull this ad off is one that's designed in exactly the same colors. I recommend that you change your page if it's built like this, unless you have a very strong reason to leave it alone (like hundreds of thousands of visitors), because it's hard on the eyes.

- ✔ **Ink:** The Ink style comes with a black background and border, and a white title, text, and URL. In other words, it's similar to the Blue Mix style, but instead of being blue and white, this one is black and white. I admit it's a little easier on the eyes, but only for short periods of time.

- ✔ **Graphite:** In my opinion, this is a boring ad style because it's gray. Yuck. But on the right Web site, the black title, dark gray text, light gray URL, and pale gray background and border might work. I don't think I've ever encountered a Web site it would work on, but stranger things have happened.

These styles are the ones that Google's created. Although Google *says* they're the most effective ad styles, people who really are making great money with AdSense will tell you that the defaults aren't usually your best option. That's okay though because Google gives you decent customization features for designing ads that *are* good options.

Tweaking the wizard

I cover the AdSense wizard in some detail in Chapter 5, but there I'm more interested in showing you how to generate the HTML you need to insert a default AdSense ad in your Web site. Now I want to show you how you can stray a bit from the beaten path so that you can come up with stuff other than the default settings.

As you might expect, you start out with the very same wizard I show you in Chapter 5. Here's how you call it up:

1. **Point your browser to** www.adsense.com **and log on to your AdSense account.**

2. **Click the AdSense Setup tab.**

3. **Select AdSense for Content.**

4. **In the new screen that appears, choose the type of ad you want to create — Ad Unit, Text only, in this case — and then click the Continue button.**

   The screen you see in Figure 7-1 appears.

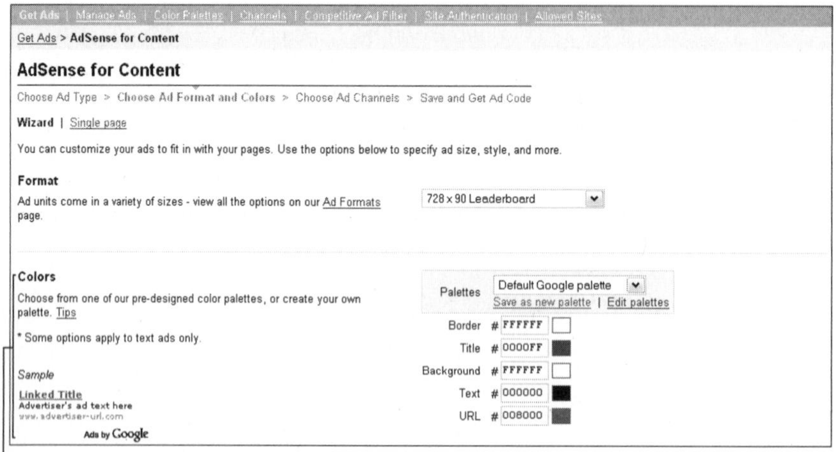

Figure 7-1:
Use the color tools to customize the appearance of your ads.

The Colors section.

5. **In the Colors section of the screen, choose one of the pre-designed color palettes from the drop-down menu on the right.**

   The Default Google palette is just as easy to work with as any other, but if you prefer one of the others over the default, that's okay.

All the colors that you can alter in the palette are shown below the palette name, as shown in Figure 7-2. Note that each color has a number to the left of it. This is the hexadecimal number that represents the color to Web browsers. (See the sidebar, "Decoding hexadecimal numbers," for more on hexadecimal numbers.)

Figure 7-2:
Google
provides a
limited number of colors
you can use
to customize
your ads.

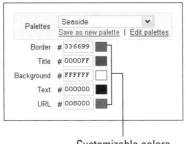

Customizable colors

6. **Use the Color Picker to the right of each ad element — Border, Title, Background, Text, and URL — to choose a new color for an element.**

As shown in Figure 7-3, when you click the *Color Picker* the nice colored square — a color palette opens from which you can choose other colors. Note that after you make the change, the sample ad in the lower-left corner of the wizard screen changes to reflect the new color.

Play with your Color Picker just a little so you can get a feel for how wild you can make your ads. I don't recommend making them wild for actual use, though. My strong advice to you will always be *the simpler, the better.* It's still kind of neat though to see how you can change your ads just by changing the color of different elements of the ad.

Click the Color Picker...

Figure 7-3:
The colors
for each
palette are
preset but
can be customized.

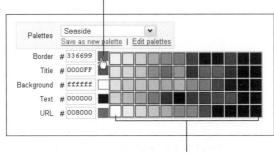

...And the color palette opens.

Here's another neat hint. If you place your pointer over one of the colors, the sample ad in the lower-left side of the screen temporarily changes to that color. Move the pointer over a different color, and the color changes again. Take it away, and the color reverts back to the original.

7. **Just below the Color Picker, use the Select Corner Style drop-down menu to specify how you want the corners of your ads to look: square, slightly rounded, or very rounded.**

   These options only actually appear on your ad if you're using a contrasting border color. If you match your border to your background, you have this option, but the corners will blend into the background like the rest of the border.

8. **Select the channel you want to use to track your ad and then click Continue.**

   Remember that channels are categories that you create so you can keep up with how specific ads perform.

9. **On the next page, enter a new name for your ad (if desired) and then click the Submit and Get Code button to generate the code for the ad.**

10. **Copy and paste the ad code generated into the HTML on your Web site.**

These steps are okay for most situations, but I admit there's one little problem with using the Color Picker to determine colors for your ad elements: Your color choices are somewhat limited. The palette that Google makes available to you shows only about 60 colors out of the hundreds that a browser can display. You're not limited to those 60, though. You can further customize your colors by entering the hexadecimal number for the color you want displayed.

"What's a hexadecimal?" you ask. I point you to the handy "Decoding hexadecimal numbers" sidebar for the full scoop, but the short answer is that *hexadecimal* numbers — the number/letter combinations you see to the left of the Color Pickers in Figure 7-2 — are part of a system for telling computer monitors how to display certain colors. Every color has been assigned a hexadecimal number, and if you enter that number into the appropriate box in Figure 7-2, your ad element takes on that color.

You may be thinking to yourself that hexadecimals look like Greek to you and you could never figure out what numbers correspond to what colors. The thing is that you don't *have* to keep all those number/color correspondences in your head. The idea here is that you want the colors of your AdSense ads to blend in with colors already found on your Web site — meaning that if you can figure out the hexadecimal numbers of colors already on your Web site, you can then plug those numbers into your AdSense wizard (refer to Figure 7-2) and then have the wizard generate code for ads that match your Web site colors to a T.

Decoding hexadecimal numbers

Hexadecimal has its roots in both the Latin and Greek languages. *Hex* is a Greek term meaning *six* and *decimal* is a Latin term meaning *tenth*. Literally translated, *hexadecimal* could mean either *six to the tenth* or *six times ten*. Either translation is correct because hexadecimal is a computer term used to mean *grouped by 16* or *base 60*.

If all that math stuff really interests you, I invite you to google *hexadecimal* to your heart's content and read all the complicated theory behind hex and deci. I cut to the chase and let you know that hexadecimal numbers are used to specify the amount of red, green, and blue present in a color.

I'm sure your 2nd-grade art teacher told you that all colors could be broken down into the component parts of red, green, and blue. This insight is what drove computer-types into using the RGB/hexadecimal number model to represent colors using the following shortcut:

    #RRGGBB

where RR tells your Web browser how much red to use, GG tells how much green to use, and BB tells how much blue.

So, to get that nice seafoam-colored border you see in Figure 7-2 (oops, I forgot — black-and-white illustrations don't show color . . . trust me, it's a nice, foamy shade of blue) you'd use the following hexadecimal number:

    #336699

For a computer to read this hexadecimal number as a color, the number sign (#) must be displayed immediately before the color code. Without the number sign, the hexadecimal code looks just like any other number, and with other symbols in front of the six-digit number, the code is read as a different type of indicator because hexadecimal code is used extensively in programming.

None of that really concerns you, though. What you really need to understand here is that hexadecimal numbers can be used by AdSense to help build ads that match your Web site perfectly. You may have to do a little experimenting or investigating to find the exact hexadecimal numbers that you need, but after you do, the results are perfectly rendered ads that look as if they belong on your Web site.

How does one determine the hexadecimal numbers of colors already on your Web site? I'm glad you asked:

1. **Point your Web browser to your very own Web page.**

2. **After your page loads, choose View⇨Source from your browser's main menu.**

   Note that you may have to choose View⇨Source Code or View⇨Page Source. Different Web browsers have different menus — the exact phrase is determined by the browser that you're using.

   A new page appears, showing the source code for your Web site.

3. **On this new page of source code, look for a line that starts something like this:**

```
<style id='page-skin-1' type='text/css'><!-- body
        {background:#ffffff;margin:0;color:#333333;
        font:x-small Georgia Serif;font-size:small;
        font-size: small;text-align:
```

This is just the beginning of this line. If you actually copy and paste the whole line into a blank document, you'll see that it's a large block of code. This code tells you the style of your Web site. Notice that throughout the code, there are different snippets that read

```
Color:#XXXXXX
```

Those numbers represent the hexadecimal numbers you're looking for.

If you look closely at your `style id` code, you'll find all kinds of tags for the colors that are used in the design of your site. For example, in the code snippet I highlight in the steps list before, the information

```
body {background:#ffffff;margin:0;color:#333333
```

tells you that in the body of the Web site, the background color is `#ffffff` (which in this case is white), the margin of the body is zero — which means there's no margin), and the color of text is `#333333` (which is a very dark gray).

If you look through the formatting for the body (that's the information you copied from that one line of source code in the steps above), you'll find the colors that you need. Aside from the background and text colors, you also need the color number for links (represented as `a:link #XXXXXX`). Simple enough to come by.

Notice that I didn't say you need the numbers for border colors and for URLs. There's a reason for that, which I expand on in the next couple sections. First, what do you do with the color numbers when you have them? You use them to help create ads that are a perfect match for your Web site.

Use the numbers you've collected to fill in the Title, Background, and Text fields of your AdSense ad design page of the AdSense wizard. All you have to do is delete the number that's there — refer to Figure 7-2 — and key in the numbers you've collected in the correct space. In the sample ad in the lower-left corner of the wizard screen, you should see the colors displayed after you click away from the color box you're editing.

What's in a color?

Surf the Internet for a while and you'll soon notice that nearly every Web page uses blue as the color for its hyperlinks. Why is that?

Answering that question requires a little background history. When the Internet first came into being, there was little you could do about page displays. The screens (or monitors) on which the pages were displayed were *monochrome* — basically black and green. Then color monitors came along, but the number of colors that could be displayed was limited.

If you wanted someone to know there was link on your Web site that led to another Web site, you had to do something that would alert the visitor to the link; thus the advent of blue links. Color limitation made it difficult to read text that wasn't black or blue, and because black was the color of most text, blue became the choice for links.

It didn't take technology long to mature to the point we're at now, with technological capabilities that allow us to generate thousands of amazing colors on a screen. There's one small glitch though — Internet users have become accustomed to seeing links in blue, so often, if a link is another color, they don't recognize it.

Fascinating, I know, but there's a point to all this. When you're designing your Web site, the most effective method of alerting users to links in your text is to make them blue. Now, your *navigational* links (on the left side or top of the page) don't necessarily have to be blue. They can blend with your page design, but *text* links should always be blue. That means that it's also a good idea to use blue for the links on AdSense ads that are integrated into your text. The color blue makes them more clickable and helps site visitors to see there's something interesting behind those words.

The borders are open . . .

Borders are made to keep people out or sometimes to keep them in. Either way, a border is like a fence. Even on paper, a border surrounds print and pictures to keep everything cohesive. So, why in the world would you want to (metaphorically, at least) fence in people by putting a border around your ads?

Borders scream, *Hey, I'm over here. I'm an advertisement. Run!* Really. I'm not even trying to be funny. Borders make ads even more ad-like than the Ad by Google logo that AdSense places on your ads — and you don't want ad-like, trust me.

The best option is to blend your ads into the background of your Web site. That means using no borders at all. There's one problem with that theory though — there isn't a No Borders option.

What you have to do instead is make the border color the same color as the ad background. Your ad background is the same color as your Web page background, right? If it's not, it should be.

Remember the Golden Rule: Blend your ads into your Web pages so they look like they belong there. That means blending the border and the background of the ad with the background color of your Web site. Use the techniques outlined in the previous section to determine the hexadecimal number of the background color of your Web site and then use the AdSense wizard to set your ad background and ad border to that color.

The easiest way to keep everything straight is to keep your Web site simple. You'll never go wrong with a white background and black text.

Camouflaging URLs

I want to move on to another topic as much as the next guy, but I need to cover one more thing about ad placement. AdSense ads consist of three zones: the title link, the text, and the URL. The *title link* is the title of the ad, and it's obvious that *the text* is the text of the ad. No rocket science here, so we can safely pass them by. The URL is what I'm concerned with here.

The URL of the Web site that the ad belongs to can be a real problem. The *URL* isn't *hyperlinked* — made into a link that leads to the Web address shown in the URL — because visitors are supposed to click the ad's (linked) title, not the ad's URL. The thing is that having a URL that doesn't transport you to a new place on the Web when clicked can confuse a visitor, especially if you've chosen not to make the (linked) title of the ad blue.

Visitors see the URL and may click it, expecting to actually go somewhere. When they *don't* go anywhere, that could alert them to the fact that they're about to click an ad. After visitors think about that fact, however briefly, they're less likely to mess with your ad at all by making those clicks.

For that reason, it's best if the URL doesn't in any way invite a site visitor to click it — and the best way to stifle that click impulse is to make the URL the same color as the text in the ad. It's usually best to have ad text black, or whatever color the surrounding text is.

My preference is to have the title linked and colored blue and have the URL black. Site visitors (at least to my site) seem to like that configuration better, and I have more success when I stylize my ads this way. Will that hold true for you? Probably, but you can always switch things around and see.

The cool thing about AdSense is that it's easy and costs nothing to tweak your ads until you find the style that works best for your visitors. So, give it a shot; change it up. Keep track of what you're doing though so that when you're done testing, there's no doubt what works best in each different area of your Web site.

Using Multiple Ads

More dessert is a good thing. More money is a good thing. Sometimes, even more people is a good thing. And guess what? More ads *can* be a good thing, too.

Wow. I'm channeling Martha Stewart. But unlike Ms. Stewart, I won't get all crafty on you, and I won't tell you that multiple ads *are* a good thing, when in fact, sometimes they're not. I just want to convey that adding multiple ad blocks to your Web pages can work well — if it's done properly.

The appeal of multiples

Having multiple ads means more chances for site visitors to click your ads. With that reasoning, many Web site owners who add AdSense to their pages automatically put as many ads as they can on their Web site. Sometimes that works for them; other times, it doesn't.

When it does work, multiple ads may improve your AdSense revenue significantly or maybe just a little. But what makes multiples work? In a word: audience.

There are no hard and fast guidelines for what works and what doesn't with multiples. In every instance, it comes down to how your audience uses your Web site and what kind of value they find in the ads that are displayed on your page.

For example, I've played with a lot of different settings for the ads on my blog in the process of putting this book together. One thing I did early on was to increase the number of ads that were shown on my blog by tweaking the blog template with code and by adding additional ad blocks using the widgets provided by my blogging application provider, Blogger. (*Widgets* are like mini-programs or additional capabilities within a program that you can add or remove at will.)

Before those changes, I was generating a few dollars each day with my AdSense ads. After the changes, the revenues dropped by a few cents each day, and I even had a few days where I generated no income at all.

In my case, it seemed that adding more ads made visitors less likely to click them. It may be the number of ads I chose to use, or it's possible that I just chose the wrong combination of ads. That's what makes testing different types, numbers, and configurations of ads so vitally important.

Using multiple ads — more than one ad unit per page — is usually a recommended practice. Having multiples gives you the opportunity to catch your site visitors in more than one location. It also allows you to include ads on your site that may appeal to different audiences. For example, the site visitors who are likely to click video ads may be a different set of visitors than those who'll click links or text ads. Figuring out the right configuration of these ads just requires testing to see how your audience responds to each type of ad.

Getting in the zone

In watching the revenue numbers for my site — in this case, the actual earnings — I could see the results of the changes I made. Those results reflected different zones that were successful for ads on my pages.

A *zone* is an area of your Web site that draws readers' eyes. Most Web sites have a header zone, a content zone, and a sidebar zone. Visitors focus on each of those areas for a different reason.

The *header zone* is where visitors look to confirm what site they're on. Later, a visitor might look to the header zone to see if there are interesting or useful links for them to follow.

The *content zone* is where visitors focus most of their attention. This is where the main content of your site is found, and that's what your visitors are looking for. Content is first, links are secondary. Don't get fooled, though. Links may be secondary, but they're still an important part of the site.

And that's exactly why there's also a sidebar zone. *Sidebar zones* are where the cool stuff is usually found. Sidebars usually feature additional information or links to other resources.

Multiple ads need to appear in one of these zones. Which zones, you ask? I can't tell you that. Try different configurations for all three zones to see what works. Test, test, test. You know your visitors, and you can deduce some facts about them and create theories for what will work. But until you actually try a specific configuration, you'll never know.

Avoiding overkill

One problem with using multiple ad blocks on your Web pages is that you can quickly overdo it. A few ads can enhance the content on your page. Too many make it look crowded and confusing. Visitors won't know what to look at first or which links to click.

If you have a blog service, you may be limited in the number of ads you can show on a page for this very reason. Blogger, for example, limits publishers to three instances of AdSense. You can place those three instances anywhere on the page, but if you place more than three ads, something won't show up.

So should you limit each of your pages to three or fewer ads? That depends on your page and how well the ads integrate into the content and surrounding elements of the page. Remember, the rule is still to make your ads as invisible as possible. By making them invisible as ads, you're making them visible as content, meaning they're more likely to attract the attention of visitors.

You don't literally want to make your ads invisible. You could, too. Changing the ads to make them blend completely into your background would certainly do the trick. But then, how would visitors click the ads? No, the invisibility superpower isn't a good one to use in this instance. Just make your ads less obviously ads.

Multiples don't have to be identical

I've already alluded to this fact, but let me come right out and say it: *Multiple ads do not have to be identical.* You can have one ad in your text and a differ-ent kind of ad at the top of your page and another kind of ad in a sidebar, if that's what works for your Web site.

In fact, that combination — one in each zone — is probably the most suc-cessful way to have multiple ad blocks on most pages. It won't work with every single Web site or even every single page on a Web site though.

When you're configuring the ads for your site or blog, you may find that ads work better on some pages and not others. That's okay. If you have a page where ads don't perform well (or even at all), remove the ads from that page and find a way to work in links to pages where ads do perform.

Play with the configuration of your ads. For my Google-Geek blog, what works best are ads between the posts. In fact, ads at the top of the page and in the sidebar don't work at all — I've never been able to generate income from them.

Ads inside the posts also didn't work for that blog, so I took them out. Ads between the posts do work, though — but not all ads. A banner doesn't per-form as well as link units do. It took a lot of testing for me to figure out these facts about what ads work, where they work at, and how well they work.

When you're testing your ads, be sure to try different configurations, but keep in mind that you do have to keep track of what you're trying and how well it works. Keep a journal or a spreadsheet, or notes on a napkin if you have to. But keep track of what you're doing so that when it comes time, you can set up your ads in a way that works best for you.

Also remember that with any kind of testing, what works today may fail you tomorrow. Your site visitors may change, the topic of your site may expand or narrow over time to suit your site visitors, and designs may get boring, so you'll need to re-do them. All I mean is that your ads might work really well right now and not work at all two weeks from now or a year from now or whatever timeframe you choose. It's not that you're doing anything wrong. It's just that things change. (You know the saying — there's nothing constant in this world except constant change.)

Testing isn't a do-it-once-and-forget-it proposition. You do it again and again and again, if necessary. Just remember, content gets stale, but so do ads. AdSense helps with this because the ads that are shown on your page change often. As your site matures, you may have to make more changes, so always be watching your revenue levels to see when the tried-and-true ways start becoming less effective.

Chapter 8

Understanding AdSense for Search

*P*eople find content on the Internet by searching for it. This is a simple fact of life. You know it, I know it, and the folks at AdSense know it. You can take advantage of this simple fact of life by installing AdSense search capabilities on your site, capabilities that allow site visitors to either search your site or search the whole Internet, all the while providing for a nice little revenue stream back to your pockets.

If yours is a site that's hundreds of pages deep, such a search capability for both the site and the Web is essential. Even if you have a smaller site though, search is an important element. Users may come to your site and find only part of what they're looking for. How will they find the rest of it? Whether it's on your site or not, you need to provide visitors with a way to find what they're looking for.

AdSense for Search gives you the search capabilities you need, but you have to use it well. You have to work through a few things, including figuring out how your revenues will be made and what kind of search options will be best for the visitors who come to your site. You also have to think about whether it's worth customizing your search box. (Hey, adding your own logo is a nice touch!) All these options make creating your search box a little more involved than creating ads for content — the stuff I cover in Chapter 7 — but I walk you through the rough parts.

Searching for Revenues

When it comes to searches that really turn up results, Google is the King of the Hill. A dozen or so other search engines are out there, and some of them even offer search capabilities for Web sites and enterprises; but none of them match the power of Google and none of them have gained the confidence of users like Google has. Google's known for results, and that's why using AdSense for Search makes so much sense.

If you've had a Web site for any amount of time, you've probably already discovered that you must have search capabilities on your site. Whether those search capabilities are only for your Web site or are for the entire Web is a decision that's best based on the amount of content you have on your site, but it's probably no secret to you that users want search capabilities. In fact, you may have already added Google Search to your Web site, using either Google's free search capabilities or the Google Custom Search Engine.

So, if you've already added Google Search to your site or you've strongly considered doing so, why not go the extra mile and add a search capability that makes you a little bit of money? Admittedly, AdSense for Search probably won't ever make you as much money as AdSense for Content, but that shouldn't stop you from trying. Why let even a little bit of potential coin surf away from your site untapped?

Here's how it works: A visitor to your site types a search query into your AdSense-enabled Google search box in hopes of finding something either on the Web as a whole or just on your Web site. You don't get paid just because the visitor used the search box on your Web site. Instead, you get paid if that visitor clicks one of the ads in the search results that are shown from the search box that you put on your page. It's a secondary-click revenue stream, which means that, with AdSense for Search, the revenues are admittedly a little harder to get to. Visitors must first use the search box and then click through an ad for you to get paid.

Just because it's not a direct click doesn't mean you should ignore the potential of this AdSense approach. The fact is that every site has visitors that won't find exactly what they're looking for. If they found your site with a search engine, they'll likely go back to that search engine and refine their search term. If they found your site directly and it doesn't contain what they want, they'll probably surf away to search for what they want.

Also, if you already have search capabilities on your site, visitors who use those capabilities are already seeing the ads that are shown in the search results. You're just not getting paid for them. If you have the capability anyway, you should at least be able to collect revenue from increasing Google's confidence level.

Besides, if the visitor will leave your site anyway to search for the information she's looking for, why not give her the option of searching from your site? The visitor benefits in time saved, and you benefit in the possible revenue stream.

Plenty of options for the types of search you can allow are available, too. Users can

- Conduct a site search
- Conduct a Web search
- Conduct a targeted search
- See results returned on your Web site
- See results returned on the Google site

It's not just plain vanilla search, in other words. You can really punch up your search capabilities so that your site visitors can search with style and find what they're looking for. You can even direct the search so that users aren't pulling information from your competition.

Search in Style

AdSense for Search is a capability that's automatically enabled if you're registered with AdSense at all. So, if you've created AdSense ads for your Web site content before now, you won't have any problems creating your first AdSense search box. (If you haven't created an AdSense ad or even created your AdSense account, flip to Chapter 2, where I cover all the details you need for getting your ads off the ground.)

It should only take a few minutes to create a search box for your Web site. I spell out the basics of setting up a search box in Chapter 5 — you know, logging on to your AdSense account, clicking the AdSense Setup tab, and then making your way through the AdSense for Search Wizard to generate the HTML code for your Web site — but I want to show you some of the tweaks available to you. For that, make your way to the AdSense Setup tab and click the AdSense for Search button. (If you need to refresh your memory on how to do that, check out Chapter 5.) Doing so calls up the first screen of a wizard (as shown in Figure 8-1) that walks you through customizing your search box. (Note that AdSense likes to keep things as simple as possible, so the customization page for search boxes is very similar to the content ad customization page.) With the first screen up and ready on your monitor, you're ready to tweak your search box however you want to. The next few sections show you how.

Figure 8-1:
The search box customization page is similar to the content ad customization page.

Web and site searches

The first decision you have to make when it comes to designing your search box is whether to allow your users to search only the Web as a whole or to allow them to search the Web as well as your site or other sites that you choose. If your site is relatively small (under a couple dozen pages), there's probably no sense in having a site search capability unless there are other, specific sites that you want search results drawn from. This is a function that works well if you have multiple Web sites and want to keep your sites in front of your site visitors as much as possible. If you have a single site, with just a few pages, it's not quite as useful.

The more pages you have, the more difficult it is for your site visitors to find what they're looking for, so you should definitely include site search capabilities in the mix. The search boxes look a little different, depending on the capabilities that you allow.

The top section of the first screen of the AdSense for Search Wizard (refer to Figure 8-1) is where you set up your Search Type options. Selecting the Google WebSearch radio button sets up the Web only search, whereas selecting the Google WebSearch + SiteSearch radio button lets you specify three specific sites to search. (You enter the URLs for your three sites in the text fields provided.)

Figure 8-2 shows the AdSense example for a search box that searches the Web as well as Web sites that you specify. You can enter URLs for up to three different Web sites that visitors can then search either individually or as part of a larger search.

Figure 8-2:
Allow users
to search
the Web
and up to
three sites
you specify.

Figure 8-3 shows the AdSense example for a search box that allows visitors to search only the Web.

Figure 8-3:
Another
option is to
allow users
to search
only the
Web from
your Web
page.

Which type of search is more effective for your site is determined by the site content and by what you hope to accomplish with an AdSense search box. If you have multiple sites, you can keep them in front of your site visitors even if your visitors don't find what they need on the current site. Use AdSense search to provide for as many of your site visitors' needs as possible even if your sites won't answer their questions.

The middle and bottom sections of the AdSense for Search Wizard's first screen (refer to Figure 8-1) let you customize the appearance of the search box itself as well as set a few other preferences. Neat stuff that I cover in sufficient detail — but not now. (I lead you back to the wizard in the "Creating an AdSense Search Box section," later in this chapter.) Right now I want to introduce you to a more high-powered way to customize your search engine with the Google Custom Search Engine page.

Creating customized searches

One other option for creating a search box for your Web site is to create a customized search engine. This isn't exactly a feature of AdSense, but instead is a separate Google capability that works with AdSense so that you can monetize the search capabilities that you give to users while directing it much more specifically.

A custom search engine is a creator-defined search capability, so you can specify which Web sites (or even which pages) you want to allow your visitors to search. The really cool thing about a custom search engine is that you can have more than the three sites that AdSense makes available for searches with an AdSense-specific search box. So if you want to allow your visitors to search 7, 15, or even 50 specific sites, a custom search engine is the way to go.

Before you can connect custom search capabilities to your AdSense account, you must first create a custom search engine. Here's how:

1. **Point your browser to** www.google.com/coop/cse.

   The Google Custom Search Engine page appears.

2. **Click the Create Custom Search Engine button.**

3. **In the new page that appears, enter your username and password in the space provided and then click Sign In.**

   You can use the same username and password you use for your AdSense account.

4. **In the new page that appears, enter the setup information for your search engine, as shown in Figure 8-4.**

   This information includes

   • **A name and description for your search engine.**

   • **Keywords that define the topic of your search engine.**

   • **The main language for your search engine.**

- **Your choice on the scope of the search.** You can limit the search to specific sites or you can also set up your search so that it either searches the whole Web or the whole Web with emphasis on the sites that you specify.

  If you've decided to specify certain sites to be included in your search parameters, you can list the specific URLs you want to allow in the text box provided. Go ahead and choose as many sites as you like. You're allowed up to 5,000 specific sites, which are also called *annotations*.

- **The specific edition of the customized search engine you want to use.** The standard edition is free but requires that you allow ads to be shown. The business edition allows you to create a customized search engine with no ads.

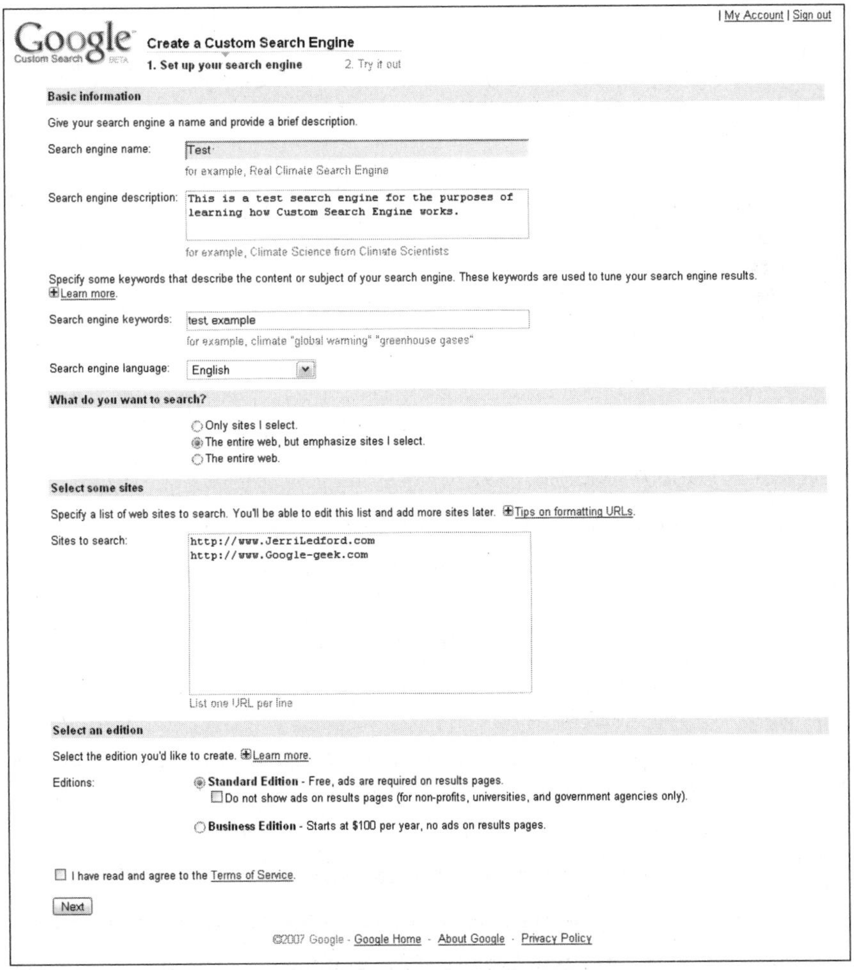

Figure 8-4:
Creating
a custom
search
engine is a
simple
process.

- **An I Have Read and Agree to the Terms of Service check box.**
  (Okay, it doesn't sound much like setting anything up, but if you don't select this check box, you're stuck in an eternal loop you'll never break out of.)

5. **After you fill in all the requested information — and agree to the terms of service — click the Next button.**

6. **On the second page of the wizard, test your search engine by running a test query.**

   The results from the test are shown on the page, as shown in Figure 8-5.

7. **After you test it, you can select the Send Confirmation Email To . . . check box near the bottom of the page to have a confirmation message sent to your Inbox.**

   The confirmation message provides links to additional information and capabilities, such as managing your custom search engine. This isn't a required option, but I suggest that you select it for at least the first search engine that you create.

8. **Click Finish to be taken to your main Google Custom Search Engine page.**

Google Custom Search Engine is a *beta* program, which means it's still in the testing phases even though it's available to the general public. Beta programs sometimes have glitches or bugs and don't work exactly as they should, so keep your eyes open for anything out of the ordinary and expect changes in the future. After the program's been sufficiently tested and improved, it comes out of beta testing and becomes a *general release* program, which means that the glitches and bugs are less likely to occur and updates to the program happen less often and on more regular schedules.

Now you have a custom search engine. Just because you have it doesn't mean that you'll start earning money from it, though. You still need to connect your Custom Search Engine account to your AdSense account before you can get paid for the ads that appear on the search results page.

1. **Point your browser to** www.google.com/coop/cse.

   The Google Custom Search Engine page appears.

2. **Click the Manage Your Existing Search Engines link.**

   If you're not automatically logged in to your account, you may be prompted for your username and password. If needed, enter your e-mail address and password in the spaces provided and click Log In.

   You'll be taken to the Manage Search Engines page, as shown in Figure 8-6.

Figure 8-5:
Results
from testing
your search
engine are
shown on
the wizard
page.

Figure 8-5:
Results
from testing
your search
engine are
shown on
the wizard
page.

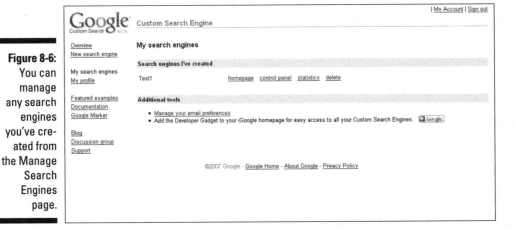

Figure 8-6:
You can
manage
any search
engines
you've cre-
ated from
the Manage
Search
Engines
page.

3. Click the Control Panel link.

The Control Panel page appears, as shown in Figure 8-7.

4. Click the Make Money link at the top of the Control Panel page (also shown in Figure 8-7).

5. In the new page that appears (as shown in Figure 8-8), select the I Already Have an AdSense Account radio button.

The Existing AdSense User form appears, as shown in Figure 8-9.

By the way, I'm assuming here that you *do* have an AdSense account. If you don't, choose the I am a New AdSense User option, which takes you to set up an AdSense account.

The Make Money link

Figure 8-7:
Connect
the search
engine and
AdSense
accounts.

Figure 8-8:
Select the
option for
an existing
AdSense
account.

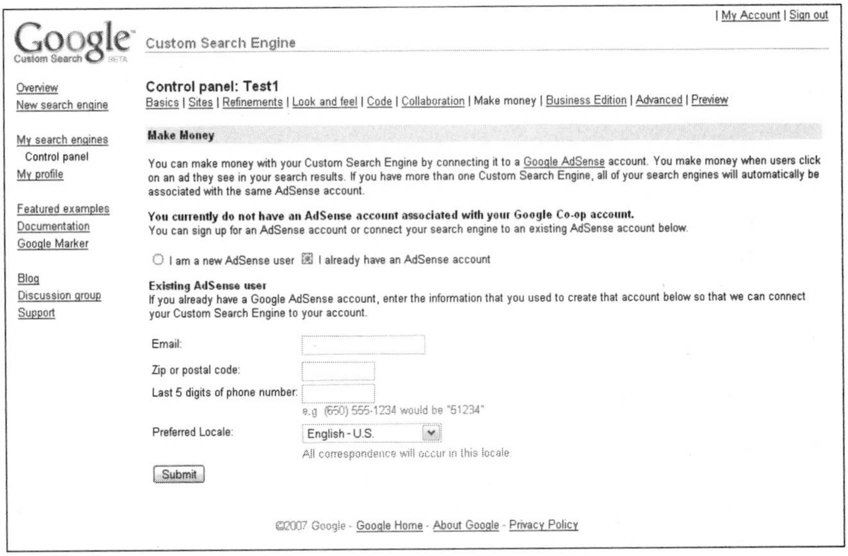

Figure 8-9:
When you
select the
option for
an existing
AdSense
account, a
new form
appears.

6. **Fill in the information requested to link your AdSense account and then click the Submit button.**

    It's simple information: e-mail address, zip code, phone number, and a drop-down menu from which you can select your location.

    If all the information matches, you receive a confirmation letting you know the two accounts are now connected. Being connected simply means that your search box not only appears on your page but also sends information about ads that appear in search results to your AdSense account. That means that when your visitors use your custom search box to search for something and then click an ad while they're viewing the search results, you get paid for it just as if you were using an AdSense for Search box.

Now, you may be wondering why in the world you'd go to all this trouble to add a customized search engine to your Web site when AdSense has similar controls built into the AdSense for Search capability. The answer is: It's all about control.

You *can* use the AdSense for Search Wizard to customize your search engine — specifying whether users can search the Web or other sites, for example, or customizing the appearance of the search engine that you make available from your site. Those capabilities are limited with AdSense though. (You can only specify up to three sites for customized searches, for example.)

If you really want to make an impact with your search engine capabilities, using a Google Custom Search Engine is the way to go. You can add more Web sites to the SiteSearch capabilities, and you can further customize the search engine to reflect your style and the design of your Web site.

Many companies or Web site owners that have a large number of pages or a complex forum system use the Google Custom Search Engine because it makes their site and their site capabilities more valuable to site users. It's really your call though. If there's no added value in creating a custom engine, don't put the time into it. I'm always an advocate for anything that adds value to site visitors because those visitors really do remember (and revisit) the sites that they find most useful.

So, that's it. Now you have a custom search engine connected to your AdSense account, providing an additional revenue stream — and you know what makes it valuable to you! You can also go back into your Custom Search Engine account at any time and tweak the search engine you created by changing the Web sites that it searches or even the look of the search engine.

To change the way your custom search engine looks, try this:

1. **Log in to your custom search engine Control Panel, as outlined in the previous steps, and then click the Control Panel link for the search engine that you want to customize.**

   Doing so opens the Control Panel page for that search engine.

2. **On the Control Panel page, select the Look and Feel link to be taken to the Customize Your Search Box page.**

   On this page, you have several options for changing the appearance of your search box, including different logo configurations and color options.

3. **In the first section of the page, as shown in Figure 8-10, select how you want the Google custom search box to appear on your page and then click the Save Changes button.**

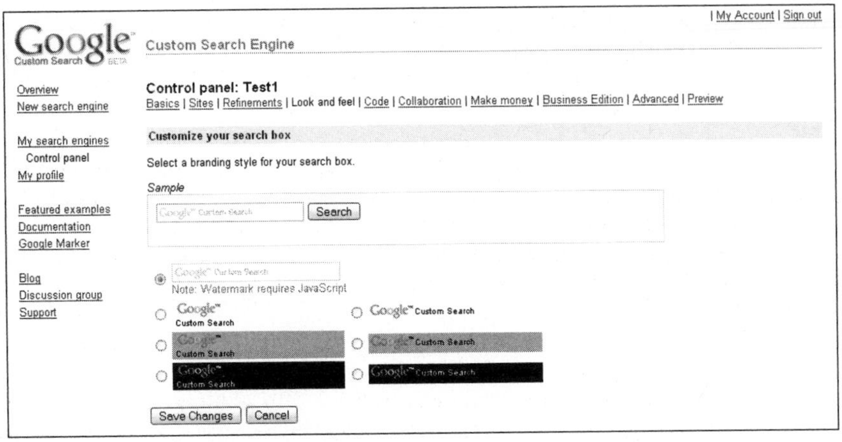

Figure 8-10:
You have
several
options for
how you
want the
Google
custom
search box
to appear on
your page.

4. **In the next section, as shown in Figure 8-11, customize the colors of the border, title, background, text, links, visited links, and cached links and then click the Save Changes button.**

   You can do this by choosing the desired colors from the *Color Picker* — the small colored boxes next to each option — or by entering the hexa-decimal numbers that represent the colors.

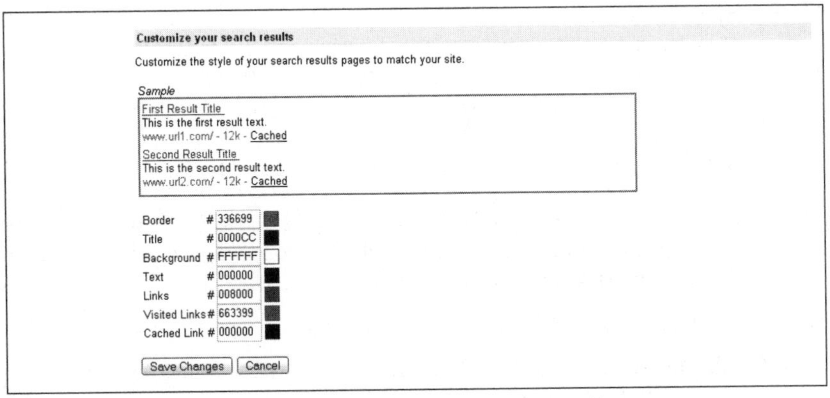

Figure 8-11:
Customize
the colors
of your cus-
tom search
engine
results
pages.

   The results of the changes you make are displayed in the sample above the color options.

5. **To add your personalized logo, enter the URL for the logo in the Image URL text box, as shown in Figure 8-12.**

   If you don't know what the URL is, you can open another browser window and go to your Web site. Then right-click the logo of your site and select Copy Image Location, flip back to the Google Custom Search Engine cus-tomization page, and paste the URL into the text box provided.

Customize your Google-hosted search results

Add a logo to your search engine's Google-hosted results page.

Sample

Test1   [   ] [Search]

     ⦿ Test1   ○ Web Search

Image URL: [http://]
(optional)   JPG, PNG or GIF; max 100px height
Link logo to URL: [http://]
(optional)   e.g. http://www.google.com/coop

[Save Changes] [Cancel]

©2007 Google - Google Home - About Google - Privacy Policy

You also have the option to link your logo to a specific Web site. For example, if you want your logo to appear on the search results page and to link back to your main Web site, then enter the main URL for your Web site in the Link Logo to URL text box.

6. **When you've entered the logo and link information, click the Save Changes button.**

   The small sample display above the logo and link text boxes displays your logo if you choose to use this option.

Although all three of these customization options are on one page, you don't have to change them all at the same time. You can change any single option on the page without affecting the other options. If you want to change the colors, but leave the logo you already have in place, or even leave it off completely, adjust your color settings and click the Save Changes button, and only the changes you actually want will take effect.

Creating an AdSense Search Box

I'm the first to say that custom search engines are pretty cool, but they're not necessary for every Web site. If you don't need a custom search engine, a regular AdSense search box works just fine.

I spend some time earlier in this chapter profiling the wizard that helps you create the search box, and filling you in on your options when it comes to specifying the types of searches the AdSense search box can perform. Now I want to show you how to create the search box from A to Z — all the way from specifying the kind of search box you want to generating the HTML code you need to place on your Web site so you can finally start earning some money from it. It's not too tough — I'd say it's fifth-grade-science-project easy — and should take you less time than brewing your first cup of coffee in the morning (unless you have a Bunn Coffee Maker — those take like three minutes, so you'd have to hurry to beat one). Here's how it's done:

1. **Point your browser to** `www.adsense.com`, **log on to your AdSense account, and then click the AdSense Setup tab.**

2. **On the Setup tab, select the AdSense for Search option.**

   Doing so calls up the AdSense for Search Wizard (refer to Figure 8-1).

3. **In the Search Type section of page, select the radio button corresponding to the type of search you want the search box to perform: Google WebSearch or Google WebSearch + SiteSearch.**

4. **In the Search Box Style section of the page, use the options to customize the look of your search box.**

   As Figure 8-13 shows, you have two options for logo styles and several different combinations of styles that can change the look of your search box.

   Your options include

   - **Google Logo:** If you select the Logo Above Text Box check box, the Google logo appears above the search box. If you leave this box deselected, the Google logo appears to the left of the text box.

   - **"Google Search" on Button:** Selecting this option ditches the Google logo and just puts the Google name on the search button.

   - **Search Button Below Text Box:** If you select this check box, the Search button (the thing a user clicks to start a search) appears under the search box. Otherwise, the button appears to the right of the search box.

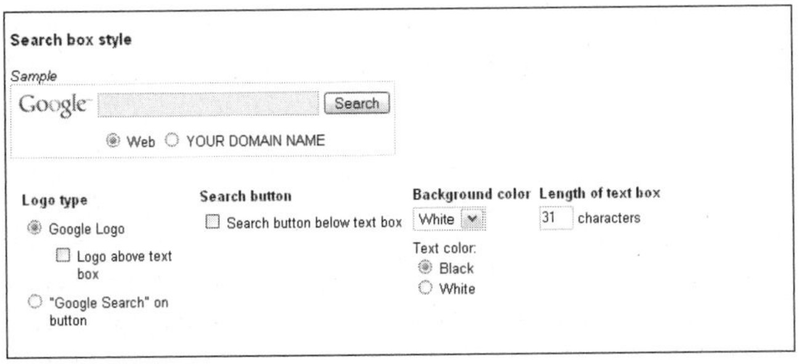

Figure 8-13:
Select the
logo style
and com-
bination of
features
that works
for your site.

- **Background color and text color:** Here you can use a drop-down menu to select the color that you want to use as your search box background — your choices here are white, black, or gray — as well as specify if you want the text to be black or white.

- **Text box length:** Here you can choose the number of characters that you want to allow in the search box. The default is 31 characters, but you can change that to whatever length suits you.

5. **In the More Options section, select the main language for your search box from the drop-down menu.**

   This setting refers to the language of your Web site. Visitors can choose to search in their own native language if it's different than the one you select, but you still have to make a choice from more than 30 selections available in the drop-down menu.

6. **Still in the More Options section of the page, choose the site encoding you'll use for your Web page from the Your Site Encoding drop-down menu.**

   Site encoding here refers to the computer language or code that your site is created in. (Even if you're using HTML, there are several versions of it.) The default is set to West European Latin-1 (ISO-8859-1). If you don't know what the encoding for your site is, leave the default in place.

7. **Select the country your domain is registered in from the Country drop-down menu and then click Continue to go to the second page of the wizard.**

   The second page, as shown in Figure 8-14, is where you customize the look of your search results page.

8. **In the second page of the wizard, select the color template you want to use for the search results page from the drop-down menu at the center-right.**

   You have six palettes to choose from, but keep in mind that you can skip the palettes and just enter hexadecimal numbers for custom colors in the appropriate text boxes — Border, Title, Background, for example — to precisely match your Web site. (Chapter 7 has more on hexadecimal numbers and how you can use them to match the colors of your search box to the colors on your Web site.)

9. **To add your own corporate logo to your search results page, enter the URL where the logo is located in the Logo Image URL text box.**

   Note: If you want your logo to appear above the search box, select the Above Search Box check box. Otherwise, the logo appears to the left of the box.

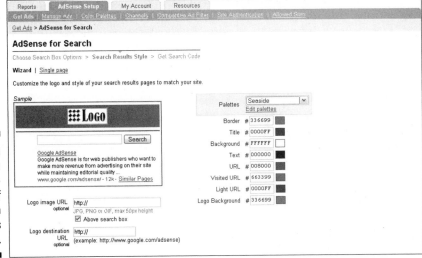

Figure 8-14:
Customize
the appear-
ance of
your search
results
page.

10. (Optional) Add a Logo Destination URL.

The Logo Destination URL is optional, but should you decide to use it, this will link your logo back to a Web page that you specify. That can be the main page of your Web site or any other page that you choose.

11. In the More Options section of the screen, as shown in Figure 8-15, select where you want the search results to appear.

Your choices here are

- **On Google, in the Same Window:** Opening search results on Google in the same window replaces your Web page with the Google page. It's streamlined — no additional windows are opened — but it also leads visitors away from your Web site. The concern with leading visitors away is that they won't click back and you'll lose them completely. The tradeoff is that opening the results on Google's pages gives your site visitors confidence that their search is being done by the best search engine on the Web.

- **On Google, in a New Window:** Opening search results in a new window is an excellent way to ensure that your site remains open for users and that the user also feels the confidence that comes with seeing Google-logoed pages. A second window (or tab, if you're using a Web browser that supports tabbed browsing) opens with the search results, but your Web site also remains open. When users finish browsing search results, they can close the window in which the search results are displayed, but your Web site will still be open. That's no guarantee that the visitor will continue surfing your site — he could close your site, too — but it does leave the possibility that he'll continue surfing through your pages.

- **On Your Own Web Site:** Opening search results on your Web site keeps the user on your site, but also strips away some of the confidence that comes with Google search results. The search results are stylized to match your site, but still contain the Google logo. They're just not actual Google pages, which could erode user confidence some.

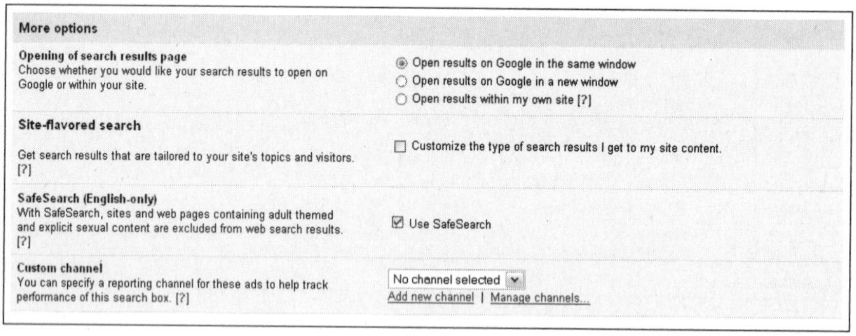

Figure 8-15:
More options allow you to specify where search results should appear.

12. **If you want to enable site-flavored searches, select the Customize the Type of Search Results I Get to My Site Content check box.**

    Site-flavored search is a progressive technology — meaning that the results get more accurate over time — that pulls search results that are related to the content of your Web site. In the beginning, search results are more general, but over time the results become more refined and better related to your site content.

13. **If you want to use the SafeSearch option, select the Use SafeSearch check box.**

    SafeSearch filters out nearly all the adult content (such as pornography) from search results.

14. **Select a Custom Channel for tracking earning results from the drop-down menu of custom channels that you've created.**

    Remember, channels are basically a tagging method that allows you to track specific ads or groups of ads.

15. **Select Continue to generate the search box code, as shown in Figure 8-16, for pasting into your Web site.**

Figure 8-16:
After you complete the cus-tomization and click Continue, the code for your search box displays.

Keep in mind when you're customizing the search results page that you defi-nitely don't want to go crazy with all the colors. The last thing you want to do is create a kaleidoscope that gives your site visitors headaches.

A better option is to stick to standard design principles and have a single color for the background — preferably one that matches the background of your Web site — and then use no more than three colors in the foreground. For example, if you have a basic white background for your Web site, that counts as one color.

Then, you can style your text in black, links that haven't been clicked as blue, and links that *have* been clicked as red. Including the white background, you have four total colors. Four colors won't jar the user, and your search results will still look very professional.

After you generate the code for your search box, copy and paste the code onto your Web page in the same way that you copy and paste AdSense for Content code. It may take a little tweaking to get the search box in exactly the spot you want it, but you can move it around with your HTML editor to ensure that it appears in the proper place.

AdSense for Search and WordPress

In many ways, WordPress is different from other kinds of blogging programs. At its core, WordPress is a good blogging program; but because it's so customizable at the code level, it has much more power than other blogging applications. That also happens to mean that some things just aren't as easy with WordPress.

Installing an AdSense search box in Blogger is pretty straightforward. You create the search box in AdSense, copy the code, and use an HTML widget to insert it in your blog. With WordPress, the process is much more difficult and requires that you edit the core code of the WordPress blog page where you want the search box to appear.

Here's an easier way — MightySearch is a WordPress plugin from MightyHitter (`www.mightyhitter.com`) that's designed to let you paste in your AdSense for Search code and it will make the code work properly on your WordPress blog. The plugin handles all the details that could take you forever to figure out if you're not a WordPress genius.

Adding search capabilities to your site just makes sense. Chances are that you won't have every detail that your site visitors are looking for on your Web site. Why not make it easy for them to find what you don't have? In the process, you can add to your AdSense revenue stream. Nothing wrong with making some money on the information you don't have on your site, too.

One thing you should know about designing your search box is that with the customization that's available, you can change the look of the search box completely. You should not, however, change the color of the search *button*. Because it's Google and people trust Google, they'll recognize the gray search button, and they're more likely to use it. If you change the search button, visitors could mistake your search box for something belonging to some other search company, and their confidence in finding what they're looking for might not be as high.

Adding search capabilities through AdSense makes sense whether you have a site of 5 pages or 500. Users may come to your site and find everything they need, but if they don't, they'll go somewhere to search out the answers they seek. Give them a search box linked directly from your site, and you'll not only help them out, but you might gain a little financial reward in the process.

Part III
Other Types of AdSense

The 5th Wave   By Rich Tennant

"Is this really the best use of Flash animation on our e-commerce Web site? A bad wheel on the shopping cart icon that squeaks, wobbles, and pulls to the left?"

In this part . . .

AdSense is so much more than just content ads and search boxes, and this part helps you understand all the options that are available to you. From video ads to referral programs, I include all the remaining AdSense options in these chapters.

I show you what AdSense for Video is, how it works, and how to make video that catches a visitor's attention. I then show you how to tap into the AdSense for Mobile market by creating mobile ads and improving your AdSense revenues. I close things out with coverage of AdSense for RSS, AdSense referrals, and how to use AdSense with your blogs. There's more than one way to earn a pretty penny!

Chapter 9

Show Me Some Video (& Other Gadgets)

*V*ideo is one of the top technologies online right now. Everyone's watching, downloading, streaming, or creating it. You find video on a majority of pages, and several services — including YouTube, GodTube, and Google Video — make it possible for people to create and upload videos of interest as well as find, watch, and/or download said videos.

No wonder AdSense is trying to tap into the video market. The popularity of online video is almost as mind-boggling as the popularity of blogs or podcasts or any other newer technology that no one expected to fly but is taking the Web by storm. The draw is entertainment. The content changes constantly and there are so many different types of video — from those created by amateurs to professional documentaries to full-length television shows and movies — that there's something to keep everyone busy.

Add to the availability of a wide variety of videos the fact that Internet users are logging on through broadband services more and more frequently, and you have a mix that just works for video. To take advantage of it, AdSense is monetizing videos in more ways than one, as this chapter makes clear.

When it comes to AdSense, consider another technology along with video: AdSense for Google Gadgets. *Google Gadgets* are cool little programs and downloads folks come up with that you can add to your Web site, blog, or desktop that help you do stuff faster. For example, Google hosts a whole slew of gadgets created by third parties that you can add to your *iGoogle* page — your personalized Google page — that help you accomplish tasks faster. I have an iGoogle page that features things like dictionaries, calculators, and weather reports.

If you have some software-writing skills and can come up with your own gadgets, you should strongly consider embedding AdSense ads into your gadgets as one way to monetize the gadgets you create to share with others. If you have a popular gadget like Weather Forecast by LabPixies or MP3 Player by Mike Duffy, it could be a very lucrative way to create more AdSense revenue.

Video and AdSense: Choosing the Right Product

AdSense, in its ongoing drive to be as accommodating as possible, actually has three options available for video. Each of these options is targeted to a different aspect of video — aspects that reach both those who create videos and those who want to advertise on a text site with video. The three types of video are

✔ **Click-to-play video ads:** Video ads are a type of ad displayed on your Web site. You must opt into image ads when you create your first AdSense for Content ads and use one of the supported formats to add click-to-play video ads to your site. The supported formats are

- 336x280 (Large rectangle)
- 300x250 (Medium rectangle)
- 250x250 (Square)
- 200x200 (Small square)
- 728x90 (Leaderboard)
- 120x600 (Skyscraper)
- 160x600 (Wide skyscraper)

✔ **Video units:** This feature allows you to add video content from YouTube partners to your Web site in a customizable player. The video comes to you packaged with text overlay ads and a companion banner above the video — that's the AdSense part. *Note:* You must have an English-language site to use AdSense video units.

✔ **AdSense for Video:** This product delivers text overlay and InVideo ads into your existing video streams. (InVideo ads are ads that actually play within videos that are embedded on your Web site.) If you have your own online video content, AdSense for Video can help you earn revenue from that content. The rub here is that AdSense for Video is in beta testing, so it's only available to a limited number of users at this time. It shouldn't be long (maybe even before you finish reading this chapter) before it's open to the general public, though.

All three of these options are viable for different types of AdSense users, and each has different uses and capabilities. How do you know which one to use for your site? That depends on how you want your site visitors to interact with the ads. (To some extent, it also depends on whether AdSense lets you use a certain type of video ad, but I get to that in a bit.)

Click-to-play

Click-to-play ads actually take the place of graphic ads on your site, but you can't control when that happens. You place a compatible graphic ad on your Web site, and when AdSense has a click-to-play video ad that fits your site, it's shown in place of the static ad. The videos don't show all the time, and there is currently no way to make videos replace static images all the time. See, it's based on the availability of videos that are appropriate to your site, but AdSense may not always have advertisers placing ads that match your site. It's only when there are matching video ads that your content ads will be replaced.

The ad formats that accommodate these click-to-play ads are

✔ 336x280 (Large rectangle)

✔ 300x250 (Medium rectangle)

✔ 250x250 (Square)

✔ 200x200 (Small square)

✔ 728x90 (Leaderboard)

    ✔ 120x600 (Skyscraper)

    ✔ 160x600 (Wide skyscraper)

If you already have one of these ads sizes on your Web site, but it's not image-enabled — meaning it's a text only ad — you can edit the settings under the Manage Ads option. To edit existing ads, follow these steps:

1. **Log into your AdSense account and go to the AdSense Setup tab.**

2. **Click the Manage Ads link.**

   The Manage Ads screen displays a list of the ads you have available, as shown in Figure 9-1.

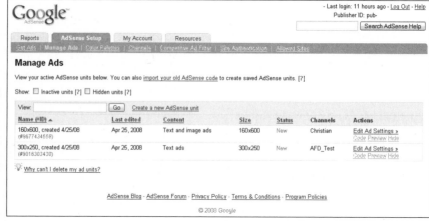

Figure 9-1: Choose the ad you want to edit from the list of available ads.

3. **Click Edit Ad Settings for the ad that you want to change.**

   The editing page for that ad appears, as shown in Figure 9-2.

4. **Use the Format drop-down menu (indicated in Figure 9-2) to select either Text and Image Ads or Image Ads Only.**

5. **Click the Save Settings button at the bottom of the page.**

   Within a couple of hours, your ads should be showing images, which can then be replaced by videos when they are available.

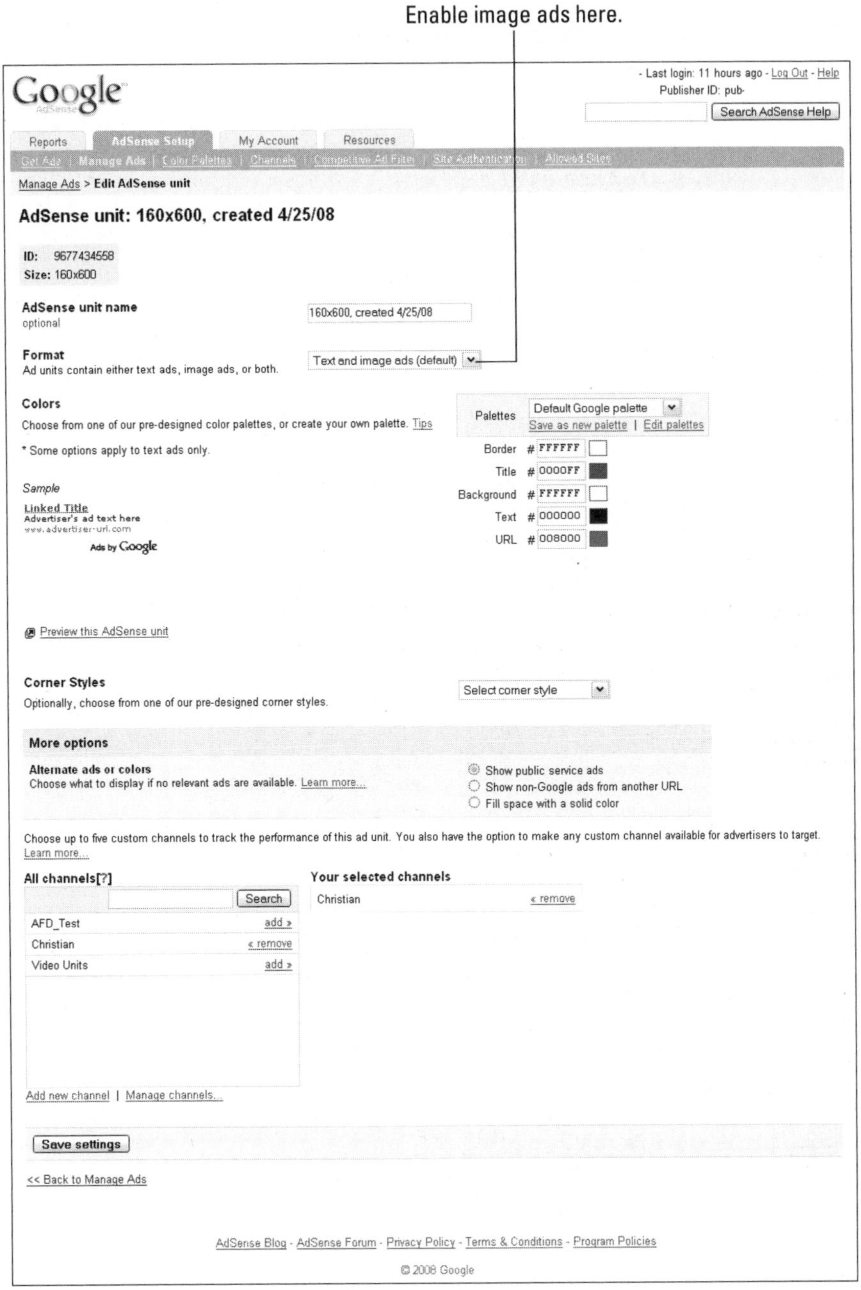

Enable image ads here.

Figure 9-2:
Use the
editing page
to change
the settings
of your ad.

Video units

Video units are ads that are partnered with YouTube videos. Such ads are displayed within your YouTube videos — both videos that you've created and videos that others have created that you have embedded on your Web site — in a couple different ways within the video player. They appear both as a banner at the top of the video player and as a pop-up link within the video player, as shown in Figure 9-3.

Figure 9-3:
Video units give viewers two places from which to click an ad.

If you don't use videos on your site, this type of ad might be a little out of place in the beginning. If you're using video on your site already, the integrations of video units are relatively smooth, and it's a great way to monetize the video content that your visitors are accustomed to.

Keep in mind that you have to have an active YouTube account to use this type of video ad and you also have to link your YouTube account to your AdSense account.

It only takes a few steps to link the two accounts:

1. **Open two browser windows and then log in to your YouTube account in one window and your AdSense account in the other.**

2. **In the window in which you have your AdSense account open, go to the AdSense Setup tab and then choose Video Units as the product.**

   Basically, act as if you're setting up a video unit for your Web site.

3. **When you get to the Video Setup page, click the Visit AdSense Video Units button.**

   Doing so takes you to the YouTube site, where you're prompted to connect your YouTube account and your AdSense account.

4. **If you already have a YouTube account and are signed in, verify your linkage request by entering the e-mail address, phone number, and postal code associated with your account.**

   This is why you signed in to both your YouTube account and your AdSense account in the first step.

5. **After you enter this information, click the Submit Confirmation button.**

   If you don't have a YouTube account, you're prompted to sign up for one. After you've created the account, the steps to connect the two accounts are the same as above.

   After you click the Submit Confirmation button, your accounts will be connected. Then you can return to your AdSense account to begin setting up video units.

AdSense for Video

AdSense for Video is the newest addition to the video family for AdSense. So new, in fact, that it's still in beta testing, and is only available to a certain number of participants. To be selected, you also have to meet certain restrictions:

✔ You must have a Flash 7 player that you can control.

✔ You must have 1,000,000 or more monthly streams — that's a million times a month that your video is viewed by site visitors. Don't let the number scare you. It's not all that uncommon for a popular YouTube video to get a million or more views in a month's time.

✔ You must be a U.S.-based Web site owner who publishes AdSense ads on your site and you must have a (primarily) U.S. viewership.

If you meet these requirements and want to display AdSense for Video ads, you also need to fill out a sign-up form (as shown in Figure 9-4) and wait to be accepted into the program. You can find the form at this URL: `www.google.com/adsense/support/bin/request.py?contact_type=video_joinbeta`.

When you do get accepted into the program, AdSense for Video allows you to place ads in *your own streaming video*. This is especially useful if you create and share videos on your Web site and other sites.

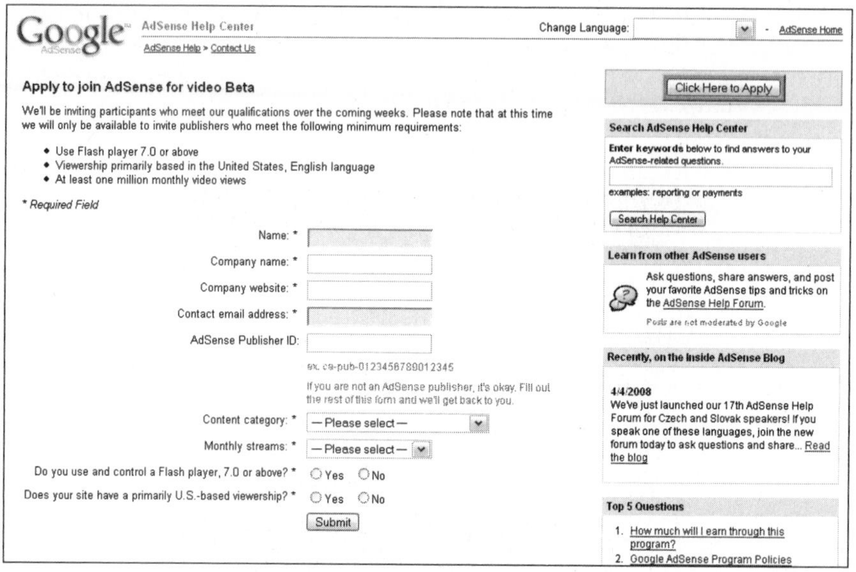

Figure 9-4: AdSense for Video is in beta testing, so users must be approved before using.

Ads can appear in one of two places in your video. Ads can be displayed *InVideo,* as shown in Figure 9-5, which means that the ads actually appear within the window where the video displays.

Figure 9-5: InVideo ads are actually small video ads within your video.

The alternative is to display ads as text overlays, as shown in Figure 9-6.

The cool thing about InVideo ads is that they're essentially a video within a video. The ads play in the lower one-third of the video player you've embedded on your site, and they're short — usually not more than 60 seconds.

While the ad is showing, the video that should be playing in the player is paused. Then, when the ad is finished, the area in which it is displayed shrinks back but still displays a link to the advertiser. The video that you have set to play should then begin on its own.

Figure 9-6:
Text overlay ads are the alternative in AdSense for Video.

Text overlay ads don't contain any actual video. They are simple text ads that overlay the lower one-third of the player. Your video plays as usual but the link remains available throughout the whole video.

There is no inherent advantage to one type of ad over the other — InVideo or Text Overlay. It's mostly a personal choice that should be governed by what you and your visitors prefer. I strongly recommend that you try each configuration separately for the same amount of time and then compare results to see which option your Web site audience likes best.

Enabling Click-to-Play Capabilities

Putting AdSense video capabilities into place on your Web site differs a little with each different type of video capability AdSense offers. The simplest path to take involves using click-to-play video ads, whereas AdSense for Video is definitely a bit trickier.

Implementing click-to-play video ads is as simple as choosing the right format (large rectangle, square, wide skyscraper, and so on) and enabling graphic ad displays. Choosing the right format for video ads isn't actually part of the video setup that AdSense offers but is part of the AdSense for Content setup (see Chapter 5).

If you made your way through Chapter 5, this choosing-an-ad-format business sounds familiar. Here's the shorthand version:

1. **Point your browser to** www.adsense.com, **log on to your AdSense account, and then click the AdSense Setup tab.**

2. **On the AdSense Setup tab select AdSense for Content.**

   The AdSense for Content Wizard appears.

3. **In the first section of the wizard, select the Ad Unit radio button and then select either Text and Image Ads or Image Ads Only from the drop-down menu to the right, as shown in Figure 9-7.**

Figure 9-7:
Select
one of the
options from
the drop-
down menu
to show
images in
your ads.

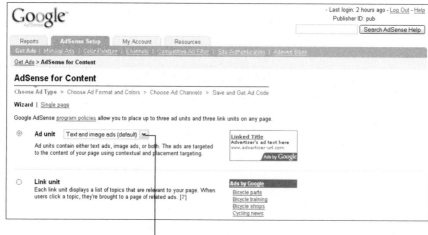

Choose an image ad option here.

Continue to set up the ad as I show you in Chapter 5. When you're finished, copy and paste the code into your Web site, and you're all set. All that remains is to wait for AdSense to place a click-to-play ad on your site.

You have no control over what videos get placed beyond enabling the graphic format that click-to-play video ads require. Ads are placed when they're appropriate for your site.

Earning with click-to-play ads is the same as earning with other AdSense for Content ads. Site visitors must click the ad and be taken to the advertiser's Web site for you to earn your payment on the ad.

When you get right down to it, nothing much different is going on in click-to-play video ads. You create and add the code for your ads in the same way you do for AdSense for Content ads. The only real difference is in the way the ad displays. If you're looking to draw a little more attention to your ads, this video format might be a good way to go about it. You can't blend video ads as well into your Web site as you can text ads, however, so test any video ads before you commit to replacing text ads that have already proven how they perform.

Getting Started with Video Units

Video units are a little more complicated than click-to-play ads. *Video units* are actually ads shown along with YouTube videos that are displayed in a specialized player you've added to your Web site.

You do have some control over what videos you choose to show in your player. You can select the video content you want by picking content categories, by selecting individual content providers, or by having video automatically targeted to your site content.

Before you can do any of that, however, you have to have a YouTube account that's connected to your Web site.

Signing up with YouTube

YouTube is a video-sharing service that's owned by Google. With YouTube, anyone can upload and share videos with others. Or, if you're not the video-shooting-and-sharing kind of person, you can browse YouTube videos to find things that interest you. Since I've been using YouTube, I've watched movie spoofs, instructional videos, and even sermons from church services. What you watch is directed by your taste in videos.

You can also find videos and add them to your Web site or blog. You don't actually download the video and then store it on your Web server; instead, you paste the code for a special URL into the code of your blog or Web site, and the video is streamed from YouTube to your site whenever someone comes to your site and starts the video.

In order to take advantage of all the fun, you *do* need to sign up for a YouTube account, which is a simple process. Start by going to the YouTube Web site at www.youtube.com. After you're there, click the Sign Up link in the upper-right corner of the page. You see a simple form, like the one shown in Figure 9-8. Fill it out, click the Sign Up button, and then wait for YouTube to send you a confirmation e-mail. After you get your e-mail, respond to it to create a YouTube account that you can use with AdSense.

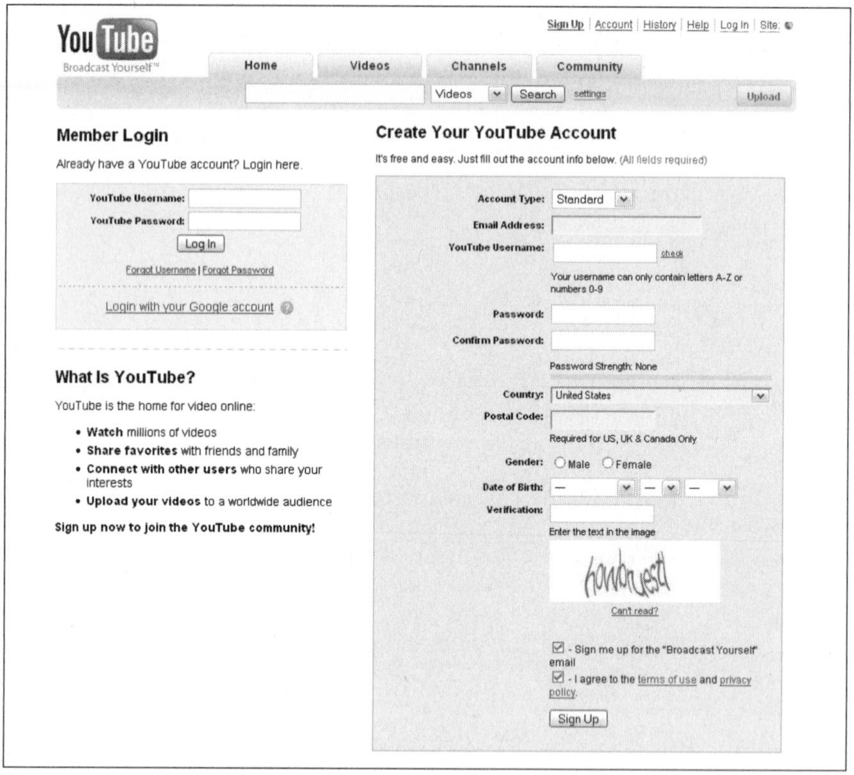

Figure 9-8:
To sign up
for YouTube,
enter the
requested
information
in the sign-
up form.

A note about the YouTube Partner program

YouTube has a Partner program that you can also use to monetize your YouTube videos. With the YouTube partner program, you can allow ads that are controlled by YouTube. Keep in mind, though, that you don't have as much control over them as you would with a standard AdSense ad. The ads are chosen for you, based on the videos that you choose to place on YouTube. That means that you won't necessarily be displaying the ads — other people will, when they display videos that you have uploaded to the YouTube service. This program can be a little confusing, and although it's not required for you to use video units with AdSense — in fact, the YouTube Partner program is a completely different entity than AdSense for Video — I want to take a minute to discuss its quirkier aspects.

To start with, signing up for the Partner program isn't difficult, *per se.* To sign up, fill out another form (see Figure 9-9) on the YouTube Web site (www. youtube.com/partners).

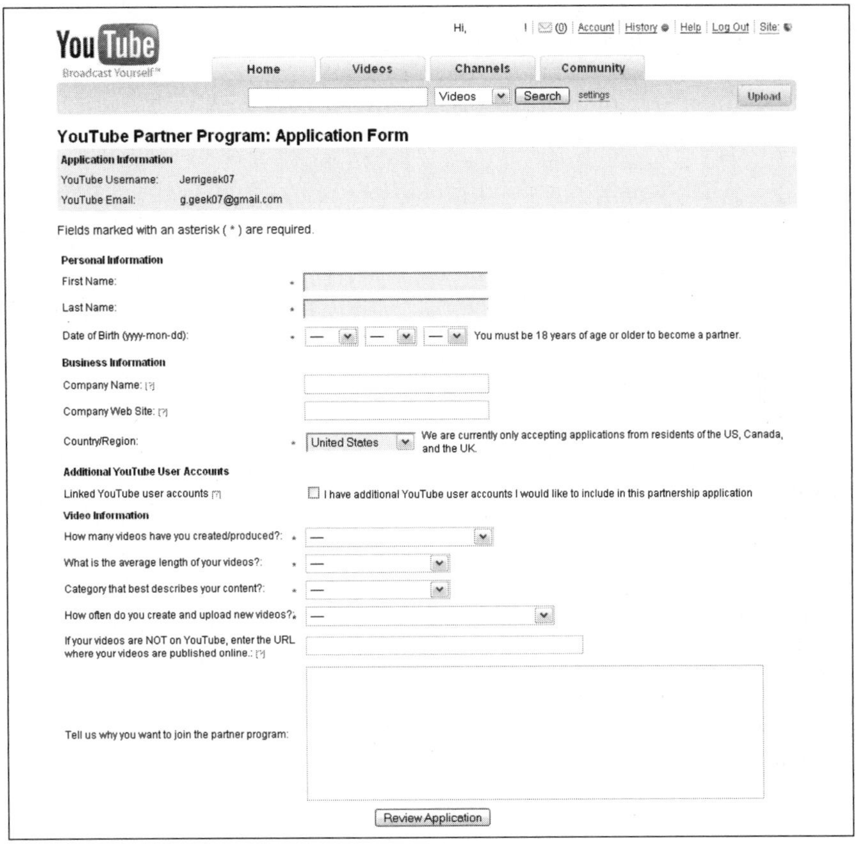

Figure 9-9:
Fill out and
submit this
form to be
considered
for the
YouTube
Partner
program.

The problem with this process isn't in the Filling Out Yet Another Form part or the Time You Spend Waiting to Find Out If You've Been Accepted into the Program part. The problem lies in the requirements to be accepted. To be accepted into the YouTube Partner program, you must meet the following criteria:

✔ You must create and upload original videos suitable for online streaming.

✔ You must own (or have express permission to use and monetize) all audio and video content that you upload — no exceptions.

✔ You must regularly upload videos that are viewed by thousands of YouTube users.

✔ You must live in the United States, Canada, or the United Kingdom.

In all, the only real issue is with the third point: You must regularly upload videos that are viewed by thousands of YouTube users. If you're new to YouTube, you're not likely to meet this criterion, so you may not be approved for the YouTube Partner program, which is frustrating when you want to start using AdSense video units immediately.

If you do meet the criteria and you're accepted into the YouTube Partner program, you have yet another method for monetizing your YouTube videos — in addition to using AdSense for Video. There is one little confusing part, though.

If you have more than one YouTube account, you could find yourself in AdSense-connection hell! In an effort to get out of that fiery Neverland, you may find that you're clicking from your AdSense account into your YouTube account, only to be sent back to your AdSense account again as you try to connect the two.

Make very sure you're logged in to your AdSense account and your YouTube account with the exact same e-mail address before you begin the connection process. If you're not, you'll be running in circles for hours trying to figure out what you've done wrong. Take my advice on this, folks. I spent nearly a whole day trying to figure out what I was doing wrong!

Creating your first video player

If you've made it this far, you deserve a medal. I don't give you one, though; instead, I show you how to create your first video player.

I make the assumption here that you've already connected your YouTube account to your AdSense account, as I describe in the previous section. That means you've received a nice confirmation message praising you for your successful linking of your YouTube and AdSense accounts. If you scroll down a bit in that message, you also see a line informing you that You Have Not Created Any AdSense Players Yet. Next to that little bit of info you see a Create AdSense Player button. Guess what I ask you to do?

1. **Click the Create AdSense Player button.**

    The New AdSense Player page appears, as shown in Figure 9-10. Use this page to build a customized AdSense player for your Web site.

2. **In the New AdSense Player page, enter a name for your AdSense player and, if you like, a short description in the text boxes provided.**

    Although the name and description are shown only to you, still enter something that helps you remember the purpose of the player, rather than some smart-alecky name whose meaning you might forget in a month or two.

3. **In the Theme section of the New AdSense Player page, select a color scheme for your player.**

    Make it something that matches well with your Web site.

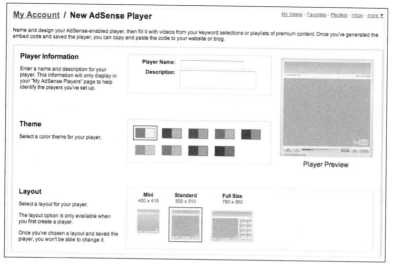

Figure 9-10:
Give your
AdSense
player a
name and
description
to help you
recognize it.

4. **In the Layout section of the page, choose a size that best suits your site.**

   Your choices here are Mini, Standard, and Full Size.

5. **After you finish making your selections, scroll farther down the page to make selections for what content you want to display in your AdSense video player, as shown in Figure 9-11.**

   You can choose to either let YouTube automatically populate your player with content, which is done by keywords — you enter the most relevant keywords for your site — or if you're like me and want more control, you can choose from a list of categories or individual providers that will be used to populate the player.

6. **After you make your selections, scroll to the bottom of the page and click the Generate Code button to get the code for your Web site.**

   When the page reloads, you'll have to scroll to the bottom of it to copy the code that's provided.

All that's left is to install the code on your Web site and then videos are fed directly into the AdSense player.

You're not limited to a single AdSense player on your Web site. You are, however, limited to one per page. If you want to create new players for other pages on your site, click the Create Player button on the left side of the screen when you log in to AdSense Video Units. Each player that you've created is then displayed on the Video Units page so that you can access it for deleting or editing at any time.

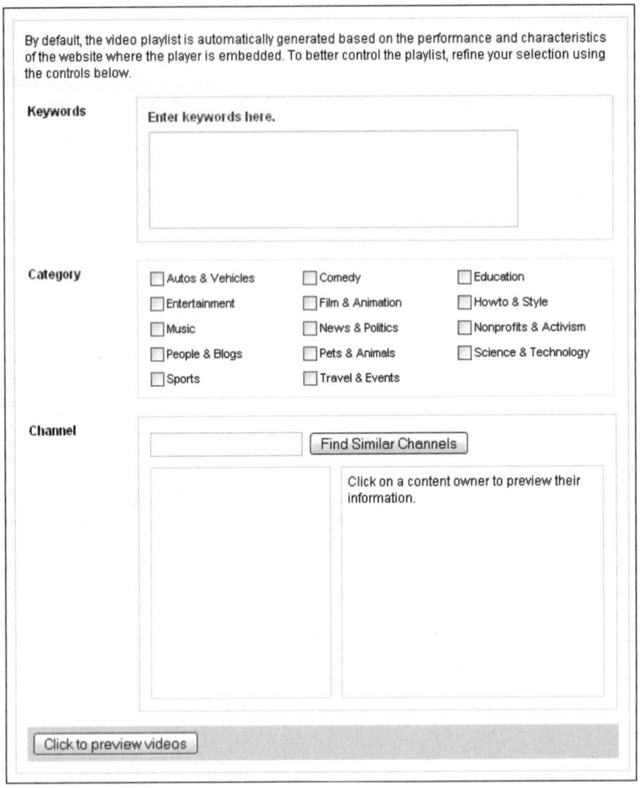

By default, the video playlist is automatically generated based on the performance and characteristics of the website where the player is embedded. To better control the playlist, refine your selection using the controls below.

Keywords

Enter keywords here.

Category

☐ Autos & Vehicles   ☐ Comedy   ☐ Education
☐ Entertainment   ☐ Film & Animation ☐ Howto & Style
☐ Music   ☐ News & Politics   ☐ Nonprofits & Activism
☐ People & Blogs   ☐ Pets & Animals   ☐ Science & Technology
☐ Sports   ☐ Travel & Events

Channel

[   ] [Find Similar Channels]

Click on a content owner to preview their information.

[Click to preview videos]

Figure 9-11:
You can
choose the
content that
appears
in your
player or
let YouTube
choose
for you.

Installing the code

Installing the code for the AdSense player is exactly like installing any other AdSense code on your Web site. First highlight and copy the code and then paste it into the HTML (HyperText Markup Language) for your Web site, between the <body> and </body> tags.

After you upload your Web site code to the server, your video units should begin showing immediately, although in some rare cases, you could experience a short delay. If your ads aren't showing within about an hour of having uploaded the new site with the AdSense code included, contact AdSense to see if you've done something wrong.

Earning with video units

Your earnings with video units aren't much different from the earnings that you generate with other types of AdSense ad units. The difference is all in the display.

With video units, you have two opportunities to earn from your placement. The first involves the banner-type ads that appear at the top of the video player, and the second comes from the text overlay ads that appear on the bottom 20 percent of the video player. When your site visitors click either of these ads, you get paid.

Some video units also have the *cost-per-impression model* — also called a cost-per-thousand-impression model because payment is based on the number of times an ad or video is viewed, divided by 1,000 — which means all that's necessary for you to get some earnings out of this is for someone to view the video. Like all cost-per-impression ads, those are doled out by AdSense to sites that generate very high levels of traffic and stringently meet the requirements that advertisers have set forth.

You never know for sure when cost-per-impression ads are displayed, so all you can do is steadily build your Web site traffic and hope that they're displayed when you're having a nice spike in traffic. If you do happen to notice when a cost-per-impression ad is displayed, you can always try to drive traffic to your site. You never know how long the ad remains on your site though, so whatever efforts you take should be ones that have quick results.

Reports for video units

After you connect your AdSense and YouTube accounts, a new report appears on your Reports page. This report is for the video units, and it shows the same information for video units that you see for other types of AdSense ads:

- ✔ Page impressions
- ✔ Clicks
- ✔ Page click-through-rate (CTR)
- ✔ Page cost-per-thousand impressions
- ✔ Earnings

You have the same capabilities with this report that you have with any of the other earnings reports that AdSense makes available, including the ability to generate the report regularly and have it e-mailed to you. (For more on AdSense reports, see Chapter 15.)

If you're already using video on your Web site or blog, AdSense video units are a good way to monetize on that video. After you work your way through the confusing parts, you can add video with the click of a few buttons. The earnings potential is there, so get started with it.

Go, Go Google Gadgets

If you've ever seen a personalized Google home page, you've seen Google Gadgets in action. *Google Gadgets* are basically little programs that you (or someone else) put together and upload to the Google Gadgets collection. Users can then download those gadgets and add them to their iGoogle home page or even to their Google desktop application.

Some serious confusion exists about how Google Gadgets works with AdSense, though, and I clear that up for you. First, a little more about Google Gadgets, what they do, and how they're created.

What's a gadget?

Google Gadgets are mini-applications that are created with XML, HTML, or JavaScript. When you create a Google Gadget, it can do anything from display the weather forecast to show you the Bible verse of the day or connect you to a useful service on a company's Web page. One example is the Wikipedia Gadget, which sits on your iGoogle page and shows a search box for Wikipedia. To perform a search, type your search string into the search box, click Search, and you're taken to the correct Wikipedia page. Cool, huh?

Gadgets are an excellent way to turn users onto your products and services by giving them a sneak peak at what you have to offer. Gadgets can be in the form of calculators, search boxes, useful tools, or whatever it is that you have to offer. The thing to remember as you plan to create a Google Gadget is that the more useful or entertaining it is, the more people will download and install the gadget, which is the key to monetizing your gadgets.

When you create gadgets, think creatively about the audience that you want to serve. What does that audience want that doesn't already exist? When you hit that sweet spot, you'll know you've come up with the right idea by the number of downloads of your gadgets.

Creating a gadget

If you have an idea for a gadget that you think will be wildly popular, create it. You can create gadgets in XML, HTML, or JavaScript. Creating gadgets is all about how you format the code that makes the gadget work.

Don't be discouraged if you don't know XML or JavaScript, though. If you know some basic HTML, Google provides all the additional information that you need to create a gadget with the Google Gadgets Editor (GGE). You use this program to write the code for the gadget. Alternatively, you can use any text editor that you're comfortable with, but GGE is specifically designed for you to work with gadgets.

To access GGE, log in to `http://code.google.com/apis/gadgets/docs/gs.html#GGE` and scroll to the bottom of the page. That's where the editor, as shown in Figure 9-12, makes its home — until you offer it a new home on your computer.

Figure 9-12: The Google Gadgets Editor is where you can create your first gadgets.

One of the most basic gadgets that you can create is the same program that everyone starts with when they're figuring out how to program an HTML site of any kind — `Hello, world!`

`Hello, world!` is a very simple program to write and requires only a few lines of code, such as:

```
<?xml version="1.0" encoding="UTF-8"?>
<Module>
<ModulePrefs title="hello world example" />
<Content type="html">
<![CDATA[Hello, world!]]></Content>
</Module>
```

I explain this line by line as follows:

```
<?xml version="1.0" encoding="UTF-8"?>
```

The first line is a standard opening line of code that tells any processor reading it that a program's coming, and it's written in *this* language with *that* protocol. In this case, the language is XML version 1.0, and the encoding protocol is UTF-8.

```
<Module>
```

The `<module>` tag indicates that a program — the gadget — is within the program.

```
<ModulePrefs title="hello world example" />
```

The third line is the module preferences tag, which indicates information about the module, such as the title, the author, and other optional features that might need to be taken into consideration.

```
<Content type="html">
```

Just as it reads, this line tells you what the type of content for the gadget is. In this case, the content type is HTML (which is why you can get away with not knowing XML or JavaScript). If you can use the tags here to get started and you know HTML, then you can use HTML as your content type and write your gadget using HTML code.

```
<![CDATA[Hello, world!]]></Content>
```

The `<![CDATA>` tag is used to enclose HTML when a gadget's content type is HTML. This tag tells the browser that reads the code that the text within the CDATA section shouldn't be treated as XML. The CDATA section typically contains HTML and JavaScript. `</Content>`, or the closing tag, is another part to this line. The *closing tag* — in this case, the `</Content>` closing tag — indicates where the content for the module ends and is a signal that the program information is complete.

```
</Module>
```

Here's another closing tag. This one indicates that the module is complete.

With that, you're finished. This is a very simple gadget, but when done properly, it appears like the one shown in Figure 9-13.

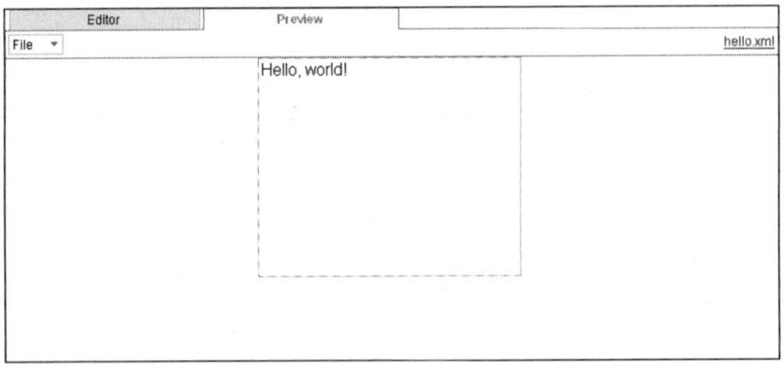

Figure 9-13:
The Hello, world! gadget is as simple as it gets.

If you play with it some more, you can tweak it considerably. For example, Figure 9-14 shows what I did with some very simple HTML tags.

Figure 9-14:
Play with
the HTML
a little and
you can
change
Hello,
world! as
desired.

Obviously, you'll want to do something a little more sophisticated than a simple Hello, world! message, but I want to give you a feel for how easy it is to work with Google Gadgets.

I'm sure you're wondering where AdSense comes into this mix, though, right? It's simple. AdSense doesn't have a module specifically for Google Gadgets. However, you can program your AdSense ads directly into Google Gadgets.

Programming your AdSense ads into Google Gadgets is just like creating a Google AdSense for Content ad. Generate the ad by using the same steps that you would if you were putting the ad directly into the content on your Web site, and then insert the AdSense code into your gadget code. (If you skipped straight to this chapter and you don't know how to create a content ad, you can jump to Chapter 5 where I address that.) You may have to play with it a little to get the styles and placement just right, but the end result is a gadget that includes an AdSense ad for everyone to see.

Except for one small problem . . .

Creating gadgets sounds simple enough, and if doing so with AdSense ads piques your interest, you'll probably want to do a little more studying on the topic because it's more involved than I make it sound here. You can read more about it by going to the Google Gadgets Web site at http://code. google.com/apis/gadgets.

There's one small issue of which you might want to be aware upfront. When you're creating a Google Gadget with the intent of embedding Google AdSense code into it, you first need permission from AdSense. AdSense doesn't usually have a problem with granting that permission, but without it, your ad probably won't show up properly in the gadget.

To get permission, you have to e-mail Google AdSense with their support form found at `www.google.com/adsense/support/bin/request.py`. Enter your contact information in the form, and then, in the text box provided for questions or statements, write a brief request to use AdSense in your gadget. If you already have an active gadget that is popular, be sure to include information about it. If you're creating a new gadget, include that information too. And don't forget a description of your gadget. Google will make the determination to allow you to use AdSense in your gadget on a case-by-case basis.

You may have to wait a few days to get a response from AdSense, so think a little ahead of the game if you're trying to meet a specific deadline.

Another issue to keep in mind when you're creating your gadgets with AdSense embedded in them is that the combination of the two isn't something that Google came up with, so there are times when gadgets and AdSense don't play well together.

This can result in either the gadget that you've created not being shown or the AdSense ad not being shown. There's no known fix for this issue right now. Google's working on it, so you'll see that your ads and gadgets display well for a time and then they'll crash. This is the nature of the beast, so be prepared with alternative plans (maybe for a gadget without ads) in the event that one program ticks off the other.

Ultimately, even without AdSense, Google Gadgets are a great investment of your time because they're a quick and easy way to draw a lot of users to your site — especially if you can nail down your audience and provide a truly useful gadget. If you can combine AdSense with your gadgets, you've really created a winning combination.

Chapter 10

AdSense for Mobile

· ·

· ·

*L*ook around on any given day and you'll probably see a few dozen people using their cell phones. Most will be talking on them, but you'll also find plenty who are texting or even using the Internet.

Despite its smaller format and scaled-down capabilities, the mobile Internet is gaining a lot of traction, especially among younger — Generation X and Generation Y — users. These kids are always on the go, and they grab what they're looking for from the Internet while they're in mid-stride. (Unlike me — I'm a little more "mature" and find it difficult to read the screen on the phone, much less search the Web!)

This younger generation also has a larger disposable income than adults — folks who have mortgages, car payments, and credit card bills to think about, not to mention the cost of providing disposable income to the younger generation!

If that disposable income is available, why wouldn't you want to tap into it? Most Web site owners do feel that urge, so they've created mobile-friendly Web sites that allow cell phone-enabled Internet users to access their content whether those visitors are sitting on the bus or climbing the Rocky Mountains. Of course, with mobile Web sites, Google will find a way to monetize these mobile-friendly sites.

Enter Google *AdSense for Mobile,* which is a program that allows you to put ads on your Web site that can be displayed on mobile browsers. Visitors surfing your site with a mobile phone can see and click these ads, and you can earn some bucks even in this smaller format.

Trying to harvest a bit of cash from mobile users *does* require some changes to your Web site, though, and it also requires that you scale down some AdSense strategies. Think small, in other words, but don't freak. Thinking small doesn't require too much retooling. This chapter contains what you need to know to target those mobile surfers and add another stream to your AdSense revenues.

The Differences of Mobility

Nearly half of all mobile Internet users use mobile Web sites only to find tidbits of immediately useful information. Mobile surfers don't usually surf just for the fun of being on the Internet — they save major surfing for when they can sit at a computer and see pages displayed more than a few words at a time. In part, that's because mobile Web sites are usually pretty poorly designed still, despite the fact that the mobile Web has been around for awhile now.

It's hard to get the hang of how a Web site should appear on a cell phone screen. Many Web site owners make the mistake of designing their Web site for the computer screen and then enabling it for mobile phones without changing site design. You can do that, but the results won't be the most useful site a mobile surfer comes across.

Enabling your site for mobile users is easy — for the most part. In most cases, it requires a small switch in the encoding of your Web site from HTML (HyperText Markup Language) to XHTML (eXtensible HyperText Markup Language) or another mobile-enabled Web design language.

Some mobile applications, however, require *PHP — hypertext processor* (I have no clue how the popular acronym gained the first *P*). PHP is a server-side processing language because *scripts* (or *applications*) are run from the server rather than from the computer that the application appears on. This makes it much easier to have rich programming on Web sites, which doesn't depend on the computer a visitor may be using.

Because of the way it works, PHP makes creating rich, detailed mobile Web sites a much easier process. The cool part is that if you have a Web site written in HTML or XHTML, changing it to PHP is often as easy as changing the extension of the files that make up the site from `.htm` to `.php`. Really.

Well, okay, it sounds easy enough. Now for a reality check — I've seriously oversimplified the considerations that go into creating mobile Web sites. The fact remains that if your site is built for display on a computer screen, mobile users won't have the same experience. For example, Figure 10-1 shows how a list of links might look on a mobile Web page. Keep in mind that there's no mouse on a mobile phone, so users have to scroll through every link on the page until they get to the one they want to follow.

Figure 10-1:
Links on a
Web site
may look
something
like this on
a mobile
browser.

Simply changing the extension on an existing site built for the Internet also
doesn't do justice to the pages that display on mobile phones. Much of the
graphics and functionality of the site is lost during the translation to a mobile
format, so while the extension change allows you to quickly enable the text
and links on your site for mobility, it doesn't make the site pretty or even
completely useful.

The hardware restraints faced by most mobile users also create serious
issues. You have to go into creating a Web site with the thought of making it
available to the largest audience possible. That's just a fact of mobile life, and
as more and more mobile adoptions take place, the mobile surfer is more of a
consideration. That means making your site friendly for both mobile and non-
mobile surfers.

Mobile content is different

When you're considering a mobile surfer as part of the audience for your site,
keep in mind the different uses for the mobile Web. Google has done a lot of
research in this area and has defined three types of mobile surfers:

- **Repetitive Now:** This is the group of mobile surfers who have a set
  of online activities that they conduct from their phones on a regular
  basis. Some of the repetitive tasks these surfers perform are checking
  the weather, reading news stories and blog posts, and checking stock
  quotes.

 ✔ **Bored Now:** The Bored Now group of Web surfers have a few minutes of downtime and don't know what else to do in such a short amount of time. Out comes the phone, and the Web browser is opened to occupy their minds for just a few minutes. This type of mobile surfer is probably the most targeted because this is the only area where true e-commerce dollars can be captured. Bored Now surfers are selecting ringtones, downloading videos, and adding themes to their phones.

 ✔ **Urgent Now:** "We need it right now" is the motto of this group of mobile surfers. These people are booking, changing, or checking airline flights, booking hotel rooms, finding directions, or locating restaurants. They need information now, so they pull out their phones to find it.

As you consider these three types of mobile surfers, think about which group you're targeting because the group determines whether AdSense ads will even be acknowledged by these users. The Repetitive Now group and the Bored Now group might click your ads. Unless there's something very compelling about them, the Urgent Now group is likely to pass right by an ad and go straight for the information they seek.

Mobile requirements

Mobile content is definitely different from the content that you find on other Web pages, and because it is, participation in AdSense for Mobile has some different requirements. Obviously, the Web site must be mobile-compliant, but it also must be developed with a server-side scripting language, such as PHP. If you're not sure what PHP is, check out "The Differences of Mobility" section earlier in this chapter to find out more about it.

If your mobile site isn't developed with a server-side scripting language, AdSense for Mobile ad code doesn't display properly on your pages. The code generated for AdSense for Mobile doesn't render properly on a normal Web site, either, so don't generate the code thinking that you can fool Google into believing that you're supporting mobile Web sites. All you'll wind up doing is generating an obvious error that your site visitors can see.

Here are some of the mobile Web page markup languages that can be used to program your Web site and still have mobile ads enabled:

 ✔ **WML (WAP 1.x):** WML, or *wireless markup language,* is a programming language that's based on XML (eXtensible Markup Language) and is designed specifically for creating Web sites and applications for mobile devices.

 ✔ **XHTML (WAP 2.0):** *eXtensible HyperText Markup Language* is an intersection of HTML and XML, meaning that it's useful for both normal Web sites and mobile Web sites.

✔ **CHTML (imode):** *Compact HTML* is an alternative to WML and XHTML, but it was designed specifically for Japanese cell phones and even more specifically for one manufacturer's products — the Japanese company DoCoMo — and the imode phone designation just indicates an Internet enabled device. So this isn't a markup language that has a wide usage outside Japan.

I know this is all pretty complicated, but it really is necessary to program your mobile Web site using a supported mobile scripting language if you want your site to be both functional and useful. Users aren't likely to return to a site that's nothing more than text and links. If you plan to have a mobile site, you should make it as functional and useful as possible. If you want to find out more about mobile scripting languages, check out *Next Generation Wireless Applications: Creating Mobile Applications in a Web 2.0 and Mobile 2.0 World,* by Paul Golding (Wiley Publishing), or *Wireless Markup Language (WML) Scripting and Programming Using WML, cHTML, and xHTML,* by William Routt (Althos Publishing).

In the preceding list, there's another abbreviation that I haven't explained yet — WAP. *Wireless application protocol* is a standard that's used to simplify how a browser sees a Web site so that mobile browsers can access the Internet. The protocol is automatically built into the programming language that you're using to create your mobile Web site. So WML sites automatically adhere to the protocol WAP 1.0 and higher. XHTML is designed to work with the protocol WAP 2.0 and higher.

In addition to the actual software language requirements that AdSense sets forth, ad placement, behavior, and accessibility guidelines are as follows:

✔ You can display only one ad unit per mobile Web page.

✔ A *double ad unit* — an ad unit that displays two different advertisers' links — can be placed only on the bottom of the page but can be located above the page's footer (including navigational links and copyright messages).

✔ Ads displayed on a mobile Web page may not be modified or obscured in any way.

✔ After an ad has been clicked, the landing page display may not be interrupted or prevented in any way. For instance, you can't display any other pages — including other advertisements — before taking users to the advertiser's Web site.

✔ The Google crawlers must be able to access your mobile Web sites for targeting purposes. If the crawler can't access your site, ads won't be displayed on your mobile pages.

If you're truly interested in creating a mobile Web site and you have content that will support mobile users, monetize the site as much as possible. These guidelines help you to do just that — put the right content in front of mobile surfers so you can take advantage of mobile ad revenues. That process is only slightly different than the one used for setting up AdSense for Content (see Chapter 5).

Setting Up AdSense for Mobile

Okay, the technical mumbo-jumbo is out of the way. I don't claim that what you've read so far in this chapter is everything there is to know about understanding mobile programming languages and protocols, and creating mobile Web sites. This is an AdSense book and it doesn't cover everything mobile. If you want to know more about creating mobile Web sites, check out *Mobile Internet For Dummies,* by John R. Levine, Michael J. O'Farrell, and Jostein Algroy (Wiley Publishing). If you really want the whole nine yards, go for Nirav Mehta's *Mobile Web Development.* It's technically dense, but you'll find everything you need to know in it.

Setting up AdSense for Mobile is a lot like setting up AdSense for Content. The differences are all related to the mobile platform and are easy enough to navigate. You have to tell the AdSense folks which programming language — or a markup language (or just markup for short) — you used for your site. You also have to tell AdSense which character encoding you used for the site.

Character encoding happens when you combine one set of characters with some other indicator, such as numbers or integers. Morse code is probably one of the best known sets of character encoding because it combines letters of the Latin alphabet with dots and dashes that are used in telegraphy. The result is that a set of dots and dashes (or *depressions*) can be sent with a telegraph machine and then decoded to represent the characters they represent. In other words, with a telegraph, you could send messages from one place to another.

Character encoding for Web sites works basically the same way. Characters are encoded with some numerical system. Then, the Web browser can decode those characters to ensure that they're displayed properly. In most cases, UTF-8 is the most commonly used character encoding for U.S. Web sites.

I'm jumping just a little ahead of the game here. To begin creating your mobile ads, first log in to your AdSense account. Then use these steps to create the ad:

1. **Click the Get Ads link on the AdSense Setup tab.**

   The Get Ads page appears.

2. **On the Get Ads page, select the AdSense for Mobile Content link, as shown in Figure 10-2.**

   The AdSense for Mobile Content Wizard appears, ready to walk you through the process of setting up mobile ads (see Figure 10-3).

3. **In the Format section of the wizard, use the drop-down menu to select the type of ad you want to display on your Web site.**

   You have two options: Single or Double. Single shows the link to one advertiser whereas Double shows the links to two, but the ads are stacked one on top of the other.

   Mobile text ads contain 24–36 characters of text depending on the language in which the ad is written, followed by a destination URL if advertisers choose to enter one. Advertisers also have the option to allow customers to directly connect to their business phones by placing a Call link next to the destination URL. If the Call link appears, visitors can click the link to initiate a call to the advertiser.

Figure 10-2:
Select the
AdSense
for Mobile
Content link
to create
mobile ads.

The AdSense for Mobile Content link

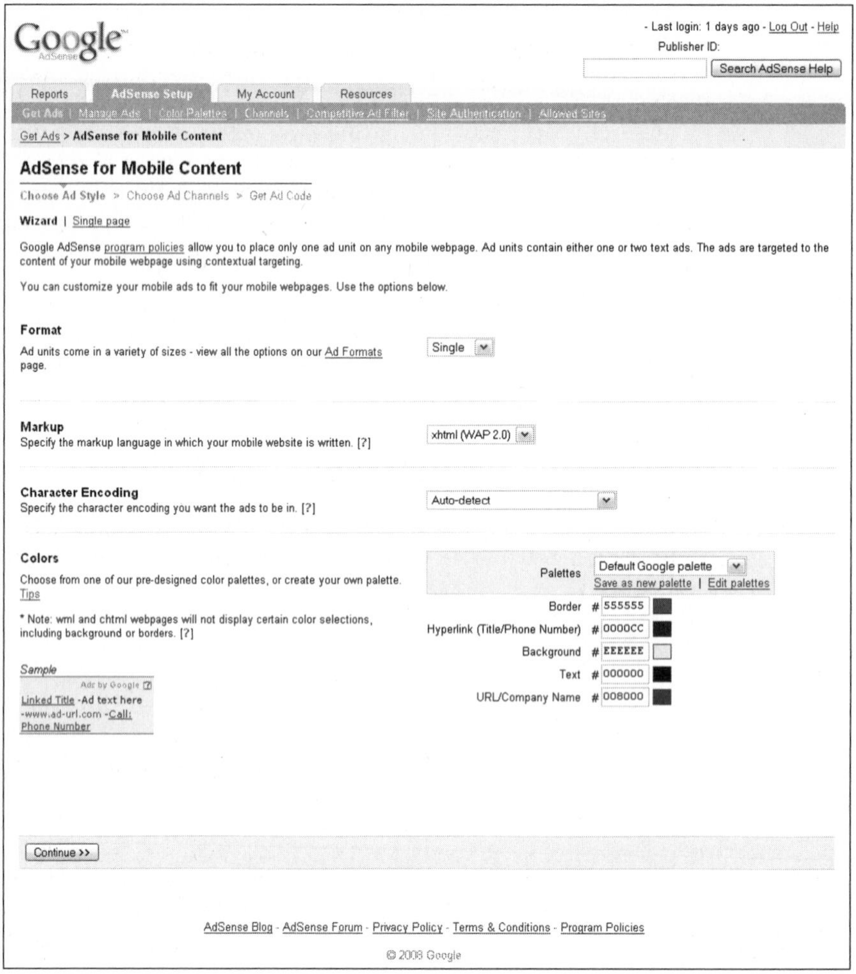

Figure 10-3:
The AdSense
for Mobile
Content
Wizard
walks you
through
creating ads
for mobile
content.

4. **In the Markup section of the wizard, use the drop-down menu to select the markup language used to create your mobile Web site.**

   Your choices are WML, XHTML, and CHTML. If you're not sure what these are, flip to the discussion about them earlier in this chapter in the "Mobile requirements" section.

5. **In the Character Encoding section of the wizard, use the drop-down menu to select the character encoding for your Web site.**

   If you're not sure what character encoding is used on your site, AdSense gives you the option to Auto-Detect encoding. Make sure that option is selected.

6. **In the Colors section of the wizard, use the color palettes to choose colors for the various elements of your ads.**

As with AdSense for Content, you want your mobile ads to blend with the pages on which they appear. Use the Color Picker (that pretty colored box) next to each element to choose the color you want to use for that element. Alternatively, you can also enter the six-digit hexadecimal number in the text box provided to further customize colors if the one you want to use isn't available in the Color Picker. However, you should know there are some markup languages — like WML and CHTML — that don't allow color customization, so your ads are displayed in the default Google palette if you're using one of these languages.

7. **Click Continue.**

   You're taken to the next page in the wizard, where you have the option of selecting or creating specific channels to track your mobile ads. Remember, channels are simply tracking tools that help you visualize how ads are performing. You can add a channel to your ad, and then when you look at your AdSense reports, you can immediately see how one channel of ads performs over another.

8. **In the new wizard page, use the drop-down menu to select a channel — or click the Add New Channel link to add a new one — and then click Continue.**

   You're taken to the Get Code page of the wizard.

Placing mobile ads to increase earnings

Placement is one problem that you'll likely encounter with mobile ads. The format of a mobile Web site is already so small, so how do you place ads that catch the attention of mobile surfers?

My suggestion is to place them near the top of the page. For example, if you're setting up your mobile Web site so that a small logo appears and then content and links for your page immediately display, ads appear between the logo and the content.

This gets the ads right in front of the mobile Web site users as quickly as possible to ensure they don't navigate away from the page before your ads are seen.

Another alternative might be to put your ads at the top of a list of links that appear on your mobile Web page. This integrates the ads into the links, making them feel a little more natural on the site. But again, they're still above the links so that users have the chance to actually see the ads before they navigate away from the page.

Ultimately, the perfect placement of your ads may take some trial-and-error. With any form of AdSense, don't take my word — or anyone else's for that matter — as gospel. Instead, begin with my suggestions and test your ads over a period of time to see where they earn the most click-throughs for your site. Only thorough testing can you really determine what works and what doesn't on your specific pages. Ultimately, what works for you is all that really matters, right?

In this last page of the wizard, you see one major difference from the AdSense for Content routine. Check out Figure 10-4, where you can see a Server-Side Scripting Language drop-down menu right above the box that contains the code for your ad.

9. **In the Server-Side Scripting Language drop-down menu, choose the language that was used during the creation of your Web site.**

    The code changes to reflect the option that you select.

10. **Copy and paste the code into your mobile Web site.**

    Paste the ad code into your mobile site in the same way you paste the code into a regular Web site. Find the location on the site where you want the ad to appear and paste the code there. Remember, however, that it can take up to 48 hours for ads to start appearing on your pages.

Select the appropriate scripting language.

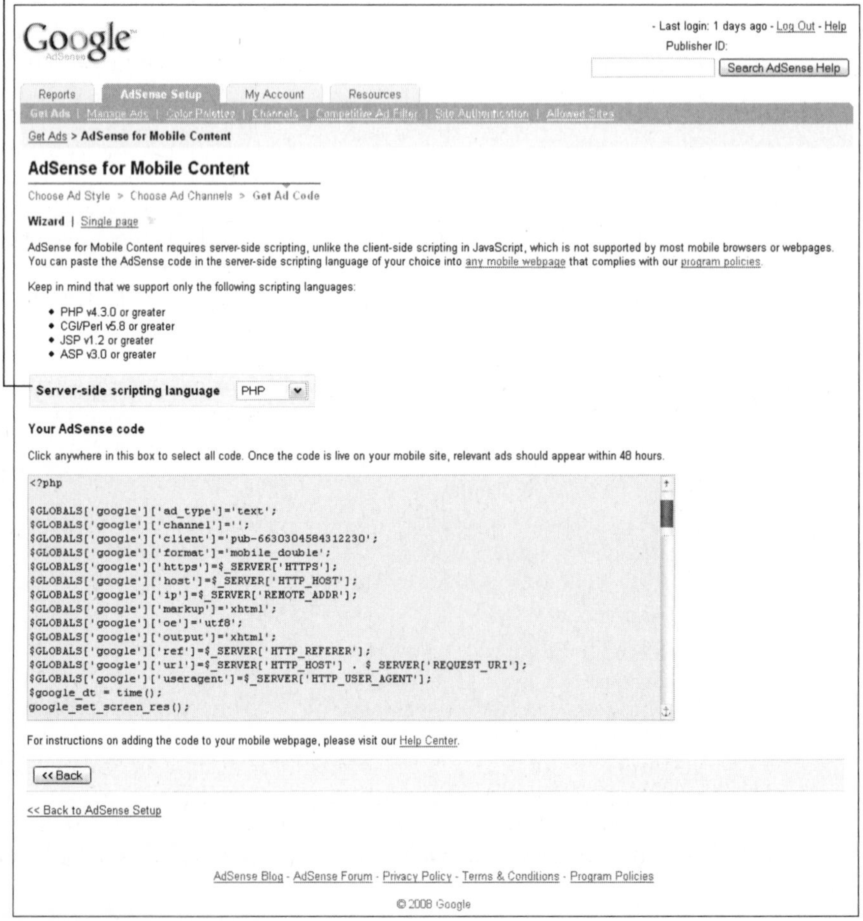

Figure 10-4:
Select the server-side scripting language used to create your Web site.

Just as you can with content ads, you can filter your mobile ads to prevent your competitors from advertising on your mobile site. To filter a site, go to the AdSense Setup tab and select the Competitive Ad Filter link. After the Competitive Ad Filter page loads, select the AdSense for Mobile Content tab and enter the URLs that you want filtered. Enter one URL per line. When you're finished, click the Save Changes button below the text box.

Earning with AdSense for Mobile

The AdSense way of doing things is pretty much the same across all ad formats — visitor clicks ad, you get money. Mobile ads do have *one* wrinkle that you haven't seen in other types of ads, though, and that's the Click to Call link. This link allows visitors to click the link and place a call to the advertiser. It's a cool feature, but one that might leave you wondering how you'll get paid for that.

Truth is that this link works just like any other link in an ad. You get paid for mobile ads whenever your site visitors click the ad links. That includes the Click to Call link. Like other types of AdSense ads, the amount of payment is determined by the payments that advertisers make when their ads are displayed. It's a formula that Google keeps closely guarded, but it works the same as AdSense for Content and other types of AdSense. Advertisers bid for the right to have their ads shown. Then, each time the ad is shown, Google gets paid whatever that winning bid amount is. In turn, Google then gives a percentage of what it is paid to you, the Web site owner who publishes the ad. But how much is the exact percentage? Google is pretty tight-lipped about it.

You can track your AdSense for Mobile earnings on the Reports page, which is the first page you encounter when you sign in to your AdSense account. Included here is a category for AdSense for Mobile Content that shows page impressions, clicks, click-through-rates, effective cost-per-thousand impressions, and earnings. Like other reports, you can show these numbers by day, week, month, or all the time. (For more on AdSense Reports, see Chapter 15.)

Mobile Web sites, and by extension mobile ads, aren't for everyone. You may not have a Web site that's appropriate for (or is even of interest to) mobile surfers. That's a call you have to make.

If your site does lend itself to the mobile lifestyle, however, consider AdSense for Mobile. It's one way to monetize your mobile efforts — and although the revenues that you generate for mobile ads might not be enough to pay the mortgage or the payment on that shiny new car you rushed out and bought when you were approved to display AdSense ads, it might add a little to the revenue streams that you're building. In my book, every little bit helps.

Chapter 11

AdSense for RSS

· ·

· ·

*E*very once in a while you stumble across a great idea that hasn't quite made it to fruition yet. That's what AdSense for Feeds is. It really is a great idea — who could hate the ability to place ads in dynamic content that's pushed out to readers? — but it's an idea that hasn't quite made its way off the production line yet.

Another way of putting this is to say that AdSense for Feeds is still just a concept. As I write this, it's in closed beta testing and there is no word from the company about when the beta testing will end and general public release will begin. (I've heard rumors that it will be open to the general public soon, but I really can't confirm any of those rumors.)

I still think covering the topic is a good idea. The program is sure to be available sooner, rather than later, and if you already know how to use it, you'll be ahead of the learning curve. Because you can sign up to be notified when AdSense releases the program for general use, you won't have to waste any time when it does become available.

Feed What? An RSS?

As the popularity of blogs grew, so did the popularity of another technology, called a *feed* or *RSS feed*. Both of these terms refer to the same thing. Feeds are content that is pushed out to registered users who have signed up to receive them. The content that's pushed out can be short teasers about blog posts, news, or podcasts or it can be a complete blog post, news item, or article.

Podcasts can't be pushed out through RSS, but you can send a teaser or blurb about the podcast. (And, if you think podcasts have something to do with the pod people from *Invasion of the Body Snatchers,* have I got news for you: A *podcast* is actually an audio recording that's available to listen to online. It's an audio version of an article, news story, or blog post.)

Pushing content

Think of feeds like the ticker tapes that were used to transmit breaking news into newsrooms around the world back in the 1940s and '50s. Only this ticker tape is faster, produces less waste, and is written in complete sentences.

The technology is different, but the result is the same — news is shared as soon as it's created. Now, I can hear you grumbling that blogs aren't news. Blog usually are news to *someone.* Does that mean that what you'll find in a blog is going to appear on the 6:00 news or as headlines in tomorrow's newspaper? Not usually. But for every blog out there, there is a host of people who read the blog and want to know when a new post goes up. To those people, those posts are news, and they wouldn't mind at all if news was updated in the timeliest fashion possible.

Because blogs have become so important in communicating in today's Internet-centric world, people often read multiple blogs every day. I know people who subscribe to feeds for a dozen or more blogs every day. The blogs vary — some like news, some like blogs in a particular niche area, and some just like the stories about other people's lives. Whatever draws a person, there is usually more than one blog for them to keep up with, and that's where feeds come in.

Despite what you may have heard, RSS doesn't stand for *Really Simple Stupid.* It actually stands for *Really Simple Syndication,* and it's a protocol by which content is delivered to a user who can read the content using an *RSS reader* or *feed reader* — programs that display the content pushed out in RSS or feeds. This content may be a small snippet — up to about 250 words — or it may be the whole article. The person who sets up the feed determines how much text is delivered to the reader.

Reading content

I've tied RSS feeds into the bloggy part of the Internet, but I have to be a bit careful here. Accessing blogs is a no-brainer — you fire up your browser, point it to the correct URL, and start reading away. RSS feeds are a bit different in that, as I mention earlier, you need a special software program — an *RSS reader* or *feed reader* — in order to access RSS feeds.

Not that it's at all hard to find a feed reader. Examples abound, including a Google variant (of course!) known as the Google Reader (`www.google.com/reader`) as well as Feedreader, a neat little product available at `www.feedreader.com`. I'm not talking rocket science here. All you need is a relatively simple software program that's been programmed to collect content from various feed-enabled sources.

Using programs like Google Reader or Feedreader is usually pretty simple. You begin with the application, which provides you with the "window" for reading the selected content. To add content to the program, you usually just have to enter a URL. The program then goes out and gets new content either on a schedule that you set or in real-time. For example, if you're using the feed reader that's built in to Outlook 2007, when you check your e-mail — or whenever Outlook is scheduled to download your mail — your feeds are also automatically updated. New feeds are updated in the Feed Display folder, just like new e-mails.

If you're using a program like Google Reader, the feeds are collected on a Web site. You log in to the site to see a listing of all the available posts — that listing is automatically updated each time someone posts a new item to the feed to which you're subscribed.

The AdSense connection

You might be saying to yourself "Self, this is truly fascinating stuff, but where does AdSense fit in to all this?" Wonder no longer. AdSense, in its infinite wisdom, is working on software that would place AdSense ads directly into the RSS feeds that are pushed out to subscribers. The idea here is that even though you have content that's pushed out to readers, you can still monetize that content with ads. This is an especially valuable concept for Web site owners out there who provide complete content in feeds.

Often, a Web site (or blog) owner will only syndicate a small portion of his content, specifically because doing so forces the readers to come to the Web site to finish reading the content, which increases the chances that those readers will click any ads that are shown on the site. Pushing your ads out with your content gives you one more opportunity to get ads in front of readers.

Beta Testing, Still

The idea behind AdSense for RSS is that you can

- Create *dynamic* content — content that changes frequently.
- Have that content pushed out to your readers.
- Place ads within the content that remain intact, *even if the reader doesn't visit your Web site.*

It's a grand idea, but the program is still in beta testing. And the beta testing is closed to new users — at least for a little while longer. So, even though the AdSense Web site advertises AdSense for RSS, you can't access it.

You can, however, sign up to be notified if and when the program moves forward. It's closed to beta testers as of the writing of this book, so signing up for updates is the only option available right now. If you'd like to receive notices about the general availability of AdSense for RSS, you can sign up at `http://services.google.com/ads_inquiry/aff`. Just enter the requested information. Then, as AdSense for RSS updates are released, you'll be notified.

Getting Started with AdSense for Feeds

In discussions with AdSense team members, I get the impression that AdSense for Feeds won't be in beta testing too much longer. If that's the case, you'll want to know how to use it once it becomes available to you. Not a problem. I have seen the future — beta tester that I am — and it is cool!

The first thing you need to know is that AdSense for Feeds needs two subscriptions. One is to AdSense (of course), and the other is to another Google program — FeedBurner. At the time of this writing, those two accounts are not the same. And unlike other Google programs, you can't sign in to your FeedBurner account using your Google Account information. You have to create a separate account. (Rumor has it that this will change in the near future, but no one can give me an exact date.)

FeedBurner is a program that lets you track how your feeds perform. With this program, you can analyze, optimize, monetize, and publicize your content feeds. FeedBurner also has an option for troubleshooting, called Troubleshootize — wouldn't want to break with the *-ize* theme.

Creating an account in FeedBurner is easy enough. All you have to do is

1. **Point your Web browser to** `www.feedburner.com`.

   Feedburner's home page loads on your computer screen.

2. **Click the Register link in the upper-right corner of the page.**

   The Create an Account page appears.

3. **Enter the requested information in the Create an Account page and then click Sign In.**

   You're automatically signed in to your new account where you'll see a bold, red message, like the one shown in Figure 11-1. This is your prompt to create — or *burn* — your first feed account.

4. **Enter the URL of your blog, podcast, or news feed into the text field and then click Next.**

   A new page appears, giving you some information about your feed.

5. **Read through the information, and then if you want, you can change the feed title or the feed address. When you're ready, click Activate Feed.**

   The information provided on the next page gives you details for the services that have been enabled. You'll see mention of *BrowserFriendly,* a service that approves the appearance of your feed in most browser windows and makes it easier to subscribe to, and *FeedBurner stats,* a service that tracks basic traffic statistics — like number of subscribers — for your feed. You also get the option to add other traffic statistics services.

6. **If you want to add other services, click the Next button. If not, click the Skip Directly to Feed Management link.**

   Assuming you click the Next button, you're taken to a page like the one shown in Figure 11-2.

7. **Choose the additional tracking options that you want to include and then click Next.**

   Click-throughs and Item Enclosure Downloads — that's podcast downloads — are two of the tracking options included. You can also choose to use FeedBurner Stats Pro, which allows you to see the number of people who have viewed or clicked the content in your feed and shows the popularity of individual items.

   That's it. You're done. Now you can begin using FeedBurner to manage your content feeds. And you can use it to include AdSense ads in your feeds.

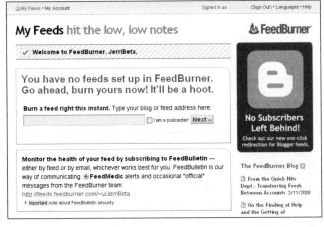

Figure 11-1: FeedBurner prompts you to create your first account immediately on sign-in.

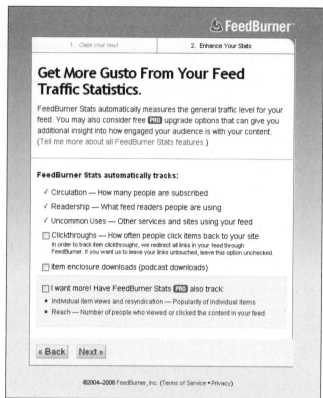

Figure 11-2:
Select from
additional
services
that are
available
on your
FeedBurner
account.

Enabling AdSense for Feeds

Just like AdSense ads that appear on other parts of your Web site, ads that
appear in your feeds are unobtrusive. They usually appear at the bottom of
the feed, as shown in Figure 11-3.

Your AdSense ad

Figure 11-3:
Ads appear
at the bot-
tom of a
feed.

Enabling your ads is easy enough, just follow these steps:

1. **Point your Web browser to** www.feedburner.com **and click the Sign In link.**

2. **In the new page that appears, enter your username and password and then click the Sign In link.**

   Your feed dashboard appears.

3. **Click the title of the feed you want to manage and then select the Monetize tab on the page that appears.**

   The screen shown in Figure 11-4 appears.

4. **In the In Your Feed section of the Monetize tab, use the drop-down menus to select how often you want ads to appear in feeds and what length of posts they should appear in.**

   You can choose to have your ads appear after every post, or after every second, third, or fourth post. You can also limit the ads that are shown according to length. Your options are to show ads in posts of any length, or only in posts that are longer than 50, 100, or 150 words.

5. **In the On Your Web Site section of the Monetize tab, select the Display Ads from AdSense Content check box.**

6. **Use the customization options of the Monetize tab to configure your ads.**

   The configuration portion of the screen, as shown in Figure 11-5, looks much like other AdSense configuration screens you've seen before now. Select the desired options for the ads that will display in your content.

   Your available options include

   Color: Select colors for the border, title, background, text, and URL, or you can use a pre-designed color template from the available drop-down menu.

   Channel: Select the desired tracking channel for your ad.

   Ad size: You have two options for size: 300 x 250 or 468 x 60.

   Ad position: This option allows you to choose to place your ad on the left, in the center, or on the right. Keep in mind, though, that this is specific to the area of your feed where ads will appear — at the bottom.

Figure 11-4:
Choose the AdSense option to create AdSense-enabled ads for your feeds.

7. **Choose your blog provider from the Get the HTML Code to Put Ads on Your Site drop-down menu.**

   A new window, like the one shown in Figure 11-6, appears on-screen. Leave this window open for just a bit. I show you how to paste the code into a Blogger blog on the next page.

8. **After that window appears, be sure to switch back to the configuration window and click the Save button to save your ad configuration in case you need to access or edit it in the future.**

After loading for a few seconds, the configuration screen appears again, but you'll notice there's a confirmation message near the top of the page. You've created your first ad for feeds.

Of course, if you could just create the ad and be done with it, wouldn't life be grand? I think it would, but you're not that lucky. After you've created the ad, you still need to copy and paste the code for the ad into your Web site or blog account. (Remember, the code is still available in another window. You didn't close that window, right?)

Different blogging programs do this differently. Here's how you do it for Blogger. (You need to have both your Blogger account and your FeedBurner account open.)

 FeedBurner actually provides specific directions for several different blogs, including Moveable Type, WordPress, and even a generic blog — one you might have created on your personal Web site or through your Web site hosting company. When you use the Get the HTML Code to Put Ads on Your Site drop-down menu to generate the HTML code for you, you get some handy instructions on how to deal with the code after getting it.

1. **Log in to your Blogger account and select the blog for which you want to include ads for feeds.**

   If you're not clear on the whole connection between AdSense and blogs, Chapter 13 should answer all your questions. Go ahead and flip over now. I'll wait . . . good, you're back.

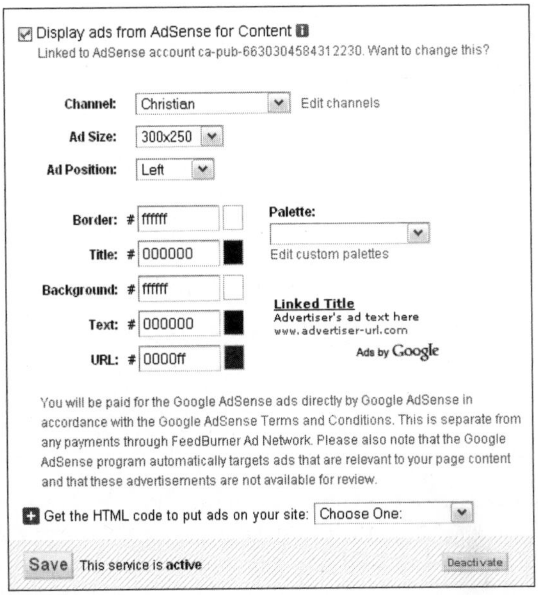

☑ Display ads from AdSense for Content 🔘
  Linked to AdSense account ca-pub-6630304584312230. Want to change this?

Channel:	Christian ⌄ Edit channels
Ad Size:	300x250 ⌄
Ad Position:	Left ⌄

Border: #	ffffff
Title: #	000000 ■
Background: #	ffffff
Text: #	000000 ■
URL: #	0000ff ■

Palette:
⌄

Edit custom palettes

Linked Title
Advertiser's ad text here
www.advertiser-url.com

Ads by Google

You will be paid for the Google AdSense ads directly by Google AdSense in accordance with the Google AdSense Terms and Conditions. This is separate from any payments through FeedBurner Ad Network. Please also note that the Google AdSense program automatically targets ads that are relevant to your page content and that these advertisements are not available for review.

➕ Get the HTML code to put ads on your site: Choose One: ⌄

Save   This service is **active**   Deactivate

Figure 11-5:
Configure the ads that appear in your feeds using familiar tools.

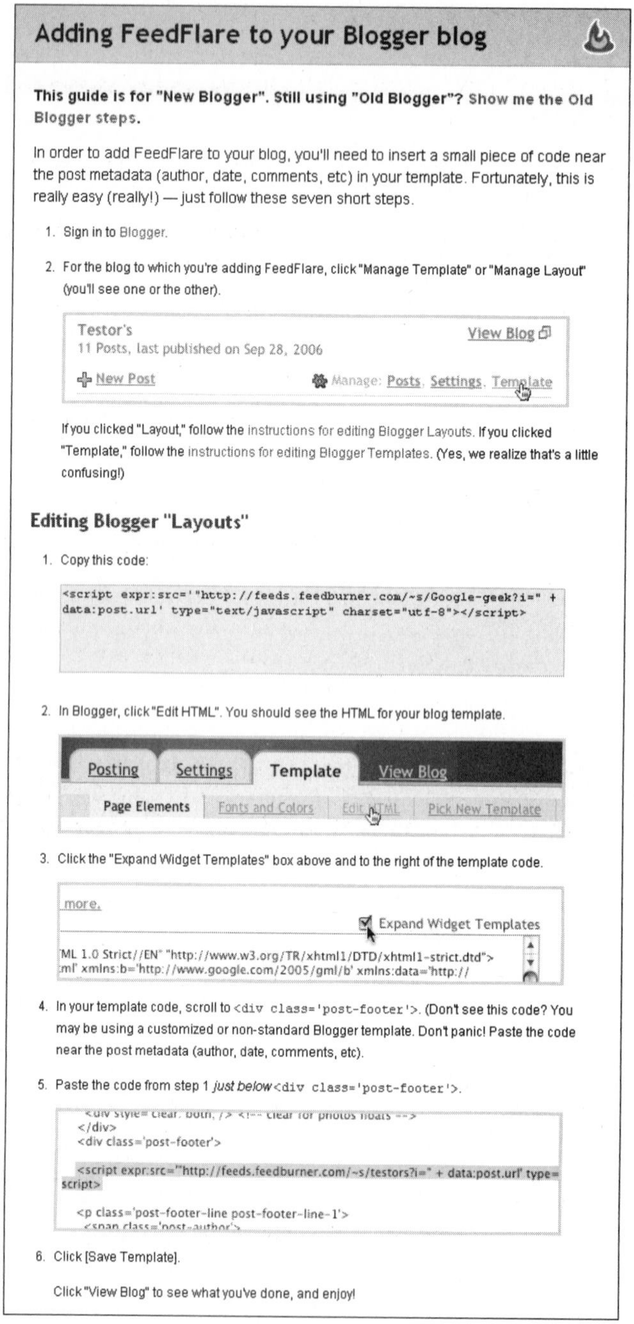

Adding FeedFlare to your Blogger blog

This guide is for "New Blogger". Still using "Old Blogger"? Show me the Old Blogger steps.

In order to add FeedFlare to your blog, you'll need to insert a small piece of code near the post metadata (author, date, comments, etc) in your template. Fortunately, this is really easy (really!) — just follow these seven short steps.

1. Sign in to Blogger.
2. For the blog to which you're adding FeedFlare, click "Manage Template" or "Manage Layout" (you'll see one or the other).

   Testor's View Blog
   11 Posts, last published on Sep 28, 2006
   New Post Manage: Posts, Settings, Template

   If you clicked "Layout," follow the instructions for editing Blogger Layouts. If you clicked "Template," follow the instructions for editing Blogger Templates. (Yes, we realize that's a little confusing!)

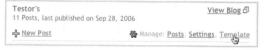

Editing Blogger "Layouts"

1. Copy this code:

```
<script expr:src='"http://feeds.feedburner.com/~s/Google-geek?i=" +
data:post.url' type="text/javascript" charset="utf-8"></script>
```

2. In Blogger, click "Edit HTML". You should see the HTML for your blog template.

   Posting Settings Template View Blog
   Page Elements Fonts and Colors Edit HTML Pick New Template

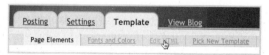

3. Click the "Expand Widget Templates" box above and to the right of the template code.

   more.
   Expand Widget Templates

```
ML 1.0 Strict//EN" "http://www.w3.org/TR/xhtml1/DTD/xhtml1-strict.dtd">
ml' xmlns:b='http://www.google.com/2005/gml/b' xmlns:data='http://
```

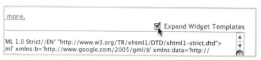

4. In your template code, scroll to `<div class='post-footer'>`. (Don't see this code? You may be using a customized or non-standard Blogger template. Don't panic! Paste the code near the post metadata (author, date, comments, etc).
5. Paste the code from step 1 *just below* `<div class='post-footer'>`.

```
  <div style='clear: both;'/> <!-- clear for photos floats -->
  </div>
  <div class='post-footer'>

  <script expr:src='"http://feeds.feedburner.com/~s/testors?i=" + data:post.url' type=
script>

  <p class='post-footer-line post-footer-line-1'>
    <span class='post-author'>
```

6. Click [Save Template].

   Click "View Blog" to see what you've done, and enjoy!

Figure 11-6: When you select your blog provider, a new window appears with the appropriate code for ads.

2. **Go to the Layout tab and select Edit HTML.**

3. **Remember that window from FeedBurner that you left open? The one with the code in it? Switch over to it now and copy the code provided by FeedBurner.**

   This code is provided when you select the blog that you're using from the bottom of the configuration page.

4. **On the Edit HTML page of Blogger, place a check mark in the box next to Expand Widget Templates, see Figure 11-7.**

5. **Read through the HTML code displayed in the Edit Template box until you find the line that reads:**

   ```
   <div class='post-footer'>
   ```

6. **Paste your AdSense code generated from FeedBurner (see the previous set of steps) immediately below this line.**

7. **Click Save Template.**

   Now you should have ads enabled in your feeds.

After you've created a feed, you can find it listed in the Review/Approve section of your My Account page at FeedBurner. At this time, there's no reference to it in AdSense, however. Even the ability to create ads for feeds is only available through the FeedBurner Web site.

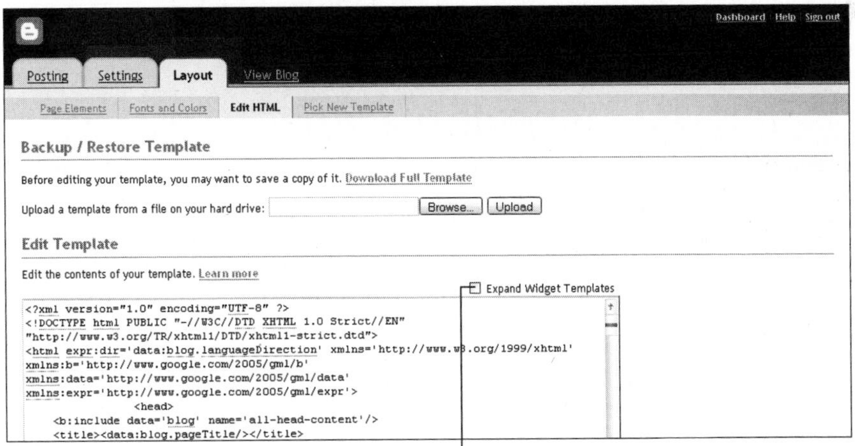

Figure 11-7: Select the Expand Widget Templates check box to see all the HTML for your blog.

Click here to see all the HTML for your site.

After the AdSense for Feeds program goes live, it's likely the way ads are tracked will change. Even the way ads are set up and installed is likely to change some. So, before you begin creating your AdSense ad, you should check out the help topics in FeedBurner's Help section to read about how the program is installed and how it works. FeedBurner's help is much like Google's, so you should be able to navigate it easily.

Style notes

One thing you'll notice as you're creating your feed ads is that the style options are very sparse. You're really limited in both the size and the display that are available for feed ads because of the nature of feeds. Most feeds are mostly black text on a while background. That limits what you can do stylistically.

The important thing to remember as you're creating your feed ads is that you want people to click through them. So, keep it simple. Black titles and text and blue links should do the job very well. Don't try to use funky colors or to make every colorized element of a feed ad a different color. Basic is better when it comes to these ads because of their location.

Ads that are displayed in feeds will very obviously be ads. Remember to eliminate the border around the ad, and blend the text of the ad with the surrounding text. It doesn't matter if your Web site has a black background with lime green lettering. Feeds will appear to readers as black text on a white background. Make your ads match so they blend in as well as possible.

Earning with Feed Ads

AdSense for Feeds doesn't currently have a designation on the AdSense Web site. In fact, if you're not specifically searching for the topic, you won't ever find it. And it's not just the information that's hard to locate. Anything related to your earnings or the performance of the ads is also non-existent.

At least for now, feed ads are tracked through AdSense for Content. I assume that will change when the program is finally released for general consumption. At that time, it's most likely that — like other AdSense programs — feed ads will have their own sections.

Until then, assigning a channel that's specific to your feed ads is the best way to track them. Since the numbers for your ads will be lumped in with AdSense for Content data, without a designated channel you'll never know what's coming from your Web site or blog and what's coming from your feed.

When it comes to actually generating revenue from feed ads, the process works just the same as with other ads — users must click through an ad for you to be paid for it.

At this time, there's no information available about whether feed ads will have the case-by-case instances of pay-per-thousand-impressions. That's something that surely will be made public when the program goes live. There's also no information about what the *revenue share* — how much you'll make when a reader clicks through your ads — will look like with feed ads. It's safe to assume, however, that it will take the same general (and vague) structure that content ads take.

AdSense for Feeds is such a great idea. There are so many instances of dynamic, feed-enabled content on the Web today that it only makes sense to monetize that content. How long it will take for the program to make the final cut and be released to the general public is anyone's guess, though. In the meantime, keep working with your other AdSense ads — and be sure to sign up to receive updates on AdSense for Feeds from the team at AdSense.

Chapter 12

The AdSense Referral Program

Google offers so many different ways for you to earn some money that it's often hard to choose what's best for your site. This chapter talks about yet another revenue method that you can add to your list of possibilities: referrals.

Referrals differ from other ads in that they allow you to recommend specific products or services that you've used and liked to your Web site visitors. You can choose from hundreds of different products and services, so you're not limited to just the obvious Google products (which tend to be the referrals that you see most often).

Although similar in some ways to other AdSense products, the AdSense referral program is also a little different in the way that you set up and choose the products that you want to recommend. Earnings and earnings potentials are also different from what you see with AdSense for Content.

This chapter outlines those differences and helps you get started with AdSense referrals to earn more from your Web site offerings.

Understanding Referral Units

Recommending products and services to others on the Web has been a concept for as long as the Web's been around. Probably one the best known *referral* programs (okay, *referring* to something in this context is the same as recommending it) is the one that Amazon.com offers for the books and other products that are available to buyers around the world. Everyone has seen the little Amazon boxes on Web sites that allow you to click through to buy the featured product.

Google AdSense offers the same type of service. The difference is that AdSense offers the ability to refer other programs or Web sites, rather than just offer the products that you like. For example, I use the Firefox Web browser, which is a personal preference, but I love it and think everyone who tries it will love it too. I include an AdSense referral button for Firefox where space allows on my Web sites. Then, each time a user clicks through that referral button and downloads Firefox, I get a small payment added to my AdSense revenues.

Referrals are a neat feature that can seriously help to bump your AdSense earnings if the referral ads are targeted well to your Web site audience. The key is in the targeting though, as you see when you get a little deeper into this chapter. There are two kinds of referral products — Google products and non-Google products — so you're not as limited in what you can refer your users to as you might be with other referral programs.

But why referrals? (Did you know I can hear you asking these questions? Well, okay, not really. But I do imagine you asking them.) The answer is simple really. Some of the best advertising that any company can ever get is based on word-of-mouth referrals.

No advertising in the world sells a product better or faster than when someone loves the product and shares that fact with others who then share it with others. If you've seen the commercials on TV with the *domino effect* cell phones, that's a really good graphical representation of the concept of word-of-mouth advertising, which is also dubbed *buzz*.

One person tells two who then tell four who then tell eight. This buzz grows exponentially until it seems like everyone is talking about the product and even rushing out to buy it.

That's the same effect advertisers hope for when they place their products in the AdSense referral program. They hope to take advantage of the buzz that's created when one person loves a product and recommends it to others who also love it and recommend it to others. As the ad-placement person, that's good for you because advertisers are willing to pay to generate good buzz.

Google products

When you're considering adding AdSense referrals to your Web pages, you have the option to refer Google products or non-Google products. Or, you can refer both if you like — up to three referrals per page.

One thing to remember is that you're limited to three AdSense ads on your page. If you have three content units, a referral unit won't appear on your page, even if you add the code. When you're choosing your AdSense layout for your Web pages, be sure you carefully consider what types of ads work best for the visitors that will see them.

In Google referrals, you can choose from among the following six offerings:

- **AdSense:** You know what AdSense is. If you love it — and who doesn't — you can add a referral button so visitors to your site can use it and grow to love it, too.

- **Firefox plus Google Toolbar:** Firefox is a Web browser from Mozilla that (in my opinion) beats Internet Explorer hands down for usability. When you add the Google Toolbar — a tool that lets you quickly access some of the most useful applications and features from Google — you have a winning combination, so why not recommend it to your users? It's a pairing made for Internet power users.

- **AdWords:** If you're advertising anything on the Web, you're probably doing so with *AdWords,* Google's pay-per-click keyword marketing program. Recommending AdWords to others with something to advertise is a great way to boost your AdSense revenues.

- **Google Pack:** Google Pack is a collection of 13 useful Google products, all of which are free — not limited trials! Included in the Google Pack offerings are

  - *Google Earth:* Offers maps and satellite images for most locations around the globe.

  - *Norton Security Scan:* A program that scans your computer to determine if your computer is free of viruses, worms, and spyware.

  - *Google Desktop:* A desktop search application that allows you to search the files on your hard drive just as you would search the Web. The program also includes program plugins, called widgets, that let you access other Google applications from your desktop.

  - *Firefox with Google Toolbar:* Firefox is a great Web browser, but with the Google Toolbar added on you get Google search access built right into your toolbar, so you don't have to go to the Google Web site to search.

  - *Adobe Reader:* This program allows you to read Adobe PDF files.

  - *Skype:* An Internet telephone service that allows you to speak to other Skype users using a microphone and speakers or a microphone-enabled headset.

  - *Star Office (including Java):* This is a complete office software suite — a free alternative to Microsoft Office.

  - *Google Toolbar for Internet Explorer:* If you use the Internet Explorer browser, the Google Toolbar allows you to access Google Search from your toolbar without going to the Google Web site.

  - *Spyware Doctor:* This program helps you find and remove spyware that may have been planted on your hard drive.

- *Picasa:* If you have a lot of digital pictures, Picasa is your organizational answer. This program helps you organize and catalog your digital pictures and also provides tools to help you edit pictures or create slide shows.

- *Google Photos Screensaver:* Use this program to create a screen saver for your computer using the photos stored on your hard drive.

- *Google Talk:* Google Talk is both an instant messaging program and an Internet telephone service.

- *Real Player:* A digital media player you can use to play MP3s and videos and to view photographs.

Each of the programs offered in Google Pack are optional, so users can choose to download 1, 3, or all 13 software applications.

✔ **Google Checkout:** Google Checkout is an e-commerce application that has two facets. One facet is for buyers who are tired of entering their information time and again into online forms when they purchase products on the Internet. The other is for sellers who want to offer products or services from their Web site — Google Checkout acts as a site's shopping cart application.

✔ **Google Apps:** One of the newest offerings from Google, Google Apps is a collection of Web-based applications and services that businesses, schools, and organizations can use to improve productivity. Among the applications and services that are available through Google Apps are

- *Gmail:* Google's Web-based e-mail application.

- *Google Talk:* An instant messaging and Internet telephone application.

- *Google Calendar:* Google's Web-based calendaring application.

- *Google Docs:* Google's answer to Microsoft Word, Microsoft Excel, and Microsoft PowerPoint. Google Docs acts as an all-in-one office suite for all your word processing, spreadsheet, and presentation needs.

- *Google Apps Security and Compliance Services:* Provides security and compliance for existing mail systems.

Did you even know that many Google products are available? Really, that's just the tip of the iceberg, but those are some of the most used Google applications and services that are available. Why not recommend them to your site visitors if you use them and find them worth the time it takes to download and configure them?

AdSense users can (potentially) see excellent earnings from some of the applications and services you can refer, something I detail in the "Earning with Referral Units" section a little later in this chapter. All I'll say for now is that you'll be pleasantly pleased with some of the referral fees that you can earn.

Non-Google products

On the flip side of the coin are the non-Google products that you can refer. Hundreds of them are spaced across 26 different categories. Browse through the Animals section or Travel section, but make sure you have a good chunk of free time available because some of those categories have more than 100 products available for referral.

Of course, when you're talking about referring a product, how do you know which one you should refer, especially when you can choose from hundreds? The easy answer is to stick with the products that you know. If you don't know any of the products that are listed (which is highly unlikely because you'll find referrals for all kinds of programs, such as SmugMug photo hosting and Boca Java Gourmet Coffee), you can always try them before you add a referral to your site.

The important thing to remember is that you're not limited to Google products. You can refer any of hundreds of different products and services, and you can tailor your choices to what is most interesting to your site visitors. Also, understand that the referral fees paid for non-Google products vary by product. You can catch a glimpse of the expected earnings range when you're selecting the products and services that you want to refer. For more on that actual selection, check out the following section.

Adding Referrals to Your Web Pages

If you've already tried a few of the other AdSense ad formats, you'll soon discover that creating referral ads is a little bit different. Succinctly put, you have lots of choices, but your choices are restricted. I know, that doesn't make much sense on the face of it, so let me put it another way: You can only do so much stylistic customization with any individual AdSense referral, but you have plenty of referrals to choose from, giving you the power to customize which products you refer to your visitors.

Even the process of creating referral ads is a little different. You don't immediately start with a stylistic choice for what kind of ad to create. Instead, you start with a location choice and then move into selecting what products you want to refer. Only after you do all that can you begin to worry about stylistic concerns. Differences in creation aside, though, setting up a referral ad is just as easy to get through as all the other AdSense types, and maybe even a little easier than some.

Referring from . . .

Remember how you created a content ad? If not, here's a quick refresher:

1. **Log in to your AdSense account by going to** www.adsense.com.

2. **Click the AdSense Setup tab to be taken to the AdSense Setup page.**

3. **On that page, click AdSense for Content, which takes you to the page where you begin to create your AdSense for Content ad.**

4. **Begin creating the ad by selecting whether to create an Ad Unit or a Link Unit.**

   Remember, the ad unit is either text and links or graphics and links, and the link unit is links only.

5. **After you make your selection, click the Continue button to move to the next page.**

6. **On the second page, choose the format for the ad that you're creating, select the colors for the ad, and decide whether to allow public service ads or other placeholders. After you make your selection, click the Continue button.**

7. **In the next page of the wizard, select a tracking channel for your ad and then click the Continue button to be taken to the final page of the wizard.**

   Tracking channels allow you to view how individual ads or groups of ads perform.

8. **On the last page, enter a name for your ad that you'll recognize if you need to come back and edit it, and then click Save and Get Code.**

   Now all you have to do is copy and paste the code into your Web site (and if you don't remember how to do that, flip to Chapter 5 for details).

The setup process for referrals is quite a bit different than the setup process for content ads, as the following steps make clear:

1. **Log on to your AdSense account and click the AdSense Setup tab to go to the AdSense Setup page.**

2. **From the list of available ad formats to create, choose Referrals.**

   You'll be taken to the Referrals page, as shown in Figure 12-1.

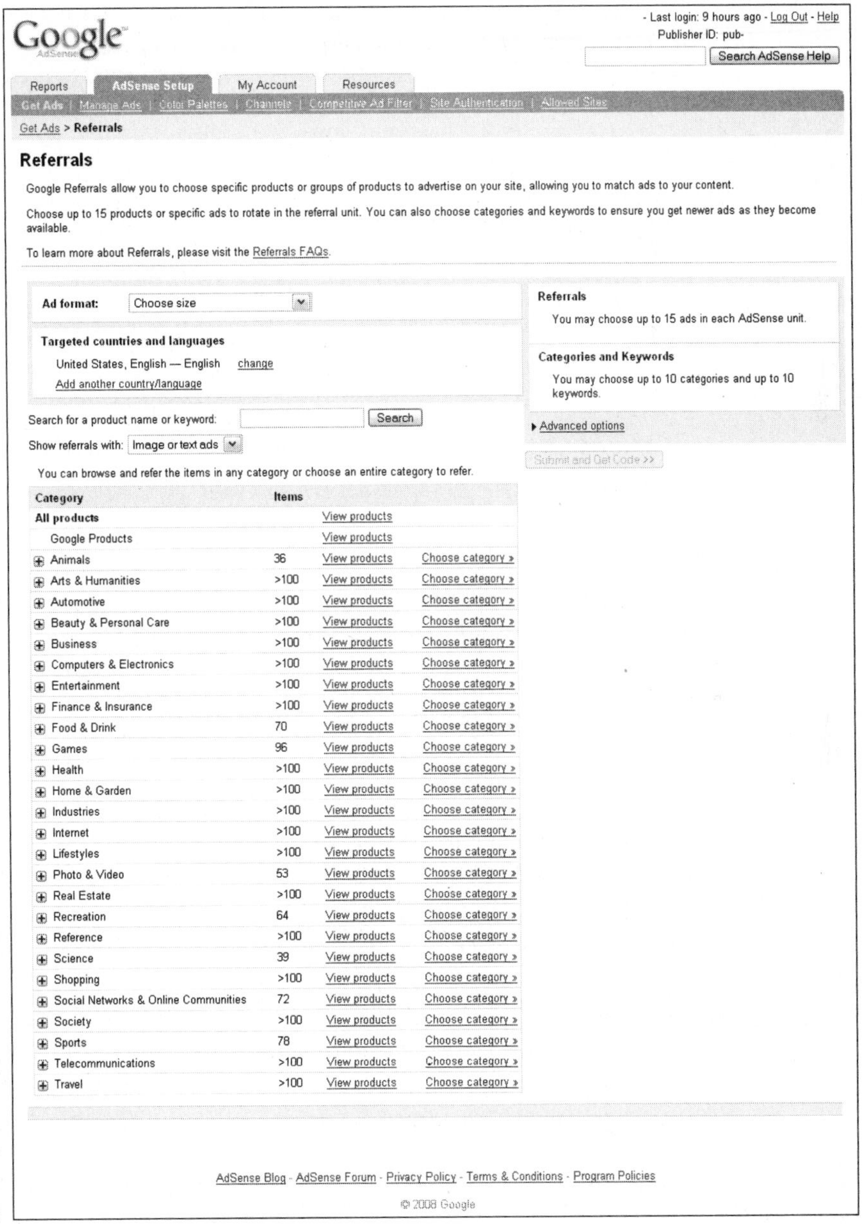

Figure 12-1:
Even the creation page for referral ads looks very different than the creation page for content ads.

3. **Select the size of the ad you want from the Ad Format drop-down menu.**

4. **If this is the first time you've tried to create a Google referral ad, select your location (country) and language preferences.**

These preferences should be based on the preferred country and language of your *site visitors,* not necessarily your own. (It's perfectly possible to have a site in one country that serves visitors from another country.) Setting country and language preferences make it possible for you to refer the most relevant products to your users.

There's a little more to it than that though: Not all referrals are available in all countries or languages. If a referral on your site targets someone in an ineligible country, you might not get credit even if that person does what he's supposed to do and takes advantage of the referral.

You can scoot right through this section of the setup process. If you do, your referrals default to the language settings you have on your account, but you can go back and change them at any time from the Creation Wizard. The language settings are on the right side of the page, near the top.

After you set the location and language for your referrals, you're all set for the next step — choosing what products to refer to your visitors. The next section turns the spotlight on that chore.

You don't HAVE to refer THAT

Write this down: You don't have to refer any product you're not comfortable with. Some people have the impression that if you set up AdSense referrals on your Web site, you're stuck with whatever AdSense puts up there. That is *not* the case. You can pick and choose which products you want to refer. (The whole idea with referrals is that you're supposed to be *recommending* something, and who recommends stuff they don't like?)

When you begin setting up your referral ads, you have to go through setting up the location, as I show you in the previous steps. After that's complete, you have two options for finding the products that you want to refer, as shown in Figure 12-2. You can either search for specific products to refer or you can browse all the available products.

Product search is available on a keyword basis. Enter the keyword that represents the products you think your visitors would be interested in and click the Search button. As shown in Figure 12-3, search results are shown in place of the categories that were listed on the page before the search.

If you don't find what you're looking for in the search results, click the Back to List of Categories link at the top-left corner of the page. This returns you to the category list so that you can search again or browse the categories.

Enter keywords to find products.

| Search for a product name or keyword: | | [ ] | [Search] |
| Show referrals with: | Image or text ads ▼ | | |

Browse items

You can browse and refer the items in any category or choose an entire category to refer.

Category	Items		
All products		View products	
Google Products		View products	
⊞ Animals	37	View products	Choose category »
⊞ Arts & Humanities	>100	View products	Choose category »
⊞ Automotive	>100	View products	Choose category »
⊞ Beauty & Personal Care	>100	View products	Choose category »
⊞ Business	>100	View products	Choose category »
⊞ Computers & Electronics	>100	View products	Choose category »
⊞ Entertainment	>100	View products	Choose category »
⊞ Finance & Insurance	>100	View products	Choose category »
⊞ Food & Drink	77	View products	Choose category »
⊞ Games	85	View products	Choose category »
⊞ Health	>100	View products	Choose category »
⊞ Home & Garden	>100	View products	Choose category »
⊞ Industries	>100	View products	Choose category »
⊞ Internet	>100	View products	Choose category »
⊞ Lifestyles	>100	View products	Choose category »
⊞ Photo & Video	39	View products	Choose category »
⊞ Real Estate	>100	View products	Choose category »
⊞ Recreation	66	View products	Choose category »
⊞ Reference	94	View products	Choose category »
⊞ Science	44	View products	Choose category »
⊞ Shopping	>100	View products	Choose category »
⊞ Social Networks & Online Communities	84	View products	Choose category »
⊞ Society	>100	View products	Choose category »
⊞ Sports	62	View products	Choose category »
⊞ Telecommunications	>100	View products	Choose category »
⊞ Travel	>100	View products	Choose category »

Figure 12-2:
To find
products
to refer,
search or
browse the
referrals
available.

One way to narrow your search results is to use the provided drop-down menu to select whether you want to search for image referrals, text referrals, or both. Image referrals result in referral buttons, which look a lot like search buttons, but text referrals are great for including in the text of a blog entry or other content on your Web site. (You can read more about the stylistic uses of these two types of referrals in the "Customizing referral ads" section, later in this chapter.) The other way to find the products you want to recommend is by browsing the available categories of products. To browse a category, click the small plus (+) sign next to the title of the category (refer to Figure 12-2). The category expands to show the available subcategories, as shown in Figure 12-4. When you find a subcategory that you want to explore further, click the View Products link to the right of the subcategory.

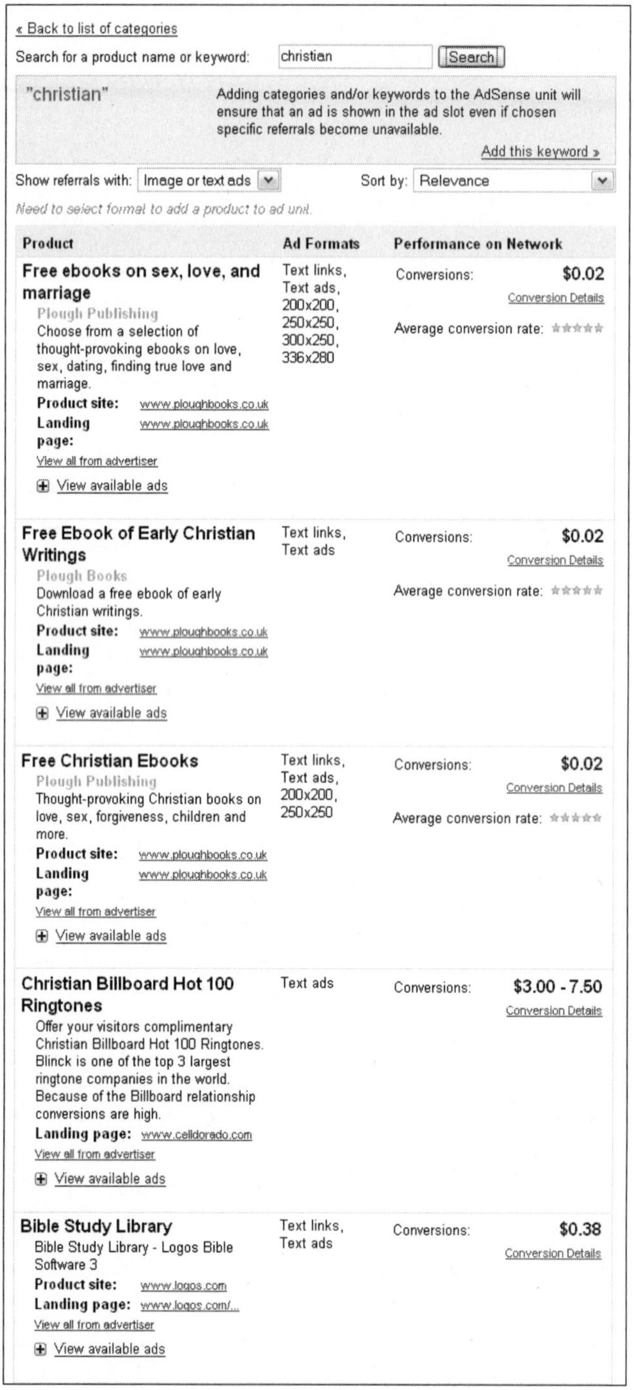

« Back to list of categories

Search for a product name or keyword: | christian | [Search]

"christian"   Adding categories and/or keywords to the AdSense unit will ensure that an ad is shown in the ad slot even if chosen specific referrals become unavailable.

Add this keyword »

Show referrals with: | Image or text ads ▾ | Sort by: | Relevance ▾ |

Need to select format to add a product to ad unit.

Product	Ad Formats	Performance on Network	
Free ebooks on sex, love, and marriage Plough Publishing Choose from a selection of thought-provoking ebooks on love, sex, dating, finding true love and marriage. **Product site:** www.ploughbooks.co.uk **Landing page:** www.ploughbooks.co.uk View all from advertiser ⊞ View available ads	Text links, Text ads, 200x200, 250x250, 300x250, 336x280	Conversions:	$0.02
		Conversion Details	
		Average conversion rate: ☆☆☆☆☆	
Free Ebook of Early Christian Writings Plough Books Download a free ebook of early Christian writings. **Product site:** www.ploughbooks.co.uk **Landing page:** www.ploughbooks.co.uk View all from advertiser ⊞ View available ads	Text links, Text ads	Conversions:	$0.02
		Conversion Details	
		Average conversion rate: ☆☆☆☆☆	
Free Christian Ebooks Plough Publishing Thought-provoking Christian books on love, sex, forgiveness, children and more. **Product site:** www.ploughbooks.co.uk **Landing page:** www.ploughbooks.co.uk View all from advertiser ⊞ View available ads	Text links, Text ads, 200x200, 250x250	Conversions:	$0.02
		Conversion Details	
		Average conversion rate: ☆☆☆☆☆	
Christian Billboard Hot 100 Ringtones Offer your visitors complimentary Christian Billboard Hot 100 Ringtones. Blinck is one of the top 3 largest ringtone companies in the world. Because of the Billboard relationship conversions are high. **Landing page:** www.celldorado.com View all from advertiser ⊞ View available ads	Text ads	Conversions:	$3.00 - 7.50
		Conversion Details	
Bible Study Library Bible Study Library - Logos Bible Software 3 **Product site:** www.logos.com **Landing page:** www.logos.com/... View all from advertiser ⊞ View available ads	Text links, Text ads	Conversions:	$0.38
		Conversion Details	

Figure 12-3: Search results replace the categories that were listed.

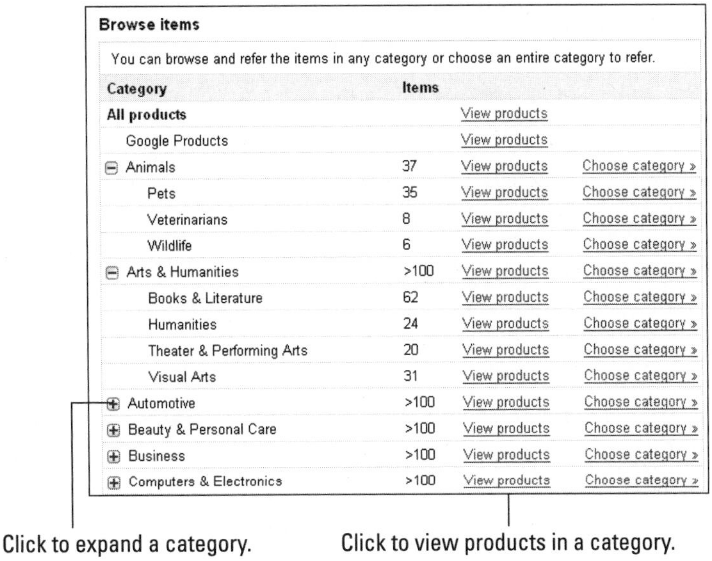

Figure 12-4:
Click the
plus button
next to a
category to
view sub-
categories.

Click to expand a category.   Click to view products in a category.

After you select a subcategory of ads to view, you see more information
about the product, as well as the available ad sizes and the monetary performance of the ads, as shown in Figure 12-5. You can use this information to
make informed decisions about the products that you want to refer.

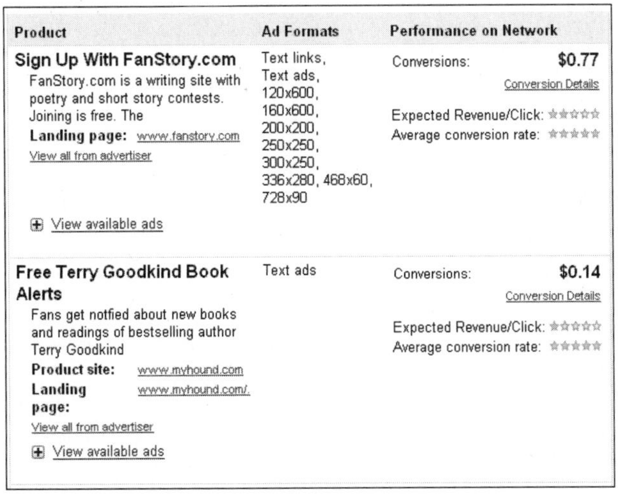

Figure 12-5:
Clicking a
subcategory
reveals
more infor-
mation
about the
available
ads.

Selecting the right referrals

Let me take a step back for just a minute and tell you a little more about what kind of decision-making information is accessible when you look more closely at the available ads. If you take another look at Figure 12-5, you see a View Available Ads link with another small plus (+) sign to the left — the universal symbol for click-me-and-I-expand. Figure 12-6 shows what happens when you take the plunge and click that little plus (+) sign. The list here fills you in on what you see:

- **Top left:** This info mirrors what you'd see in the unexpanded version, in Figure 12-5. You get a short description of the product, a link to the product Web site, and a View All from Advertiser link. If you click this link, only the available referral ads from *that* advertiser are shown.

- **Top center:** This is a list of the available ad formats. You're not limited to a referral button with most of these products. (Again, you see this in Figure 12-5 as well.)

- **Top right:** This information indicates the average performance you can expect from this referral. The dollar amount shown is the maximum, meaning you can earn up to that amount, and there's a Conversion Details link that leads to more info on the conversion requirements. (*Conversion requirements* spell out what has to take place for you to actually get paid. I explain all about conversion requirements in more detail a little later in the "Understanding conversions" section of this chapter.)

- **Bottom left:** Here's where you see a graphical representation of the referral ad, as it will appear on your Web site. For some products, you get text links, text blocks, and graphical ads to choose from; for others, you may only have one choice. One thing you should know about what you see here is that, for the text links and graphical ads, this is exactly how your referral ads will look on your Web site — no ifs, ands, or buts. The text blocks are a bit more accommodating, in that you can customize the colors a tad. (I talk more about stylistic concerns in the "Choosing between button and text" sidebar and the "Customizing referral ads" section, later in this chapter.)

- **Bottom middle:** Here you find an explanation of the referral type: text links, text boxes, and graphical formats and sizes.

- **Right side:** The Choose Ad link appears in this section of the expanded block. This allows you to select single ads rather than selecting categories or even advertisers, both of which are possibilities.

Product	Ad Formats	Performance on Network	
Sign Up With FanStory.com FanStory.com is a writing site with poetry and short story contests. Joining is free. The **Landing page:** www.fanstory.com View all from advertiser	Text links, Text ads, 120x600, 160x600, 200x200, 250x250, 300x250, 336x280, 468x60, 728x90	Conversions: **$0.77** Conversion Details Expected Revenue/Click: ★★★★★ Average conversion rate: ★★★★★	

⊟ Hide ads

writing site		Text Link	Choose ad »
poetry contests		Text Link	Choose ad »
poetry feedback		Text Link	Choose ad »
writing contests		Text Link	Choose ad »
short story contests		Text Link	Choose ad »
Feedback for your poetry		Text Link	Choose ad »
contests with cash prizes		Text Link	Choose ad »
feedback for your writing		Text Link	Choose ad »
feedback for everything you write		Text Link	Choose ad »
Over 30 writing contests are available on FanStory.com		Text Link	Choose ad »
Writing Contests Free Writing Contests For Poets and Short Story Writers FanStory.com		Text Block	Choose ad »
Writing Feedback Feedback For Your Poetry Feedback - Poetry Contests - Fun! FanStory.com		Text Block	Choose ad »
Writing Contests Get feedback for your writing Feedback - Writing Contests - Fun! FanStory.com		Text Block	Choose ad »
Writing Contests Join writing contests. Great Prizes Get feedback for your writing too! FanStory.com		Text Block	Choose ad »
Poetry Contests Join poetry contests. Great Prizes! Get feedback for every poem posted. FanStory.com		Text Block	Choose ad »
		468x60 pixels	Choose ad »
Get Feedback For Your Writing		468x60 pixels	Choose ad »
		468x60 pixels	Choose ad »
Writing Feedback! Writing Contests! Fun!		468x60 pixels	Choose ad »
		468x60 pixels	Choose ad »

Figure 12-6: Click the plus sign next to the View Available Ads link to see additional information about the ads that are available.

When you're selecting your ads, notice some of the restrictions on the number of ads that you can select. Here's how the restrictions work: Referral ads can be static or dynamic on your site. *Static* referrals are those where — no matter whatever format you choose to display — you get a single referral ad and nothing more. You can accomplish static referrals in one of two ways: You can either select an ad that doesn't rotate — like a Google Ad — or you can choose a single ad from the list of other products that are available.

You can, however, go the dynamic route by rotating the referrals that you're offering, just to keep things from getting boring. If you decide that you want to jazz up your referrals, you can show up to 15 specific ads or you can select 10 keywords and 10 categories from which your ads are selected. The advantage of choosing the specific ads is that you have complete control over what's shown. If you select the Keywords and Categories options, the referrals that are shown rotate *any* of the ads that are available in those keywords and categories. Big difference.

After you decide on the ads and/or keywords and categories that you want for referral ads, you can move on to customizing your referral ads to work on your Web site. The following section shows you how.

Customizing referral ads

The odd thing about creating referral ads, to me at least, is that all the actions for creating the ads are on the same page. When you begin the customization process for referral ads, you have the ads that you're selecting from displayed on the left, but after you select an ad or category of ads, the customization abilities expand on the right.

When you first open the ad-creation pages, not much appears available for customization — you only see information boxes on the right side of the page for Referrals and Categories and Keywords. After you select the products, keywords, or categories that you want to refer, you begin to see customization capabilities on the right side of the page — Referrals, Categories and Keywords, as well as Alternate Ads or Colors. Additionally, a new section appears under the Advanced Options heading — AdSense Unit Name.

To see how this works, go ahead and select an ad — one of those ads you tracked down with the techniques spelled out in the previous section. Selecting an ad brings up the customization section of the AdSense Unit Wizard, as shown in Figure 12-7.

First things first, choose an ad format. (Ad format selection is the top option on the customization section of the page.) To view your options, click the Ad Format drop-down menu — formats listed in black are available, whereas formats listed in red are unavailable. Feel free to choose any of the available options you feel suit the space you have available on your Web site.

After you get formatting out of the way, the menu on the right expands with additional customization options. You see these sections: Referrals (which list the referral ads you've selected), Categories and Keywords (which list the categories and keywords you've selected), and Alternate Ads or Colors.

Figure 12-7:
Use these options to customize your referral ads.

The Alternate Ads part of the Alternate Ads or Colors option is where you choose what should show on your site instead of the referral ad in the event that a particular advertiser reaches its budget limit and its ad can no longer be shown. You have three options here to select from:

✔ **Automatically Choose Fallback Referral Ads:** This option leaves any fallback ads up to AdSense. If your chosen advertiser hits its budget limit, AdSense substitutes another ad.

✔ **Show Non-Google Ads from Another URL:** If you're using more than one advertising program, you can have Google show ads from that other program if your chosen advertiser hits its budget limit. (How generous of Google!)

✔ **Fill Space with a Solid Color:** Rather than show any additional ads, AdSense blanks out the ad space you have set aside with a solid color. The only problem with this option is that as long as your ads are blocked (because advertisers' budgets are limited), you have no potential to make money from this spot that you've set aside.

I select the first option for each of my ads. I have yet to see a time when alternate ads needed to be shown, but I'm sure that it does happen. (I guess I'm just not picking the most popular ads in the referral program!) If you have another option or you don't trust that AdSense will show ads of which you approve, the other options are just as viable.

Choosing between button and text

You have to decide whether you want to use a text ad or a button ad, or whatever other format is available from the Ad Format drop-down menu. Typically, Google referral ads are available only as text and button ads, but other advertisers can offer their referrals in any ad format that's available for content ads.

When you have to choose between the text ad and the button (or graphical) ad, which one works best? Good question. In my humble opinion, text ads work best when they're surrounded by text. For example, if the referral ad that you plan to place in your text is for Google AdSense, one of the text options available to you is Sign Up for Google AdSense. Work that line into an article and then use the referral ad as the link.

One catch here, though — you can't change the text of the ad. No matter how you place that text within your text, the ad that's displayed in the preview is exactly what will appear on your Web site. If you're using the Google AdSense referral that reads `This site monetized by`

`Google AdSense`, you can't change that text. Working a sentence like that into an article is a little more difficult. In other words, if you choose to use text ads within text on your Web page, be sure to choose a text ad that blends well with the surrounding text.

Graphical ads, including button ads, are better suited for the outer edges of your pages, such as on the sides, top, or bottom of your site. Remember that ads on the top right, above the fold, tend to work best, but with referral ads, you can move them down the page and even to the bottom of the page. Referral ads appear more natural than other types of ads in those locations, so you don't lose as much performance as you might with a different type of ad.

Your ads perform better if you place them correctly, so be sure to test different placements before deciding on a permanent home for your referral ads. (For my general thoughts on AdSense ad placement, check out Chapter 5.)

As for your colorizing options, remember that these are only available for text block ads, not text links or graphical ads. To see your options, click the Advanced Options to expand the Customization menu so it includes a Text Block Color section and a Custom Channel section. The Text Block Color option is the very first option that appears under this link.

The options in the Text Block Color section are limited to those included in the drop-down menu in this block, as shown in Figure 12-8. Choose an option from the drop-down menu, and a preview of that option appears immediately below it.

Figure 12-8:
Select
a color
scheme
for your ad
alternative
from the
drop-down
menu.

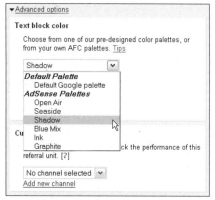

When choosing colors, try to get as close to the color scheme used on your Web site, but resign yourself to the fact that you just can't match it perfectly. Because you can't, stick with colors that are complementary to your site. Don't do something dramatic just to draw attention to the box. If you do, you end up with a referral box that looks completely out of place and isn't aesthetically pleasing, which (believe it or not) could cause your visitors to avoid clicking the box even if they're interested in the referral.

Aesthetics, or the appealing look of an ad, are important. If visitors see a small portion of your site that looks out of place, they're more likely to avoid it because humans, by their nature, need harmony. If your referral box is out of harmony with the rest of your site, it sends a subliminal message to visitors to avoid it. Don't let a referral stand out like a sore thumb. Instead, keep the colors of your referrals similar or complementary to the rest of your site.

One of the last options that you have in the Advanced Options section — and this has nothing to do with the appearance of the referral ad on your site — is what channel you want the ad to be tracked with. I talk a lot about using channels in Chapter 14, but for now, you need to know that channels help you track ad performance on your pages or even on whole Web sites so that you can keep track of which ads are generating the most revenue.

If you don't know how to create a channel yet, don't worry. You can always create an ad without one and add the channel later — maybe after reading Chapter 14. Or, you can click the Add a New Channel button, enter a name for this channel in the text box that appears, and click OK. Then you have a channel that you can use to track the referral ad.

The last option in the Advanced Options section allows you to give your ad a specific name. By default, ads are named according to their size and the date created, but if you have a bunch of different ads and referrals on your Web site, keeping track of what's what might be a little difficult if you leave the default name in place.

Consider creating a more descriptive name that helps you remember what the ad is and its purpose. When you see reports — once a week or once a month, depending on your preference — you can quickly decipher which of your ads is performing well and which should be removed or replaced. (Not sure what kind of reports I'm talking about? Check out Chapter 15. You'll be glad you did.)

All you have to do is highlight the default text and type the name you want to use. When the code for the site is generated, the indicator that tags that ad with the name you've created is added automatically to the code.

Adding the code to your Web site

After you select your ads and customize them to your tastes, all that's left is to generate the code and then paste that code onto your Web site. To do that, click the Submit and Get Code button at the bottom-right of the Referrals page.

The site processes for a few moments and then you're taken to a page similar to the one shown in Figure 12-9.

Copy the code and paste it into the HTML of your Web site, making sure you place it between the <body> and </body> tags of the site. (Okay, I know there could be a lot of real estate between the <body> and </body> tags on a site. Exactly *where* between those tags you place your code is determined by your profound study of AdSense ad placement principles, as outlined by yours truly in Chapter 5.)

Every HTML editor is a little different, and the code for every Web site is different, so I can't tell you exactly where in the text between the <body> and </body> tags to put the code, but you can play with the placement until you get it just right.

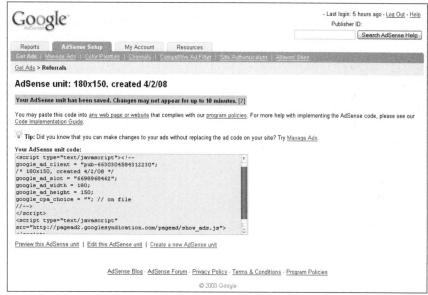

Figure 12-9:
The code for referral ads looks very similar to the code for other types of AdSense ads.

When you're done, upload your Web site and you should immediately begin to see your referral ad. Well, okay, you might temporarily get public service announcements, but in most cases, the referral ad shows right away. However, if it doesn't appear on your site within 48 hours, you may have done something wrong in the process and you'll need to try again.

Promoting Referral Ads

Referral ads seem to be different than other AdSense ads in more ways than just how you create them. For example, it's perfectly okay to promote your referral ads — to a point. Although AdSense definitely doesn't want you to do anything to draw attention to your AdSense for Content ads, you have a bit more freedom when it comes to highlighting other AdSense products:

- ✔ **AdSense for Search:** Feel free to mention to your site visitors that you have a search box they can use to find whatever.

- ✔ **Referrals:** Refer away. It's always best if you've actually used the products you're referring so that what you tell your visitors is accurate. Tell them your thoughts about the products and share your stories of how the product has performed for you.

You're absolutely not allowed under any circumstances to draw attention to the referral by telling readers to click it. Click Here graphics pointing to the referral box and anything resembling a directive to click the button are not allowed. Oh, you also can't claim sponsorship — as in, *This Web site sponsored by that product.*

Go ahead and write an article about the product that you're sponsoring and leave the referral text within the article as well as a referral graphic on the right side of the page. You can even tell your visitors that you recommend the product that you're referring. Just don't tell them to click the link or the graphic, and don't try to force a visitor to pay attention to the referral ad. Let referrals naturally occur, based on your good experiences with the products that you're referring.

Earning with Referral Units

If you think things have been a little different with AdSense referrals up to this point, you'll really see the differences in the earnings department. Here's where everything that you've read about AdSense so far changes a little bit.

Earning with AdSense referral ads requires some action on the part of your Web site visitors. Earning with referrals isn't as simple as clicking through a link, or even searching and then clicking through search results. AdSense referrals have *conversions* — which are specific actions that must take place before you get paid for displaying the referral ad.

Even after a conversion takes place, the payments are a little different than what you see with other AdSense ads. All referral ads are paid on a flat fee. However, the fee that you're paid can be influenced by your location. Each advertiser sets country-specific goals, so you're paid *up to* the maximum amount shown for each of the referrals that you make from your AdSense referral ads.

To further complicate things, there's a validation period when you first add a referral to your Web site. This validation period is put in place to help AdSense validate that conversions that take place through your referral ads are genuine. During this period, you earn the minimum payment for conversions, with the amount increasing after the validation period is over.

Here's the frustrating part — the validation period has no time limit on how long it lasts. On the AdSense Web site, Google states:

> *"For most publishers, the validation period should end quickly, but it will vary by publisher due to differences in the time it takes to collect the necessary account data."*

In other words, how long you're paid the minimum instead of the maximum is determined by how much traffic your site generates and how often your site visitors take advantage of your referrals. That's not exactly something that you can change or influence in much of a big way.

When you're looking at the available referral ads, the amount shown in the upper-right corner of the referral information box may be a single dollar amount or a dollar range. When you see a dollar range, you notice this principle of minimum versus maximum the most.

For example, I looked at an ad that had an earning range of $1.73–$15.38. The lower figure is the minimum, which is what you can expect to earn during the validation period after you place the referral ad on your site. The higher figure is the maximum, which you work up to earning as the validation period continues (until it ends) for any future referrals made from the ad.

I find the whole process a little frustrating, but I do understand why AdSense has the validation period in place. Without it, publishers could add referrals to their sites, ask all their friends to click through, do whatever is necessary for conversion, and rake in the dough. For a few days, the referral numbers would be really nice for the advertiser and the publisher, but then referrals would drop dramatically.

The validation period dampens this type of activity, making the actual number of referrals more realistic — which isn't such a bad thing. With realistic numbers, you can know exactly what to expect from your referral earnings, and advertisers can know exactly what to expect from their referral spending.

Understanding conversions

Until now, I kept the whole concept of referral conversions a bit vague. Let me see if I can now give you a clearer picture. A *conversion* is an action or a set of actions that have to happen before you get paid for a referral ad. It's not enough for you to place the ad on your Web page and have your visitors click the ad. Something else — a download, a registration, or something similar — has to happen before you get paid.

Here's the part that might make you think twice before including referrals on your site — some of those conversions take time. A conversion requirement that visitors sign up for a membership on a Web site and remain a member for a certain amount of time — usually 30 to 60 days — isn't unheard of.

Some conversions are simple — sign up for a newsletter, request information, and become a forum member. Others require a monetary investment from the visitor who followed the referral link — buy a product, purchase a membership, and donate a sum of money. The conversion details vary by product.

For example, the conversion details for a referral ad to Google AdSense are these:

> *"When a publisher that signed up for Google AdSense through your referral earns their initial $100.00 within 180 days of sign-up and is eligible for payout, we'll credit your account with $100.00.*
>
> *A Google AdSense referral is counted only for publishers never previously enrolled in Google AdSense. Google AdSense referral payouts do not count towards $100.00 threshold."*

Pretty complicated, huh? They're not all that complicated, though. For example, here are the conversion requirements for the Ghirardelli referral ad:

Purchase/Sale — $3.00–$11.54

Purchase Online

Really. That's all there is to it. A visitor clicks through your referral ad, makes a purchase from the Ghirardelli Web site (It's chocolate, folks! Who doesn't love chocolate?), and you're paid the referral fees. Of course, exactly how much you'll be paid is still a little murky because nothing explains exactly the percentage of sale that's credited to the publisher, but it's still simple enough to understand. Visitors buy chocolate, you get paid, everyone's happy!

The only way to know for sure what the conversion requirements are for a referral ad you may have selected is to look. When you're examining ads (remember, I talk about this earlier in the chapter), you see a blue Conversion Details link. Click this link, and a small box appears that details what the conversion requirements for that specific ad are, as shown in Figure 12-10.

Click the link...

Figure 12-10: Click the Conversion Details link to find out what has to happen for you to get paid.

...Details appear here.

Invalid conversions

One more aspect of conversions that you should pay attention to is the possibility of conversions being considered invalid. An *invalid conversion* is any conversion that AdSense deems isn't the result of genuine interest on the part of the Web site visitor who clicked the referral ad. Most usually, invalid conversions are caused by Web site owners clicking their own ads, but they can also be the result of automated clickbots, clicking contests — where you offer a prize to the person who clicks an ad the most often or who clicks the most ads — or other forms of click fraud.

Because I already know that you're not using those methods to generate AdSense revenues, consider this a refresher. Don't participate in any such fraudulent activities. They're not good for the ad programs and can have nasty results for you. Place your ads on your pages and allow visitors to naturally click through them. Don't try to inflate your numbers by requesting clicks or convincing your friends to click through your ads.

Just let click-throughs happen. If you follow the principles I lay out in this book and work diligently to create a Web site that has true visitor value, earnings will happen. Then you can truly enjoy the revenue stream that you've generated without worrying about when AdSense will catch on to your less-than-honest methods.

Tracking conversions

If you place referral ads on your page, you'll want to also track how they're performing. AdSense gives you some tools to do that. After you set up your AdSense referrals, a new report becomes available in the Reports section of your AdSense account. Right there on the front page is the new Referrals report. If you click this report, you're shown some stats based on the performance of your referral ads.

For each referral ad you display, you see the following stats:

- **Clicks:** This number indicates every time that a site visitor has clicked your referral ad even when a conversion doesn't follow.
- **Sign-ups:** When a referral product — like AdSense — requires a sign-up, and your site visitors actually do sign up, that number is displayed in this column.
- **Conversions:** When your visitors click through your referral ads and complete the required conversion, this is where that fact gets recorded. Conversions are listed by product.
- **Earnings:** Here's the line that interests you the most, I'm sure. This line tells you exactly how much you've earned from your referral ads, by product.

Outside the reports offered by AdSense, you can't track the actual conversion of your AdSense referrals in any other way. This report is enough to help you see quickly which of your referral ads are working and which are not. The report also helps you understand what you're actually earning from those referrals that *are* performing.

The earnings breakdown

The earnings you can expect to make for referrals will vary depending on the product you're referring. They may also depend on the location of the user you've referred the product to. Some referrals pay more when users are U.S. residents, whereas others pay more when users are located in other countries. The difference is determined by where the company you're referring is located and the target market the company is trying to reach.

Earnings are determined by the product owner or company that offers its products for referral. For non-Google products, individual advertisers decide the actions they want visitors to complete and how much they're willing to pay for those actions as a result of clicking through the referral ad. You're credited for non-Google referrals if a user clicks through your referral ad and completes the advertiser's conversion criteria within 30 days of clicking.

For Google products, the earnings schedule is a little different. Well, okay, it's not really different, it's just lain right out there so you can see it without having to wonder or search for what earnings you can expect to make. Your earnings for Google referral products are defined as follows:

- **AdSense:** When a user who signed up for Google AdSense through your referral first earns $100 within 180 days of sign-up and is eligible for payout, you're credited with $100. Note that it's only when the user *first* signs up and earns $100. If a visitor has been a member of AdSense in the past, you don't receive this payment. Also, this applies only to referrals located in North America, Latin America, or Japan. All others are counted as invalid referrals because AdSense doesn't support other countries at this time.

- **Firefox plus Google Toolbar:** When a visitor you've referred to Firefox with Google Toolbar runs Firefox for the first time, you'll receive up to $1 in your account, depending on the visitor's location. Your referral must be a Windows user who hasn't previously installed Firefox in order for you to receive credit.

- **AdWords:** When an advertiser you refer first spends $5 on AdWords ads within 90 days of sign-up, you earn $5. This is in addition to the first $5 that AdWords gives new users. So, technically speaking, users have to spend the $5 that AdWords gives them and $5 of their own money before you're paid. If that same advertiser spends $100 within 90 days of sign-up, you're credited with an additional $40.

> If in any 180-day period you refer 20 advertisers who each spend more than $100 within 90 days of their signing up, you're awarded a $600 bonus. Note that bonus payments are limited to one payout per year.

> ✔ **Google Product Pack:** When you refer a Windows user to the Google Pack product and he downloads and installs it, you receive up to $1 in referral fees.

> ✔ **Google Checkout:** When a user signs up as a buyer and completes a transaction through Google Checkout within 90 days of sign-up, you're paid $1. Note, however, that the transaction *must* be at least $10 for you to receive payment.

> ✔ **Google Apps:** When a visitor signs up for a new Google Apps account through your referral, you earn $.05. However, if the visitor creates a Google Apps Standard account and opens one or more Google Apps e-mail accounts that remain in use for four consecutive weeks, you earn $5. If the visitor signs up for a Google Apps Premier account, you earn $10 for each user license purchased.

Your Payment History page is where you see the monthly totals for all the referral fees that you earn — from both Google and non-Google products. The payment schedule for referral fees is just as it is with other AdSense ads. You're paid once per month after your account reaches a $100 balance. Note that the exception to this is the AdSense referral bonus. If you earn $100 in AdSense referral fees, those fees don't count toward your account minimum for payment, so you have to earn an additional $100 in AdSense revenues to receive that payment.

Also, the $600 bonus that's paid when you reach the outlined requirements for AdWords is a once a year bonus. You can only receive it one time per year, so if you earn it more than one time in a given year and you've already received the bonus, you won't receive that payment.

In general, AdSense referral ads are a pretty smart addition to your Web site if you have room to add them. Referrals are a relatively easy way to boost your AdSense income, but keep in mind that you do have to meet the conversion requirements for each ad that you show, so choose your ads wisely. Also keep in mind that the better targeted your ads are, the better they'll perform.

Chapter 13

AdSense Your Blog

- -

In This Chapter

▶ Understanding how AdSense works in blogs

▶ Adding AdSense to your blog

▶ Using the best techniques for blogs

- -

*I*nformation is the purpose of the Internet. People use the Internet to share the information that they have and to find the information that they need. It doesn't matter whether you're an individual or whether you're part of a company with thousands of employees. If you or your company has a Web site, the sole purpose of that site should be to share information with site visitors.

Those site visitors might *just* be seeking information, or they might be seeking products or services. The products and services, however, are secondary to the information because before someone purchases your products or contracts your services, he wants to know that his money will be well-spent. He wants something and he wants to know he's getting the best deal possible.

Constantly updated information comes in handy here. *Content* — information — on your Web site needs to be regularly updated to get people's attention. Equally important for you as a site owner, regular updates are what it takes to keep a search engine interested — and rating your site highly.

The Blog Explosion

Even as little as five years ago, search engines were loaded with information that had been the same for years. Many people never bothered to update the material on their Web site because there was no penalty for not doing so. Today, however, search engines look at information freshness as part of the formula to determine where a Web site ranks in search results. Web sites with highly relevant and regularly updated information rank higher than those sites that have had the same content for 3 (or 2 or 15) years.

To increase their ratings, most companies as well as many individuals now employ blogs as a way to put the most current and most relevant informational tidbits in front of people as quickly as possible. Blogs, by their very nature, are publishing on demand. Writers no longer have to put together a piece just to wait three to six weeks, or even months, to have that information in front of people. Blogs allow writers — whether personally or corporately driven — to put their thoughts and collected facts in front of a reader in an instant.

For example, consider the Web site and blog Woot.com. Woot's concept is to provide potential customers with a single product of high value every day. The company doesn't keep a huge back stock of products stored in a warehouse somewhere. Woot gets a limited number of a single product every day. That product gets announced and placed on the Web site at a very special price, but when it's gone, it's gone. No more. You're out of luck.

The concept only works, however, because the company's established a system of constant contact with its customers by using blogs. Notice the plurality there — blog*s*. More than one blog and multiple blog posts per day.

The value in having multiple blogs — and having multiple blog posts each day — is that there's *more* information you can keep in front of your site visitors. The assumption is that it's *relevant* information. Now, add AdSense to that, and you can see that the potential for income is amazing. All you have to do is create a high-demand blog, populate it with relevant information, and add AdSense to the mix.

Creating Blog Buzz

Blogs are everywhere. I subscribe to more than 24 blogs and I skim the posts every single day. When I find useful information, I take the time to read the entire posts, to follow links in the posts, and in general to gather as much information as I can from the *snippets* of daily information I find in the blogosphere. Those snippets are the very information that makes blogs of all kinds useful to me and to a large percentage of the world's population.

Without useful information, blogs are worthless. Sure, you can blog about your daily antics with Aunt Betty and her hairless pugs, but what's useful about that? Not a darn thing. That translates to three whole subscribers — your mom, your Aunt Betty, and maybe your best friend. The chances of generating any kind of cash from those endeavors are exactly zero.

But, say you blog about how to use technology to generate big bucks in business. Now, that topic will garner you some traffic. If you don't believe me, check out all the blogs that come up in the results when you search for something like *making money in technology*. Astounding what's out there.

Hot topics work because they *mean* something to subscribers, they cover valuable information that people are looking for, and they create *buzz*. Think of buzz like the *conversations* that take place in a bee hive. One worker bee goes out to gather nectar. Along the way, he comes across a field of the most flavorful flowers of the season. Mr. Worker Bee gathers his share of the nectar and returns to the hive to share his good fortune.

Upon his return, Mr. Worker Bee tells everyone he comes in contact with what a great field he's found and provides directions to the other bees in the community. Within seconds, there's *buzz* of both sound and activity. Welcome to Internet buzz, which works exactly the same way.

You generate a post on the Web that contains secrets for how to make real, living, growing slugs in your bathtub, and then along comes a visitor who was searching for that very thing on the Internet. He reads your post, decides it's worthy, and immediately shoots off an e-mail to everyone he knows who has the same interests. Those people then visit your site, and they share the news with all their friends. Before you know it, *buzz* about your post is everywhere.

Buzz only works though if the information that you're sharing is valuable to more people than your immediate family. Your first step in creating blog buzz is to choose a topic that other people find useful — and there are thousands of such topics. You can write about nearly anything and find an audience for it, but the idea is to find a topic that interests a large number of people over a long period of time.

A good way to figure out a great topic is to pay attention to the media. Yes, you have to wade through all the blather about the latest hot celebrity, but the media doesn't spend *all* it's time on the newest starlet's latest psycho-drama. For example, you'll probably find a lot of economic issues and trends. When you break down economic topics, you come up with everything from making money to saving money and investing money.

Now, take that topic and divide it a little further. What do you do that helps you make money, save money, or invest money? For me, I could write a blog about making a very good living writing about technology. And I have, in fact, written such a blog in the past, which was quite successful, thank you very much. I don't write it anymore because of time constraints, but it was a topic that I know well and could help others with.

Choosing a topic that other people want to know about is relatively easy. (Hey, getting rich off the stock market sounds like it might be a popular topic!) The hard part comes when you have to figure out enough about that topic so that you're in a position to give useful advice to other people. That doesn't mean you have to be the best-known expert on the topic. You do have to know enough to share useful information and to figure out what you don't know though.

After you have a blog in mind, all you have to do is create it. Fortunately, creating a blog is easy. Dozens of services allow you to create a blog for free, and it takes just a few minutes to set up one. Look at several different services to find the one that's right for you. The top three are

- ✔ **Blogger:** Blogger is Google's answer to blogging. It also happens to be the easiest way to add AdSense to your blog. If you're going to start a blog, I suggest you start here.

- ✔ **WordPress:** WordPress is also a pretty powerful blogging tool with free accounts. Here's the rub though — if you want to have AdSense on your account, you have to pay for the premium account and even then it can be a difficult chore to put the code in the right place.

- ✔ **TypePad:** TypePad is a hugely popular blogging application that allows you to use AdSense ads in the footer of blog posts. It's also not difficult to use, which makes it another good option for a blog that includes AdSense ads.

As I mention earlier, dozens of other blogging services are out there that you can try. Some companies offer business-specific blogs, and others offer blogs as part of a larger community of users. But for your purpose, I look at blogs that you can use AdSense with, and the service that's most AdSense-friendly (of course) is Blogger. So, the remainder of this chapter focuses on how to put AdSense on your Blogger blog.

Adding AdSense to Your Blogger Blog

Okay, so you signed on to Blogger, set up your blog, and got the word out. You're getting some visitors, and the great response you're getting makes you think it might be time to put AdSense on that blog. Let the fun begin.

The one drawback with adding AdSense to your Blogger account is that you can show only three AdSense units on your blog at any given time. So, when you're placing ads on your blog, be very selective about where you place them. Now, if you paid attention in Chapter 3, you know that your most effective ad placement is above the fold, at the very top of the page, on the right-hand side (preferably in a sidebar), or within the text on the page. With these guidelines, you can place your ads for the most attention and the best results.

AdSense as a page element

You can place AdSense in your blog in one of two ways. The first (and probably easiest) way to add it is as a *page element.* Page elements are like the building blocks of your Web site. You can choose which elements you want to appear in your blog template by pointing and clicking the desired element.

Here's how to ad AdSense with this method:

1. **Point your browser to** `www.blogger.com` **and log on to your Blogger account with your username and password.**

   You're automatically taken to the dashboard — essentially the Control Panel — for the blog.

2. **From the Dashboard, select the Layout tab for the blog that you want to add AdSense to.**

   You can have more than one blog with Blogger.

3. **On the Page Elements page (see Figure 13-1), click the Add a Page Element link.**

   The Choose a New Page Element dialog box appears, as shown in Figure 13-2.

Figure 13-1: Page elements are different capabilities you can add to your blog page.

Click here to add AdSense.

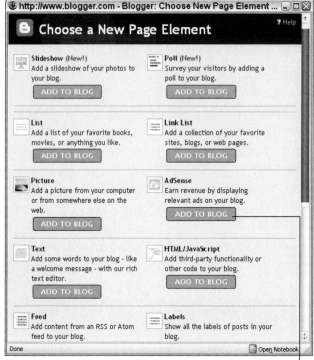

The AdSense widget

Figure 13-2:
Locate
AdSense in
the list of
available
widgets.

4. Locate AdSense in the list of available elements — or *widgets* — and click the accompanying Add to Blog button.

The Configure AdSense dialog box appears, as shown in Figure 13-3.

5. Make your selections in the Configure AdSense dialog box and click Save Changes.

Here's where you can tweak things like ad size or colors. You can even change your publisher ID, the number that identifies your AdSense account so that you're properly compensated when visitors click your ads.

Clicking Save Changes closes the Configure AdSense dialog box and you're returned to the Blogger layout page. You can see your new AdSense widget immediately below the Add a Page Element link.

After you create the widget, you can move it around by clicking and dragging it anywhere — anywhere on the sidebar, above the footer, or below the header, that is. You can't move the widget to the main post area of your blog.

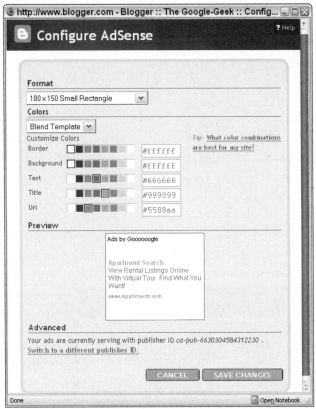

Figure 13-3:
Configure
AdSense
with the lim-
ited options
available.

If you want to place ads within the area that's reserved for your blog posts, you have to do it through the settings for the post page. Here's how:

1. **Log in to your Blogger dashboard (see the previous steps) and select the Layout tab under the blog you want to change.**

   You're taken to the Page Elements page of your blog layout.

2. **Locate the Blog Posts section of the layout page and select the blue Edit link, as shown in Figure 13-4.**

   The Configure Blog Posts dialog box appears.

3. **Select the Show Ads between Posts check box, see Figure 13-5.**

   Additional options for configuring inline ads become visible immediately below the check box, as shown in Figure 13-6.

4. **Configure your ad preferences — size, color, and publisher ID — and then scroll to the bottom of the dialog box and click Save Changes.**

   Ads now appear between your blog posts, according to the preferences that you selected.

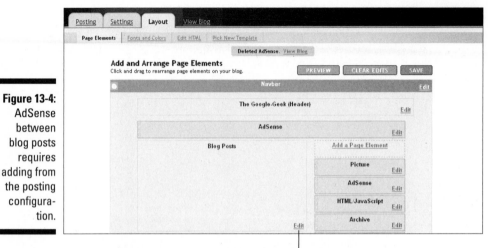

Figure 13-4:
AdSense between blog posts requires adding from the posting configuration.

The Edit link

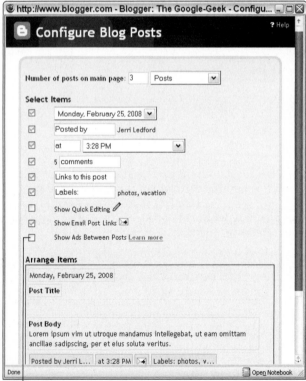

Figure 13-5:
The Show Ads between Posts option.

Select this option to place ads between posts.

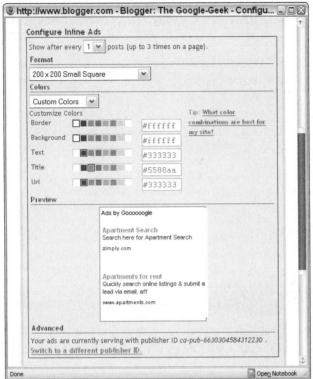

Figure 13-6:
Your
AdSense
configura-
tion options.

You can't use these gadgets to put ads directly in the text of your posts, but you can use them to put ads between your posts.

One other method for adding AdSense code using widgets that gives you a little more flexibility is to add the code using the HTML/JavaScript widget. The HTML/JavaScript widget works in much the same way as the AdSense-specific widget.

1. **On the Layout tab, make sure you're in the Page Elements view and then select Add a Page Element.**

2. **Select HTML/JavaScript from the list of available widgets.**

   The dialog box changes to a text editor, as shown in Figure 13-7.

3. **Open AdSense and generate the code for a new ad.**

   If you need a reminder on how to create ads, I covered that in Chapters 6, 7, and 8.

4. **Copy the ad code.**

5. **Return to the Blogger HTML/JavaScript editor, enter a name for the ad — this can be whatever name makes sense to you — then paste the ad code from Step 4 into the Content text box.**

6. **Click the Save Changes button.**

   The dialog box disappears and you're returned to the Page Elements view of your blog, except now you should see an element labeled HTML/ JavaScript.

   You can move this element around the header, footer, or sidebar of your blog, just as you would any other element, by clicking and dragging it to the desired location.

That's all there is to it. The big difference between using the HTML capabilities and Blogger's built-in AdSense capabilities is what you can do with the ads. Blogger's AdSense customization elements are pretty slim. By using Blogger's HTML capabilities, on the other hand, you can create more customized ads on the AdSense Web site and then paste them into your blog.

Monkeying with the code

Plopping down an AdSense ad right in the middle of a blog post — rather than *between* posts — is a little more involved than just adding it using the widget feature, but it can be done. The result is an ad that floats off the left side of the post, above the fold.

I may as well come right out and say it: Getting an ad to float off to the side of your blog post requires that you monkey-around with the HTML template of your blog. Sounds a bit dicey, I know, and if you're not careful, you could really mess up your blog, but I'm here to show you the way.

Before you make *any* changes at all to your blog, save a copy of the template to your hard drive, in case you mess up royally. I messed up the first time I tried to put the code into my blog. Fortunately, I had saved the template, so all I had to do was upload it and nothing was lost.

To save your template to your hard drive, follow these instructions:

1. **Log in to your Blogger account and go to the Layout tab.**

2. **Click the Edit HTML link below the tab, as shown in Figure 13-8.**

   The Edit HTML screen appears.

3. **In the Edit HTML screen, click the Download Full Template link.**

   A Save As dialog box appears.

4. **Using the Save As dialog box, save the template to a place on your hard drive where you can find it.**

Figure 13-7:
Blogger's
text editor.

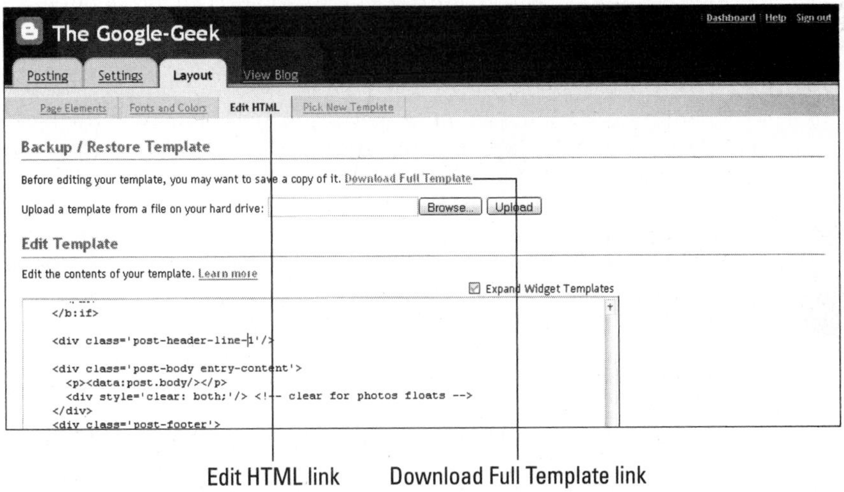

Figure 13-8:
Download
the full
Blogger
template
before
making any
changes.

Edit HTML link   Download Full Template link

After you've saved the file to your hard drive, you can play around with the template without fear of irreparably damaging your hard drive. Time to get elbow deep in HTML!

The HTML page that's displayed when you click the Edit HTML link is everything that makes up your blog. It's a monster document that could keep you busy for hours if you don't know what you're looking for. Don't worry though; I know what's what. Follow me and you won't lose your way.

1. **Go to AdSense and generate the code for the ad unit you want to place in your posts.**

   For the purposes of this illustration, I use the 125x125 square format.

   By the way, Chapter 5 gives you all the gory details on generating code.

2. **Open NotePad (or any other text editor) and paste this code into a new document:**

   ```
   <div style='float:left;'>
   AdSense Code
   </div>
   ```

3. **Copy the code generated by AdSense and paste it into the document in place of** AdSense Code.

   Replace those two words completely. When you're finished, the complete piece of code looks something like this:

   ```
   <div style='float:left;'>
   <script type="text/javascript"><!--
   google_ad_client = "pub-00000000000000";
   /* 125x125, created 2/25/08 */
   google_ad_slot = "000095560";
   google_ad_width = 125;
   google_ad_height = 125;
   //-->
   </script>
   <script type="text/javascript"
   src="http://pagead2.googlesyndication.com/pagead/show_
           ads.js">
   </script>
   </div>
   ```

   Your code won't look *exactly* like that, but it should be very similar. In particular, some of the numbers will be different, and the design of the ad may also be different.

4. **Open a Web browser, surf over to your Blogger account, and log in.**

   This should be second nature by now.

5. **Go to the Layout tab and then click the Edit HTML link below the tab.**

   The Edit HTML screen makes an appearance.

6. **In the Edit HTML view of your blog, search for the following line of code with the search function on your browser:**

```
<div class='post-header-line-1'/>
```

You could scroll through pages and pages of HTML code to find what you need, but here's an easier way. In Firefox and Internet Explorer browsers, press Ctrl+F to open a search box on your browser. When it appears, search for the line of code above.

7. **When you find your little snippet of code, go back to your text editor, copy the code that you put together, and then paste that code immediately below the line you located.**

When you're finished, your code looks like this:

```
    <div class='post-header-line-1'/>
<div style='float:left;'>
<script type="text/javascript"><!--
google_ad_client = "pub-6630304584312230";
/* 125x125, created 2/25/08 */
google_ad_slot = "9092795560";
google_ad_width = 125;
google_ad_height = 125;
//-->
</script>
<script type="text/javascript"
src="http://pagead2.googlesyndication.com/pagead/show_
        ads.js">
</script>
</div>
    <div class='post-body entry-content'>
```

Notice in this code that the first and last lines are exactly what you see in your template. That's because those two lines were pre-existing. Everything in between is what you've pasted from your text editor.

8. **Before you save the template, click the blue Preview button.**

This opens a new window that displays the results of the changes you made to the template.

9. **After you preview the results of your cut-and-paste job and you're satisfied with the results, click the Save Template button to make the changes to your blog permanent.**

With the code in the previous steps list, you're adding AdSense to all the posts that are displayed on your main page. The only problems that you might encounter are if you have more than two or three posts displayed on the page, or if you have multiple ad units displayed in different places on your site. AdSense allows only three ad units to be displayed on any one page, so if your configuration puts you over that golden number, some of the ads won't display properly.

For example, if you have an AdSense widget in your sidebar and at the top of the page, when you use this method to add AdSense to your posts, some posts will have blank spaces where the ads should be. To combat this blank space, either remove AdSense widgets or reduce the number of posts that you show on the main page of your blog.

Part IV
AdSense Administration

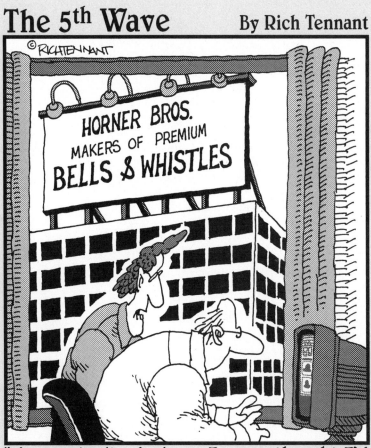

The 5th Wave   By Rich Tennant

"As a web site designer I never thought I'd say this, but I don't think your site has enough bells and whistles."

In this part . . .

This part of the book is dedicated to helping you understand the administrative functions of AdSense. These
functions are essential to helping you visualize and
increase your AdSense income.

Here you'll find out how to track AdSense responses with
programs like AWStats or Google Analytics. I also cover
setting up channels — a great way to figure out what's
working with your AdSense ads. I then walk you through
the reports that AdSense provides and how to better manage your account. I wind things up by detailing everything
you need to know in order to get paid — how to set up
your payment account, make changes to it, or put your
payments on hold.

Chapter 14

Tracking AdSense Responses

Anytime you track how well your AdSense strategy is actually doing, you're relying a little bit on science and a little bit on magic. True, the only surefire way to determine what your AdSense revenues will be is to wait until they're processed and show up on the AdSense administration pages. But that doesn't tell you what works (and what doesn't work) with the way that you've set up your ads or the placement that you're using for the ads. If you want to know what trends seem to be influencing your revenue, here's another way to go about it. Tracking your Web site traffic — more specifically, tracking what brings people to your site, what takes them away, and what they do while they're on your site — is the best way to get a feel for the trends that affect your AdSense revenues. To track all that, you have to put in some work or find a really good program.

Which of those options you decide to use is determined by you. What are you more comfortable with? You can track everything and extract all that information from the logs that are available on your server, or you can let someone else do all the hard work for you so that all you have to do is take a look at the data that's been gathered.

Both ways have advantages and disadvantages. Ultimately what it comes down to is whether a service (like Google Analytics) can provide all the data that you need. Such a service might not, and if that's the case, you have only one option: Roll up your sleeves and do it on your lonesome.

Understanding Server Logs

Let me put it to you straight: The most difficult way to track traffic on your Web site is through your server logs. Server logs are also the only way to get certain types of in-depth detail about your site. I guess you need to know what sever logs are though before I get too deep into what you can do with them.

A *server log* — more accurately a *Web server log* — is a group of files automatically generated by a server that tracks statistics about the traffic on your Web site. This group of files might contain information on where a user came to your site from, what pages on your site she visited, how long she spent on each site, and even more detailed information like what country she lives in (or the country her Internet access account is registered in) and some of the specifications about the browser she's using.

Server logs are a complicated mess of facts and information that most people just can't read. Seriously. You have to be one step above a NASA geek to understand all the gibberish contained in a server log.

Because most people won't ever reach that level of geekiness, some programs — *log analyzers* or *log parsers* — take all that data, analyze it, and then spit out more understandable statistics. Programs like AWStats (which is free, available at `www.awstats.sourceforge.net`) and Summary (which is free to try but can be costly to own, available at `www.summary.net`) can give you the information you seek from the raw data that the server collects.

Even though these programs are easier to use than trying to figure out server logs on your own, they're still not the easiest programs available. With AWStats, for example, you get to track your Web site statistics, but you have to have access to your Web server to use it. It's also requires a little more technical knowledge than some of the other Web site statistics programs that are available — like Google Analytics. Still, if you're ready to take on this program, it can potentially provide very in-depth analyses of the data that is collected in your server logs. I'm not ready to jump too deep into this pool right now, though. You'll find more information on AWStats in the "Installing AWStats" section, later in this chapter.

I'll be honest with you. Working with log analyzers can sometimes seem nearly as complicated as just trying to use the raw data coming from the server. Most log analyzers require that code be added to your Web site or Web server and then the reports have to be programmed before you can receive them.

On the flip side, server log analyzers can allow you to parse server data in ways that some other programs won't let you. With this technology, you can design reports that meet very specific needs (if you know how). For example, if you need a report that not only tells you what page of your Web site that visitors entered on but also what time of day they came to your site most often, you can program a report to divulge that kind of information.

If you're using a program like AWStats, the first thing to understand is that log analyzers count visitors differently than analytics programs do — one like Google Analytics, for example. AWStats looks at the *IP address* — the unique numerical address of a computer on the Internet, kind of like a street address for your house — of each site visitor. If one person visits your site a number of different times, AWStats counts that as only a single visitor. By comparison, a program like Google Analytics tracks computers by placing a cookie on the hard drive. That means that if a user clears out his browser *cache* — that's a record of the sites the user visited using that computer — or if the user logs in from another computer, Google Analytics counts him as more than one visitor. Looking at IP addresses is a little more accurate because even if a user clears his cache, the IP address for his computer remains the same. (Logging in from a different computer is still a problem, but as far as I know, there's no way around that kind of user being counted more than once with any stats program.)

Next, understand that programs like AWStats are more about the numbers than what can actually be extrapolated from those numbers. For example, with AWStats, Web crawlers are identified according to a list of crawlers defined by the log analyzer. Usually, a person creates the list, and the program then compares data against that list to determine which visits are from Web crawlers and which are from real people. The problem with this approach is that if the list of Web crawlers is not all-inclusive, a crawler could be counted as a visitor. The result, then, is that the number of visitors can be skewed. Because AWStats doesn't look at things like where a visitor comes from, it's hard to tell what's a crawler and what's a visitor if the crawler doesn't appear on the list of excluded IP addresses.

On the other hand, Google Analytics *does* look at where visitors come from. And Web crawlers have very specific origins, so it's usually pretty easy to tell which of your visitors are people and which are programs that are designed to crawl a Web site.

Installing AWStats

AWStats is a free program that's available from SourceForge. To download the program, go to `http://awstats.sourceforge.net`. After you download it, install it.

If you're planning to use AWStats to track your Web site traffic statistics, you must have access to your Web server. Unless you own that server (or your company owns the server), you probably don't have that access. If you're purchasing a hosting package from a Web site host, AWStats isn't the right program for you to track your statistics. If that's the case, you need to use a program, such as Google Analytics, that tracks your statistics without you having to get access to your Web server.

Assuming you do have access to your Web server, here's what you'd do to install AWStats:

1. **After you download AWStats (from** `http://awstats.sourceforge.net`**), find the file and extract the AWStats package.**

   Whatever extraction program (for example, WinZip — available at `www.winzip.com`) you use will have different instructions for the extraction process, so refer to that program's documentation if you're not sure how to use it.

2. **If the installation process doesn't start automatically (it should with Windows Installer but it won't with any other operating system), locate the AWStats Tools Directory and double-click the** `awstats_configure.pl` **script to begin the installation process.**

   `Awstats_configure.pl` tries to determine your current log format from your Apache Web server configuration file, `httpd.conf`. (The script asks for the path if it can't find the file.)

3. **If you use a common log,** `awstats_configure.pl` **suggests changing that log to the** `NCSA combined/XLF/ELF` **format.**

   You can use your own custom log format, but this pre-defined log format is often the best choice and makes setup easier.

   If you answer yes, `awstats_configure.pl` modifies your `httpd.conf` file, restarts Apache to apply the changes, and then creates a new file called `awstats.`*mysite*`.conf` by copying the template file `awstats.model.conf`.

   These actions should occur automatically (though they may require your confirmation in some areas).

4. **To verify that the main parameters of your new configuration file match your needs, open** `awstats.`*mysite*`.conf` **in your favorite text editor — the file should be located on your hard drive and you can use the search function of your computer to locate it — and make the following changes, as required:**

   Verify the LogFile value. It should be the full path of your server log file.

   Verify the LogType value. It should be `W` for analyzing Web log files.

   Check the LogFormat. It should be set to 1, although you can use a custom log format if you don't use the combined log format.

   Set the SiteDomain parameter: It should be set to the main domain name or the intranet Web server name used to reach the Web site you want to analyze (for example: `www.mysite.com`). If you have several possible names for the same site, use the main domain name and add the others to the list in the HostAlias parameter.

5. **When you've finished editing these elements, save the file to its original location.**

   Installation and configuration are now finished and the wizard should close automatically.

You may have to wait a couple days to see results from the log analyzer — and you still have to figure out how the program works if you want to get your results! After a couple days, however, you can begin creating stats reports by going to www.*myserver.mydomain*/awstats/awstats.pl — it's a Web-based program. Just remember to replace *myserver* and *mydomain* with your own server and domain information. It's a pretty complicated process, though, so I suggest that you read more about using the program by going to http://awstats.sourceforge.net/docs/awstats_setup.html.

Because Web crawlers change, a log analyzer can occasionally misinterpret a Web crawler as a real person. It's not a major mistake, but one of which you should be aware.

Tracking Stats with Google Analytics

If you're asking my opinion about the best programs to use for tracking Web site statistics — go ahead! Ask. — Google Analytics is definitely #1 on my list. It's easy to use, it's free, you don't need access to your Web server, and you don't have to be an ubergeek to use it. Google Analytics also provides all the statistics that I think you need. (I've been known to be wrong a time or two, but just keep that between you and me.)

Google Analytics started life as Urchin Analytics. Urchin was one of the premier Web site traffic statistics programs available on the Web — at an expensive price. Then Google bought Urchin and made the program available for free. The number of people who adopted it during the first few days of release was overwhelming. Google actually had to close the program to new users for a time to catch up with demand.

It's no surprise that demand for such a powerful stats program was very high, especially at a cost of exactly nothing. The statistics that are available through Google Analytics will satisfy almost everyone looking for Web site stats and are certainly enough to help you understand how your AdSense ads are performing.

Understanding Google Analytics quirks

The thing about Google Analytics that's different from a log analyzer like AWStats is the way that visitors on your site are tracked. Log analyzers tend to track visitors by IP address. Google Analytics actually tracks visitors by placing a *cookie* — a small snippet of code that acts as a kind of software ID collar — on the visitor's hard drive. Then, each time the visitor comes to your site, that cookie is recognized by Google Analytics.

The more Web-savvy among readers will immediately see the problem with relying on cookies to get the job done. A cookie is only trackable as long as it's on the visitor's hard drive. So, if a visitor comes to your site, clears out his Internet history, and then returns to the site in the same day, that user is tracked as two different users. Numbers can get a little screwy.

Most people don't clean out Internet histories on a daily basis — some never clean out them at all — but that's one of the issues you should be aware of.

Google Analytics also can be fooled by people who set their browsers to not accept cookies at all. It's a privacy issue. Some believe that when a company (any company) is tracking their movements on the Web, their privacy is invaded. On principle, they edit their browser preferences so that the browser won't accept any cookies. (Editing your preferences is a snap to do, in case you're wondering.) I don't necessarily buy into that school of thought, but I can understand why some people would feel that way.

Regardless of whether you understand the anti-cookie stand of some folks, the fact still remains that a percentage of your site visitors may have set up their browsers to reject cookies. If that's the case, Google Analytics can't track those people. It's a small percentage, but again, enough that you should be aware it's a possibility.

Even with these issues, Google Analytics remains my favorite Web site traffic statistics program. Because it's free and easy to install, I recommend that everyone at least try it for a month or two. If you don't like it, you can always move on to something else.

Intrinsically, the difference between log analyzers and programs like Google Analytics mostly involves methodology. Which program you use is determined by what you're looking for. I much prefer programs like Google Analytics over log analyzers because, as far as I'm concerned, the information that I need is covered by Google Analytics. You may not feel that way, and that's okay. Just choose the program that works best to meet your specific tracking needs.

Installing Google Analytics

Google Analytics, like all Google programs, is easy to install. It requires that you register for the program and then install the tracking code. Easy-peasy. Here are the basics for getting started with the program:

1. **Point your browser to** www.google.com/analytics.

   The Google Analytics home page appears.

2. **Click the Sign Up Now link.**

   A sign-up page appears.

3. **If you already have a Google account, sign into Google Analytics with that account. If you don't have an account, register a new account with Google.**

4. **After you sign in, click the Sign Up button (as shown in Figure 14-1).**

   You're taken to the New Account Signup page.

Figure 14-1: Even after you sign in with a Google account, you need to set up an analytics account.

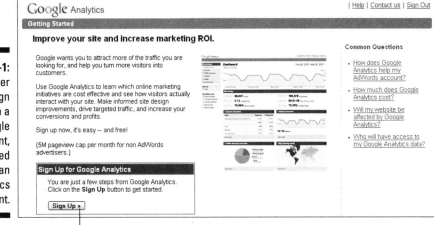

Click here to sign up.

5. **In the New Account Signup page, enter your Web site's URL, an account name (this can be any name you choose), your time zone location, and your actual time zone into the appropriate text fields and then click Continue.**

6. **In the new page that appears, enter your contact information (including name, telephone number, and country) and then click Continue.**

   The User Agreement page appears.

7. **Read through the user agreement, and if you agree with the terms of service, select the Yes, I Agree to the Above Terms and Conditions check box and then click Create New Account.**

   You now have an Analytics account, but you're still not quite done. A new page appears, displaying your tracking code, as shown in Figure 14-2. This snippet of code is how Google Analytics tracks the visitors to your Web pages.

8. **Copy the code provided and paste it into the HTML of your Web site immediately before the** `</body>` **tag of the site.**

   Now, you're *really* finished.

After you place the tracking code on your Web site, it could take a couple days before you begin to see any statistics about the site on Google Analytics — stuff like number of visitors, where they came from, and how long they stayed on your site. Even then, the statistics aren't really valuable beyond telling you who's been to your site. There's nothing historical to compare the statistics against.

Getting the real value of Google Analytics takes at least 30 days — long enough to have enough information to compare timeframes and see what a normal baseline for your site is.

After you allow enough time to establish a baseline, you can really tell what tweaks are valuable in terms of bringing in more site traffic — and seeing what may be pushing traffic off your site. For example, if you have a high percentage of your visitors leaving your site on a specific page, you know that there's something about that page that could be turning your visitors off, so you can tweak the page to try to hold them on the site longer.

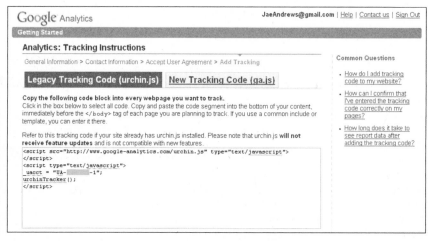

Figure 14-2:
Copy the
provided
code and
paste into
your Web
site code
to enable
tracking.

Google Analytics with Google AdWords

One very cool feature of Google Analytics is that it has reports that are specifically created for people who use AdWords to advertise. If you use AdWords (and many people who publish AdSense ads do), you can take advantage of reports, such as AdWords Campaigns, Keyword Positions, and Audio Campaigns, which allow you to specifically track your AdWords results.

AdWords is all about drawing new traffic to your site, so there's no better way to track your success with AdWords than to use a Web site traffic statistics program. Google Analytics, being a Google program, is a natural choice. (If AdWords sounds intriguing, check out *AdWords For Dummies* by Howie Jacobson [Wiley Publishing].)

Analyzing Analytics

After you set up your Google Analytics account and have a few days to collect numbers, the true value of the program starts to shine through. This section shows you how to put that value to use.

When you log on to your account from the `www.google.com/analytics/` page, the first screen that you see is a Dashboard overview of your available stats, as shown in Figure 14-3.

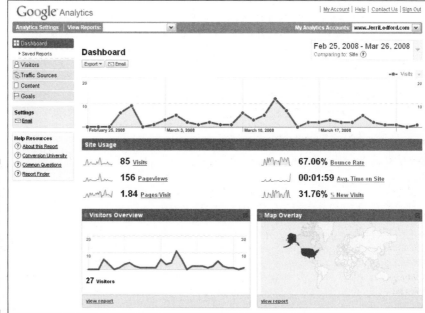

Figure 14-3: The Dashboard is an overview of the most important stats on Google Analytics.

These stats are, by default, the stats most folks consider important when it comes to Web site traffic numbers. You may not be like most folks though, which is why you're free to add other snapshots to the Dashboard if you'd rather see something there. One thing you can't do, however, is remove or replace the Site Usage stats that you see at the top of the page. These are fixed permanently in place.

You *can* change the *dates* shown in the Site Usage section — the default dates always show the previous month.

You'll find a handy navigation menu on the left side of the page, right under the Dashboard heading. This menu collapses and expands, according to where you click it. As shown in Figure 14-4, clicking one of the headings in the menu expands the menu so you can see additional reports that are available under that heading.

Headings expand to
show additonal reports.

Figure 14-4:
Click a
menu
heading
to expand
the head-
ing to see
additional
reports for
that section.

Of all the reports that are available to you, the most useful ones in terms of tracking AdSense info are found under the Traffic Sources and Content headings. Under Traffic Sources, for example, you can access the following reports:

✔ **Referring Sites:** This report, as shown in Figure 14-5, shows which other Web sites referred visitors to your site. This is important to your AdSense earnings because in addition to placing the ads on your page, you should also be marketing your site. One way to market your site is through other Web sites. This report tells you how successful those marketing efforts have been.

✔ **Search Engines:** The Search Engines report shows you which search engines sent visitors to your site. Because you know that your site is search engine optimized by keyword, this gives you a glimpse into how well your keywords are helping search engines list your site in search results.

✔ **Keywords:** The Keywords report shows which are the most popular keywords that bring visitors to your site. No better tool is out there for finding out if you've chosen the right keywords for your site. You can then use this information to ensure that your site is targeted accurately to the keywords that bring people in. In turn, your AdSense ads will be further optimized to the correct keywords.

Figure 14-5:
See where
visitors
to your
site come
from in this
report.

In addition to the Traffic Sources reports, the Content reports also contain some useful insights. All these reports are related to the content on your site, so if you want to know what's working and what's not, this is where to find out. The most useful reports from this section include

- **Top Content:** This report lists the most viewed content on your site. Do you want to know what visitors to your site are looking at or how long they're spending on specific pages? This report tells you. The report, as shown in Figure 14-6, lists the top URLs. You can then click each of the URLs to view more in-depth information, such as the time users spend on the page and the number of visitors that exit from that page.

- **Top Landing Pages:** *Landing pages* are where a visitor first "touches down" on your site. The Top Landing Pages report shows you exactly which of your pages those are. This is useful in a couple different ways. First, if you're conducting marketing with a specific entry page, you can track how effective that marketing is. Second, this information is helpful when you want to know what pages users seem to be finding on their own, especially if you're not conducting any marketing campaigns.

Figure 14-6:
See the most viewed pages of your Web site in this report.

✔ **Top Exit Pages:** Similar to the Top Landing Pages, this report shows you information about how users move about your site. The Top Exit Pages report shows you where users jump away from your site. If you're an AdSense user, this information can be invaluable. Most AdSense users don't put ads on every page on their site. Instead, they place ads on certain, optimized pages. This report, as shown in Figure 14-7, lets you know if those pages are where visitors are leaving your site. It's not a guarantee that your ads are working, but it's definitely an indicator that your ads could be performing well. You can use this information along with the data provided in AdSense reports to see which pages seem to be working better for ads.

✔ **Site Overlay:** For AdSense information, the Site Overlay is my favorite of all Google Analytics reports. The Site Overlay report literally overlays your Web site with a graphic that shows you which links on the site are most clicked, as shown in Figure 14-8. Above all other reports, this one is the most telling of how well your AdSense ads actually work.

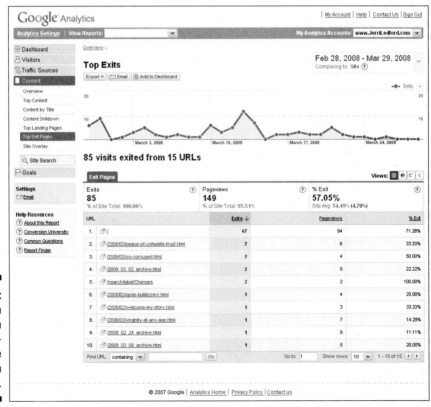

Figure 14-7: See from which pages visitors leave your site in this report.

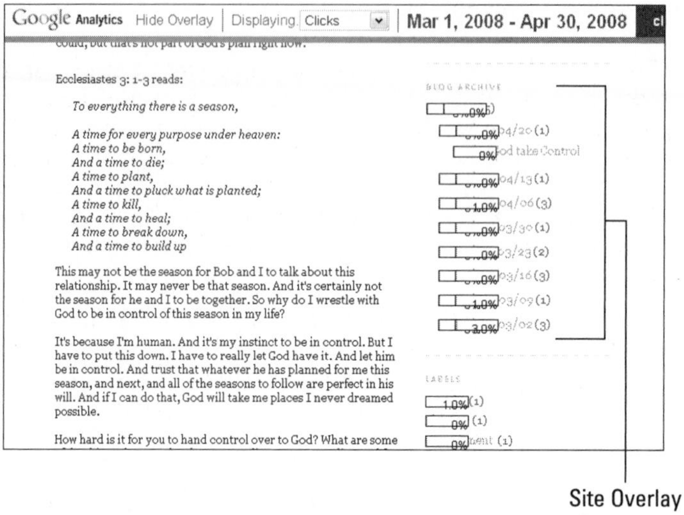

Google Analytics | Hide Overlay | Displaying Clicks ▾ | **Mar 1, 2008 - Apr 30, 2008** | cl

could, but that's not part of God's plan right now.

Ecclesiastes 3: 1-3 reads:

To everything there is a season,

A time for every purpose under heaven:
A time to be born,
And a time to die;
A time to plant,
And a time to pluck what is planted;
A time to kill,
And a time to heal;
A time to break down,
And a time to build up

This may not be the season for Bob and I to talk about this relationship. It may never be that season. And it's certainly not the season for he and I to be together. So why do I wrestle with God to be in control of this season in my life?

It's because I'm human. And it's my instinct to be in control. But I have to put this down. I have to really let God have it. And let him be in control. And trust that whatever he has planned for me this season, and next, and all of the seasons to follow are perfect in his will. And if I can do that, God will take me places I never dreamed possible.

How hard is it for you to hand control over to God? What are some

BLOG ARCHIVE

□ 0% (1)
□ 0% 04/20 (1)
□ 0% God take Control
□ 0% 04/13 (1)
□ 1.0% 04/06 (3)
□ 0% 03/30 (1)
□ 0% 03/23 (2)
□ 0% 03/16 (3)
□ 1.0% 03/09 (1)
□ 2.0% 03/02 (3)

LABELS

□ 1.0% (1)
□ 0% (1)
□ 0% ent (1)

Site Overlay

Figure 14-8:
The Site Overlay shows what percentage of clicks is received on each link.

Each of these reports is presented in graphical format. At a glance, you can see the most basic information for the report. You can also dig deeper into the report and further segment the data by using drop-down menus (when provided) and by clicking blue, linked text. Each report has a different set of capabilities, so take some time to get to know the finer side of each report.

Remember that Google Analytics alone won't tell you *everything* you need to know about how your AdSense ads perform. Combine your AdSense stats — the ones found in your AdSense reports, which I cover in Chapter 15 — with your Google Analytics stats and then you can get a clear picture of what's working and what's not.

Keep in mind that it takes some time to establish a baseline from which you can determine which efforts seem to be working and which don't.

Channeling with AdSense

When you're tracking what works and what doesn't in AdSense, you soon discover that no single tracking method works best. Instead, a combination of tracking technologies helps you gather all the data you need. In addition to a Web site traffic statistics program, such as those I discuss earlier in this chapter, AdSense offers another method of tracking that can help you determine which ads perform best — channels.

Google explains channels this way:

> *Channels enable you to view detailed reporting about the performance of specific pages and ad units. By assigning a channel to a combination of pages or ad units, you could track the performance of a leaderboard versus a banner, or compare your motorcycle pages to your automobile pages. You can even create a channel to track each of your separate domains, so you can see where your clicks are coming from. While channels can be used to track performance and revenue, they won't have any effect on your earnings or ad targeting.*

The way you use channels is determined by how you want to track your ads and by the revenues generated from those ads. You can track them by ad, page, and even Web site — whatever works best for you. When you have that information, you can cross-compare it to your Web site traffic statistics to figure out even more about what's working and what's not.

Understanding AdSense channels

AdSense offers two different types of channels: URL channels and custom channels. *URL channels* track your AdSense ads by URL. You can track either single pages or you can use the top URL (www.*sitename*.com) to track every page within a Web site.

Custom channels allow you to track specific ads, according to parameters that you define. You can use a single custom channel to track multiple ads on multiple Web sites, as well.

When using channels to track your AdSense ads, the code that's generated for your ad differs slightly from what would be generated if you weren't tracking the ads with a specific channel. However, the code should still be pasted into your Web site or blog in the same manner that you added code that isn't tracked by channels.

Creating effective channels

One very useful facet of using channels is that these differentiators allow you to track the effectiveness of changes that you might be testing in your ads. For example, if you're running two sets of ads on your page, one with borders and one without, you can assign different channels to these ads to see which performs better.

Here's a hint: Ads without borders nearly always perform better than ads with borders. Taking the border away seems to make some site visitors more willing to give an AdSense ad a try — maybe because it doesn't really *look* much like an ad.

The first thing you need to do when you decide to use channels is to figure out exactly what purpose the channels have. Why do you want to use channels? Do you want to see how well a specific ad design is performing? Or do you want to track how effective ads on a specific page of your site are?

After you determine what you want to track with channels, you can begin to create the channels that will serve your needs. You can create up to 200 different channels in your AdSense account, and after you create a channel, you can rename, deactivate, or delete it completely if you're no longer using it. The next few sections give you all the details.

When you start to create a new channel, the process is set to create channels for AdSense for Content ads. You have the option to create channels for Referrals and Mobile Content, too. If you choose to create a channel for one of the other types of AdSense, click the blue linked tab for that option. AdSense for Search is the only type of ad that you can't create a URL channel for.

Creating URL channels

Creating AdSense channels is an easy enough procedure. When you're creating URL channels, have the specific URL that you want to track. If you want to track a whole site under a single URL, the top-level Web address is the one that you need to use. If you're tracking a specific page on your Web site, be sure you have the exact URL for the page that you want to track. With that information in hand, here's how you can create your first URL channel:

1. **Log in to your AdSense account and go to the AdSense Setup tab.**

2. **Click the Channels link on the AdSense Setup tab.**

   You're taken to the Channels overview page, as shown in Figure 14-9.

3. **Click the URL Channels link.**

   The page view refreshes to show URL channels that have been previously created (if there are any).

4. **Click the + Add New URL Channels link.**

   The page refreshes to show a form for entering URLs, as shown in Figure 14-10.

Figure 14-9: Create new channels from the Channels overview page.

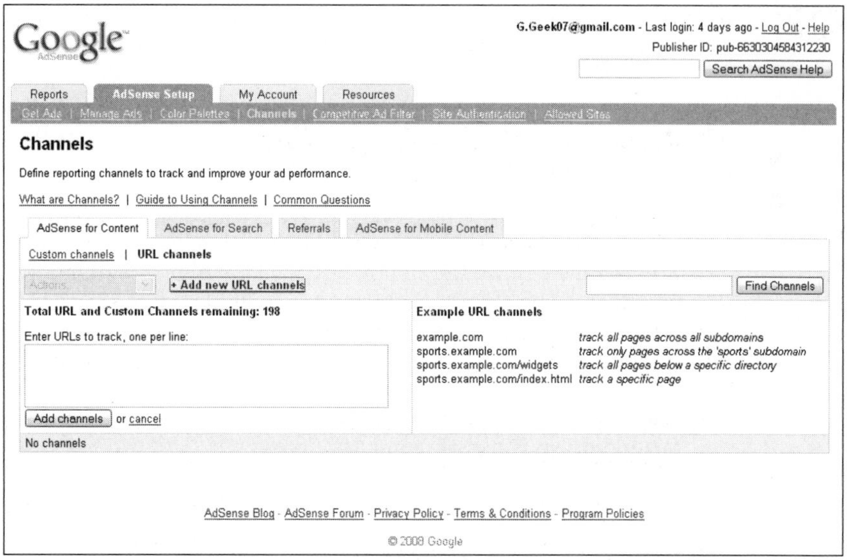

URL Channels link

Figure 14-10: Use the form that appears to add new URL channels to track.

5. **Enter the URLs that you want to track in the text box provided.**

   Make sure you only enter one URL per line.

   To track a single page: Enter the full URL (example.com/sample.html)

   To track a script that generates multiple pages: Enter the full path of the script, without the ? (example.com/sample.asp?keyword=one)

To track all pages below a specific directory: Enter a partial URL (example.com/sample)

To track only pages across a specific subdomain: Enter the subdomain (sports.example.com)

To track all pages on a domain: Enter the domain name (www.example.com)

To track all impressions and clicks across the domain (including any existing subdomains): Enter the domain name without the www (example.com)

6. **After you enter the desired URLs, click the Add Channels button.**

   Now you have URL channels available to you if you want to use them to track your ads.

Adding older ads to a channel

After you create a channel to use for tracking, the ads that already exist on your Web site aren't automatically tracked. Instead, you have to update those ads or create new ones. To edit ads:

1. **Log in to your AdSense account and go to the AdSense Setup tab.**
2. **Click the Manage Ads link.**
3. **On the Manage Ads page, select the ad that you would like to edit.**

   You're taken to a page that looks like the original setup wizard for the ad except that it's all contained on a single page, rather than on several pages.

4. **Make the changes that you want to make — in this case, you're choosing a channel from the drop-down menu.**
5. **When you're finished, click the Save button at the bottom of the page.**

That's it. Editing your ads really is that easy. And if it's new ads that you're working with, you can find more information about creating a new ad in Chapter 2.

Creating custom channels

You create custom channels pretty much the same way you create URL channels. The difference is that with custom channels, you use a specific channel name rather than a URL. When you're creating your custom channels, use descriptive names for the channel. For example, if you're testing large rectangles against link units, you can create two channels, naming one Large Rectangles and one Link Units. When it's time to see the reports broken down by channel, there's no doubt what each channel refers to.

Here are the steps for creating custom channels:

1. **Log in to your AdSense account and go to the AdSense Setup tab.**

2. **Click the Channels link at the top of the tab.**

   You should be taken automatically to the Custom Channels page, but if you're not, click the Custom Channels link.

3. **Click the + Add New Custom Channels link.**

   You're taken to a channel creation page, like the one shown in Figure 14-11.

4. **Enter the desired name for the channel and then select whether to allow the channel to be shown to advertisers as an ad placement.**

   If you choose to allow the ad placement option, the channel is shown as available for advertisers to place *cost-per-impression* ads — ads for which you'll be paid based on the number of people who see the ads.

5. **If you choose to show the channel to advertisers, the form you're filling out expands, as shown in Figure 14-12. Enter the requested information and then click the Add Channel button.**

   If you don't choose to show the channel to advertisers, you can move on to the next step.

   You're returned to the front channel page where you began, but now you see the channel you created listed below the + Add New Custom Channels option.

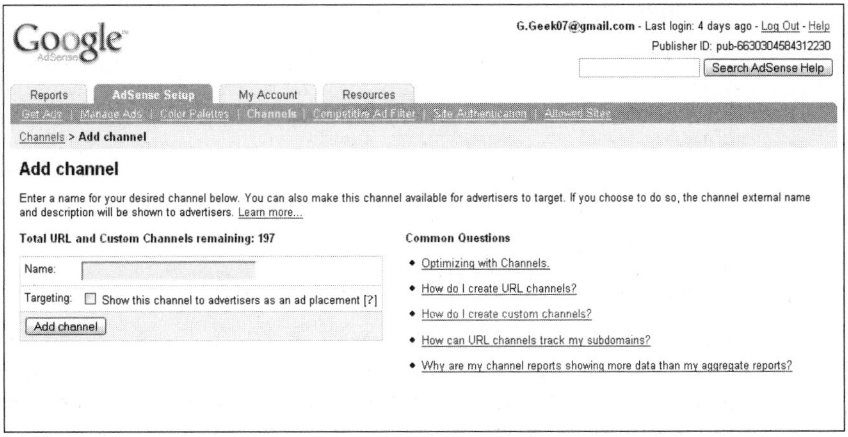

Figure 14-11: Creating custom channels requires different information than is needed to create URL channels.

Figure 14-12:
Additional information is required to show channels for advertiser placement.

After you create a custom channel, you can go through the same process you used for URL channels to add ads customized to the channel or to edit existing ads. (See the preceding section, "Creating URL channels," for more info.)

Tracking your AdSense results should be a regular part of your AdSense activities. Through tracking these results, you discover your successes — and failures. As with any technology, throwing it on the Web without thought of what works and what doesn't isn't likely to get you anywhere. But with some consistent effort, and tracking, you'll figure out what works and what doesn't. Then you can make the most of your AdSense efforts.

Chapter 15

Using AdSense Reports

In This Chapter

▶ Understanding quick, custom, and advanced reports

▶ Using report templates and the Report Manager

▶ Setting up automatic reports

▶ Stay on the crawler's good side with site diagnostics

▶ Managing your AdSense account

*W*eb site owners who publish AdSense ads on their sites tend to be obsessive about checking their numbers to see what levels their revenue is reaching. If you find yourself logging in to AdSense 15 times a day to see how many people have clicked your ads, there's an easier way to keep track of things.

With Google's set of AdSense reports, Google provides you with the tools you need to see exactly where you stand — all in just a few minutes. Some of the reports can even be automated, so you don't even have to log on to the Web site. Setting up these automated reports can save you time; time that you can spend creating better content, adding pages to your site, or tweaking the keywords that you use to help the AdSense crawler target ads to your site.

The Overview

Google makes it easy for you to automatically know how much you're earning on any given day, just by signing in to your AdSense account — you know, that little gold mine you keep at www.adsense.com. When you log in to the account, the first page you see is the Overview report, which provides you with a quick look at your daily earnings. In fact, right there in bold print (and it's probably the very first thing you see) is the Today's Earnings heading. In green, next to the heading, you see the amount of money that you've earned that day.

A little farther down the page, you see a table with details about how you've earned that money. The table lists the different types of AdSense ads you're showing as well as the following statistics, all designed to help you understand quickly what's working and what's not:

- **Page Impressions:** This is the number of people who have viewed your ads on a given day. This number represents all the visitors to your site, whether they stayed on the site or bounced right back off.

- **Clicks:** This column adds the number of times folks have clicked one of your ads.

- **Page CTR:** Short for *Page Click-Thru-Rate,* Page CTR shows the percentage of people who came to your site and then clicked through your AdSense ads to the advertiser's page. The higher your percentage, the better your ads are performing.

- **Page eCPM:** Don't ask me how they get *Effect Clicks Per Thousand* out of eCPM. (The acronym has something to do with the metric version of measurement, which really doesn't matter to you one bit.) What you *do* need to know is that this figure is arrived at by dividing your total earnings by the number of impressions in thousands. For example, if your site earns $100 from 10,000 impressions, your eCPM is $100/10 or $10. This represents the amount that you're making per thousand impressions, however, and doesn't represent exactly how much you're making. Instead, it's a measurement that you can use to compare results across channels or advertising programs.

- **Earnings:** The actual amount that you've earned over a given timeframe is shown in this column. Specify the timeframe you want to examine with the View drop-down menu, shown in Figure 15-1. You can view results by Today, Yesterday, Last 7 Days, This Month, Last Month, and All Time.

Figure 15-1:
Use the View drop-down menu to change the report timeframe.

View menu

The Overview page shows more than just how much money you're making. This page also contains notes from the AdSense team, messages that you can view — stuff like the monthly optimization report that's sent to AdSense advertisers — as well as links to quick reports. "What are they?" you ask. Read on and become enlightened.

Understanding Quick Reports

AdSense calls reports that you've preset certain variables for — dates, for example — *Quick Reports*. These reports are easy to get to. When you log in to your AdSense account, the page that you land on is the Main Report page. You'll find the Quick Reports section at the bottom of that page. These reports are already set up for you — basically —, so all you need to do is click the link for the report, and a new page loads with those variables already in place.

When a new report loads, notice the customization options shown at the top of the page. (They're above the fold; you actually have to scroll down the page to see the report data.) These customization options allow you to change dates, products, and even ad unit information to further customize your report view. I give you more information on how to use custom and advanced reports a little later in this chapter.

Figure 15-2 shows your Quick Report options for AdSense for Content ads. Here's what each report entails:

- **This Month, By Day:** If you select the This Month, By Day report, you get pretty much the same information as shown in the Overview report, such as page impressions, clicks, and earnings, but you get that info for each day of the current month.

- **Last Month, By Day:** Instead of displaying the current month's data, this report lets you look a bit deeper into the historical data to see what trends might be emerging. (Okay, *deep* here is a relative term; I'm only talking last month.) For example, are certain days better for generating AdSense income? If you can see those patterns and use them to develop useful theories and scenarios, you can test those theories in an effort to further increase your AdSense earnings.

If you use AdSense for Search on your site, additional reports may provide further statistics about your AdSense revenues. Even though AdSense for Search is a little different than AdSense for Content, the reports should have the same outward appearance. The functions of ads are different than the functions of searches, but you end up tracking the same information — clicks, impressions, earnings, and so on. Like AdSense for Content, you have reports for This Month, By Day and Last Month, By Day, This Month, By Channel & Day, Last Month, By Channel & Day, but you also have an additional report — Top Queries.

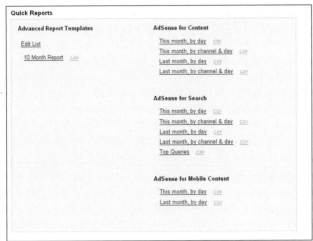

Figure 15-2:
Pick a Quick
Report,
any one.

Remember, channels are just tracking capabilities. In the reports listed above, By Channel just means that each different channel — or tracking group — you've created will have its own section on the reports.

All the remaining report options are pretty self-explanatory, except for the Top Queries report. That report actually shows the same information as the other reports, but the information is ranked from most popular to least popular, based on search queries that visitors conduct from your site with the search box that you placed on your site.

If you don't use AdSense for Search on your Web site, these reports just return empty, without any data.

Keep in mind that all such reports, whether they're for AdSense for Content ads or AdSense for Search ads, come to you already pre-defined. You still have the option to change any of the variables in the report so that you can further *segment* (or separate) data that concerns your AdSense activities. That's where custom and advanced reports are useful — so useful, in fact, that they deserve their own section.

Using Custom and Advanced Reports

Custom and advanced reports start out just like any other report that you run from AdSense Quick Reports except no data is preset for display.

When you select the Advanced Reports link on the Reports tab — remember, that's where you land when you log in to your AdSense account — a page loads displaying your options when it comes to creating reports, as shown in Figure 15-3. These options allow you to define custom reports that feature the information that you actually need at the moment, rather than information that someone else decides you might need.

Figure 15-3:
Create custom and advanced reports with the options provided.

> **Choose product**
> [AdSense for Content ▼]
>
> **Choose date range**
> ◉ this month - February [▼]
> ○ [Feb ▼] [1 ▼] [2008 ▼] - [Feb ▼] [11 ▼] [2008 ▼]
> * Date ranges are based on Pacific Time
>
> **Show data by** [?]
> [Page ▼]
>
> **Show**
> ◉ Aggregate data
>   Channel data   manage channels »
>
> [Display Report]

By picking and choosing among the various options, you can tailor a report to your precise needs. Your options are as follows:

✔ **Product:** With the Choose Product drop-down menu, you can specify which AdSense product you want to use as the basis for your report. Products here include AdSense for Search, AdSense for Content, Video Units, Referral Programs, and any other type of AdSense ads that you've allowed.

Only those products you've enabled in your AdSense account show up as options in the drop-down menu. Your Choose Product drop-down menu, therefore, may be different from mine.

✔ **Date range:** If you use this section's first radio button, you get to choose from preset date ranges that mirror those available in the quick reports (Today, Yesterday, Last 7 Days, This Month, Last Month, and All Time).

But hey, why go with the standard date range? I don't run my weeks according to Google's schedule, so I take advantage of the customized date ranges associated with the second radio button. The drop-down menus there allow you to specify the exact date range you want to use. If you need a report for a three-day period or a three-week period, or if you just want a report from Monday through Sunday, you can create it.

✔ **View options:** Another feature of the advanced reporting capabilities that you might find useful is the ability to change the way your data is shown. By default, the Show Data By drop-down menu is set to Page, which means that your data is sorted according to page impressions — the number of times your page is viewed, whether users click links on the page or not. Only there's a catch — isn't there always? It doesn't matter how many different ads or types of ads are shown on your page; each page counts as only one impression. If you're thinking about your impression figures in terms of having multiple ads on your page, they may seem low.

Another choice here is to show data by Ad Unit. This data display shows your page impressions according to the number of ads that are on your page. So, if one visitor comes to your site and clicks all the 15 ads that you have on your page, you'll see 15 page views for that single visitor. Now you have the opposite problem from the Page option. Instead of having page impressions that appear low because each visit counts only for one impression — no matter how many ads you have — now only one visit can create multiple impressions.

Using both of these Show Data By measurements can be useful in that you can see how many visitors have seen your ads as well as how many ads your visitors have seen. If, for some reason, AdSense is displaying a single ad in the place of a large rectangle, for example, you can see immediately what's happening. And it does happen from time to time when AdSense doesn't have enough matching ads to fill the rectangle, which can usually hold several ads.

A final option in the Show Data By drop-down menu — the Individual Ad option — changes your view of the data even more. When you use this display, you see how many impressions your site gets according to the number of actual ads that are displayed. Some ad displays show only a single ad — banners are one; you get one ad in a banner, nothing else — but others, like rectangles or link units, show more than one ad. When you view your report data with the Individual Ad option, you see multiples of impressions, based on the number of actual ads that are on your site.

At the Individual Ad level, you can see your ads by what type of ad targeting is used: contextual or placement targeting. Contextual ad placement is when ads are placed within your content because the ad jibes in some way with the subject of the content. Placement targeted ads are those ads that are placed on your site because the advertiser chooses to have its ads shown on your page. This is an additional detail you don't see in any other view.

You also have the option to show aggregate data or channel data. *Aggregate data* is just a collection of the tracking information for all your ads. *Channel data* is a collection of the tracking information for ads broken down into the channels that you have selected to use to track individual ads or groups of ads.

When you've finished selecting the options that you would like to display for your ads, then all you have to do to see the report is click the Display Report button. The page reloads, and your desired information is displayed.

Each different data display shows the impressions on your site slightly differently. Because the data is considered differently in each view, you see changes in your eCPM measurements as well. The fewer impressions shown, the higher your eCPM is.

Page impressions, clicks, and other report data, along with these different data views, allow you to compare ads and see which ones perform better than others. It takes some time to gather enough stats to be able to make any real determinations — if you have plenty of people visiting your site, a week might be enough; low traffic requires a little longer. With this data readily available to you, you can test different ad placements and types to discover what works best on your Web site.

Using Report Templates

The basic reports AdSense provides are useful enough for most purposes, but at times — recurring times — you need a report with a specific set of information and you don't want to have to re-create it every time you want to run that report. No sense in reinventing the wheel, right?

Report templates allow you to set up reports, based on your specific needs. Each time you want to run that specific report, all you have to do is select the template, rather than re-creating the report each time that you need it.

Here's the rub: You can't create reports that are any more sophisticated than what you can do with the advanced reporting capabilities I talk about in the previous section. What you can do, however, is create the report once, fashion a template based on that report, save the template, and reuse it whenever you want. (The idea here is to keep the template on hand so you don't have to go through setting up the report every time you need it.) Here's how you save a report as a template:

1. **Log on to your AdSense account.**

   The Reports page appears, with your Today's Earnings prominently displayed.

2. **On the Reports tab, select the Advanced Reports link.**

   Your report options appear. (Refer to Figure 15-3.)

3. **Create the report that you want to use as a template.**

   Set date ranges, choose the type of report — aggregate or channel data display — and choose the product (AdSense for Content, AdSense for Search, Referrals, and so on).

4. **Click the Display Report button to run the report.**

   When the report has processed, you see a Save as Report Template text box at the top of the report, as shown in Figure 15-4.

5. **Enter a name in the Save as Report Template text box and then click Save.**

   You see an orange confirmation box displayed if the report was successfully saved. If the confirmation box doesn't appear, go through the creation process again in case you've forgotten steps or there's a problem with the service.

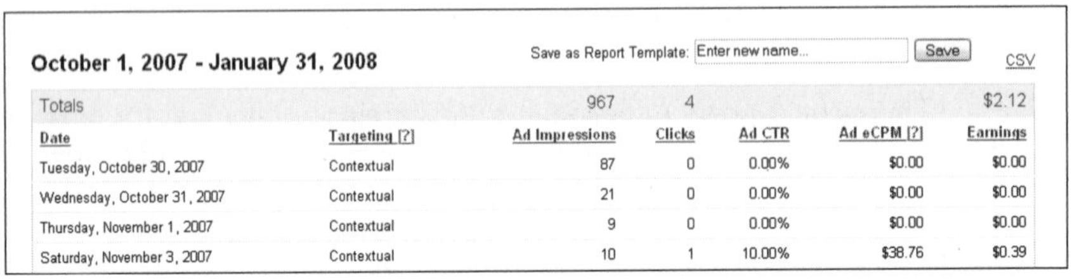

Figure 15-4:
Enter a
name in the
provided
text box to
save the
report as a
template.

October 1, 2007 - January 31, 2008		Save as Report Template: Enter new name...			Save	CSV
Totals		967	4			$2.12
Date	Targeting [?]	Ad Impressions	Clicks	Ad CTR	Ad eCPM [?]	Earnings
Tuesday, October 30, 2007	Contextual	87	0	0.00%	$0.00	$0.00
Wednesday, October 31, 2007	Contextual	21	0	0.00%	$0.00	$0.00
Thursday, November 1, 2007	Contextual	9	0	0.00%	$0.00	$0.00
Saturday, November 3, 2007	Contextual	10	1	10.00%	$38.76	$0.39

That's really all there is to it. After you create an advanced report, it's saved as a template in case you want to run it again in the future. When you're ready to run the same report again, select it from the Advanced Reports section on the Quick Reports screen. You still have to change the date range, but your other selections are automatic.

Working with the Report Manager

Each time you generate a report, it's automatically saved to a little corner of the AdSense world — the Report Manager. To get your hands on reports saved to the Report Manager, click the Reports Manager link on the Reports tab. Reports are collected here so that you can view them online or download them in CSV *(Comma Separated Value)* format, the standard used by most spreadsheet programs. To download the report, just click the CSV link, and use the Save As dialog box that appears to choose the location you want the report saved to and to choose a name for the report. When you've entered this information, click Save.

After you download a report and save the file to your hard drive, you can open it in Microsoft Excel or any other spreadsheet program that opens CSV files — Google Docs & Spreadsheets, for example.

For example, here's how to open the file in Microsoft Excel:

1. **Launch Excel and then choose File⇨Open.**

   The Open dialog box appears.

2. **In the Open dialog box, browse to the file you saved to your hard drive, select the file, and then click Open.**

   Excel's Text Import Wizard appears, as shown in Figure 15-5.

   The file that's provided by AdSense is a *delimited* file — the columns of data are literally separated. On the first screen of the wizard, you don't need to change anything.

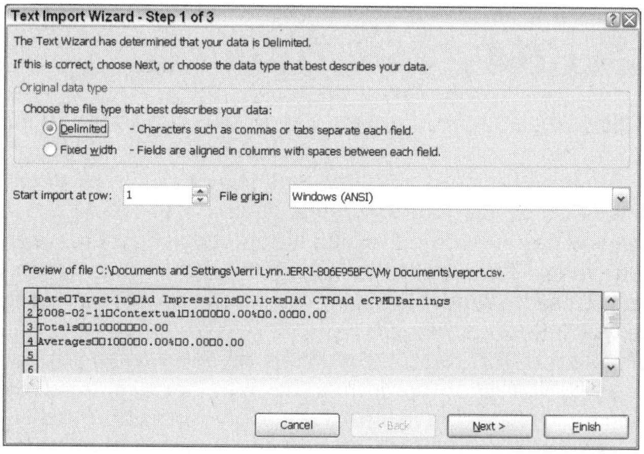

Figure 15-5: The Text Import Wizard walks you through opening the file properly.

3. **Click Next.**

   The second page of the wizard appears.

4. **In Step 2 of the wizard, select the *delimiter* — what separates each column of the spreadsheet you're importing — and then click Next.**

   In this case, the delimiter is a tab (because you usually tab from one column to the next). That's probably already selected in the wizard.

5. **(Optional) In the final page of the wizard, feel free to change the formatting of the columns that you're importing by clicking anywhere in the column and then selecting the proper formatting from the options in the upper-left corner of the wizard.**

   For this file, the formatting for all the columns should be General.

   You can see your formatting without clicking each column by looking at the very first cell at the top of each column. This cell doesn't appear on the spreadsheet, but in this wizard view, it shows you what type of formatting is already in place.

6. **After you check or adjust the formatting, click Finish to complete the importing process.**

   The Excel spreadsheet opens. If you want to keep it in Excel format, you have to resave the file as an Excel workbook.

   If you really don't want an offline copy of the report, you don't have to save the file to your hard drive. Truth is, you can access your reports from the AdSense Web site for quite a while — about a year, in fact. After that period of time, reports get deleted from the site.

Scheduling Automatic Reports

One real timesaving feature of AdSense reports is the ability to schedule said reports to run automatically, rather than having to manually set up the report and run it on the site each time you need it. To take advantage of automatic scheduling of reports, though, you have to create a report template before you can schedule it to run automatically. (If the whole idea of templates sounds a bit fuzzy to you, check out the "Using Report Templates" section, earlier in the chapter.)

After you create a report template, you should see it as an option in your Report Manager. (If it's not there, then the template wasn't successfully created and you need to go through the creation process outlined earlier again.) Follow these steps to schedule the report to run automatically:

1. **Log on to your AdSense account.**

   The Reports page appears.

2. **On the Reports tab, click the Report Manager link.**

3. **On the Reports Manager page, scroll down until you see the Saved Report Templates section.**

   The Saved Report Templates section shows you all the reports that you've saved as templates. Next to each report is a Frequency column, a Send To column, and a Format column, as shown in Figure 15-6. (More about these columns in a bit.)

Figure 15-6:
Use the
tools pro-
vided to
schedule
reports to
run auto-
matically.

Format column

4. **Using the Frequency drop-down menu, select how often you want the report to run.**

   Your choices are Never, Daily, Weekly, and Monthly.

   After you select a frequency, the default e-mail address is displayed for your account in the Send To column. That's where the report will be sent unless you change it.

5. **To change the default e-mail address, select an address from the Send To drop-down menu.**

   If the address you want to send the report to isn't listed in the drop-down menu, do the following:

   a. *Click Edit Addresses.*

      You're prompted to save your changes before you continue.

   b. *Save the changes or click OK.*

      A form opens into which you can type new addresses.

   c. *Add the new e-mail address.*

      You can add multiple addresses, too. Enter the addresses one per line.

   d. *Click Save Addresses.*

      The new e-mail address(es) appear in the Send To drop-down menu.

6. **From the Format drop-down menu, select the format for the report that you want to send.**

   Your choices here are CSV or CSV-Excel. (CSV Excel is just a report format that's specifically set for Microsoft Excel.)

7. **Click Save Changes.**

   You're done!

Your report is set to run automatically, but here's a disappointing fact: You can't automatically send the report to more than one person. You could set up multiple reports that are the same and send each one to a different person, but it's much easier just to forward the report after you get it to those who need to see it. Maybe Google will add a Multiple Addresses feature in the future, but for now, you're stuck with one address per report.

Using Site Diagnostics

In order to track down all the data needed for ad placement — as well as tracking down all the data that goes into the reports I talk about in this chapter — AdSense needs to be able to crawl your Web site. The crawler — not the same crawler that Google uses to include your site in search results, by the way — visits your site once each week to check for content, design, and usage information. I cover how this works in a lot of detail in Chapters 2–4, so if you need a refresher, you can flip there. I'll wait.

Done? Good. The AdSense crawler visits your site once each week. During that visit, the crawler looks at all the pages on your Web site to ensure that your ads are properly targeted. If the crawler encounters a problem, such as a page that's redirecting unexpectedly (and without the proper redirect information in place), or if the crawler is denied access to the site, it flags that issue in the Site Diagnostic area of your AdSense account.

To get to the Site Diagnostic area, do the following:

1. **Sign in to your AdSense account.**

2. **From the Reports tab, choose the Site Diagnostics link.**

   When that page opens, a list of problems that were encountered with your site is displayed.

   If the crawler didn't encounter any problems, the list is mostly blank, displaying only the You Currently Have No Blocked URLs message in light gray.

   If you do have issues — if the crawler can't get to your site for some reason — the reason is displayed in the table provided along with the date of the last crawl attempt on your Web site.

It's possible (though highly unlikely) that when you updated your site, Google was trying to crawl your site at the exact same time. Sometimes, if you're uploading files, the crawler can't access the site at the same time. If that's the case, the date of the last crawl reflects that.

Far more likely, however, is that a flaw in the site design or some other problem is keeping the crawler off your site. If that's the case, the error displayed helps you to figure out what needs to be done to allow the crawler to have access.

In a lot of cases, the problem is simply that you have a `robots.txt` file that denies access to certain portions of your page. (Remember this little bugger? I tell you all about him in Chapter 3.)

Sometimes, you deny a crawler access to a page on your Web site for good reason. For example, if you have several pages that are essentially the same, you might not want a crawler to look at all the pages. The redundancy could cause your search result rankings to drop. Usually, if you've designed your site well and with the Google Webmaster Guidelines in mind, you have no reason to keep the crawler off any pages of your site.

Sometimes, though, the errors that the crawler encounters aren't directly related to that `robots.txt` file. If that's the case, you see the exact error listed on this diagnostics form. You can then repair the error. After you do, however, it might take up to a week for the crawler to hit your site again. You may have to be patient to see the results of your repair.

A good example here is when a crawler can't navigate your site because of broken links. If the crawler can't follow the site navigational links, it will leave your site and come back at another time. If you fix the broken links, the next time the crawler comes through you shouldn't have any problems.

Managing Your Account

No two ways about: Part of your day-to-day site administration involves managing your AdSense account. Now, with any Google application out there, managing the application or program is pretty straightforward. AdSense is no exception.

To manage your account, log in to AdSense and then select the My Account tab. From this tab, you have several options for account maintenance, including: Account Settings, Account Access, Payment History, and Tax Information, as shown in Figure 15-7. I cover each option in greater detail in the next sections.

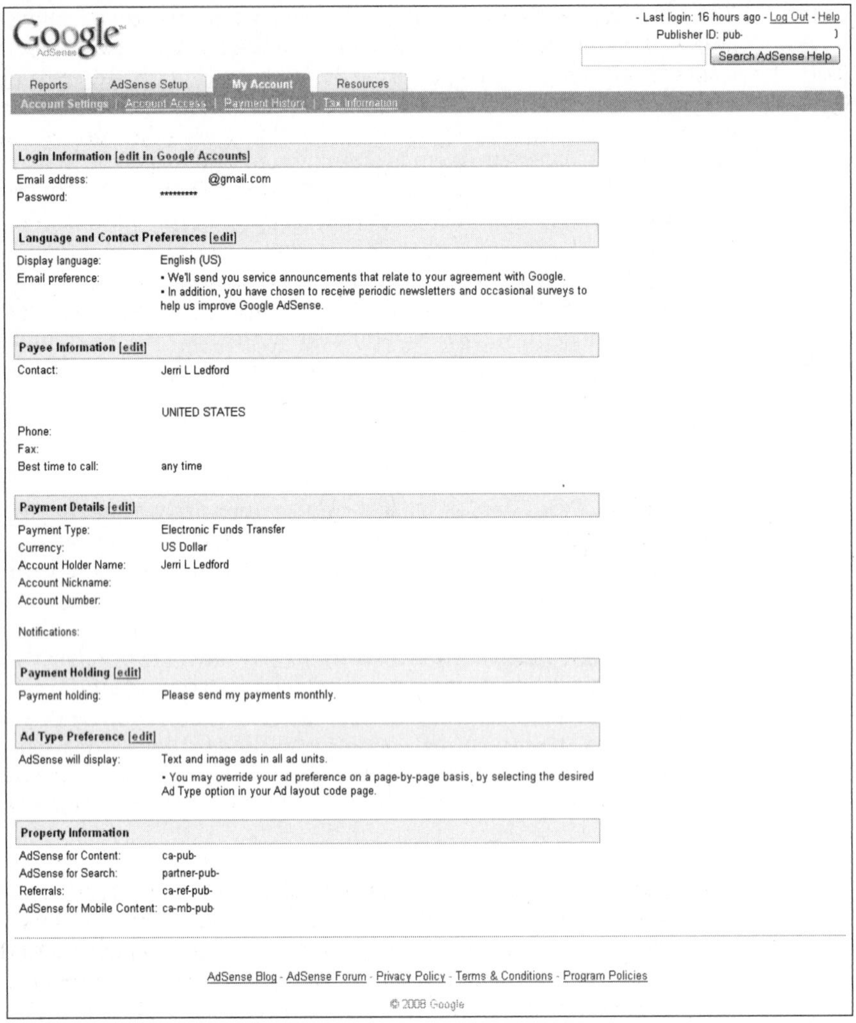

Figure 15-7:
Use the My
Account
tab to man-
age your
account
information.

Your account settings

The Account Settings section of the My Account tab lets you add or change e-mail addresses and passwords, update your address and payment information, and/or change your ad type preference.

To change any of the settings here, click the blue Edit link next to the header for that section. When you click this link, a new page opens from which you can change the information that's pertinent to that segment of the Account Settings section. After you make whatever changes you want to make, click Save to update your account settings.

The Account Settings section has a Property Information area. The numbers shown here are your account IDs for each area of AdSense that you choose to use. For example, if you're using AdSense for Search, AdSense for Content, and AdSense Referrals, you have three different IDs shown. In most cases, you don't need to know these IDs. Google keeps up with them for you and includes them in the code that's generated for the ads you display.

However, if you ever do need to know them (say, if you're having trouble with your AdSense account and you call tech support), this is where they're located. Don't share those ID numbers with anyone, though. They're specific to your account, and if you give them out, someone else could gain access to your account.

Granting and denying access

The Account Access area on the My Account tab is where you can see who else has access to your AdSense account. Unless you specifically grant an organization or another person access to the account, you should have no one else listed here.

If you're using Blogger or some other applications (such as FeedBurner) with AdSense, that organization needs to have access. Keep in mind that the company can't see your earning statements or make changes to your account beyond the changes that you authorize while setting up or changing ads. They're still listed as *hosts* in your Account Access area — someone who is hosting your blog, RSS feed, or other aspect of the Web site on which you have ads displayed.

You can disable any and all hosting applications at any time by clicking the blue Disable Access link to the right of the hosting company's name. After you click that link, however, the account no longer has access to the elements of your account needed to allow you to show ads through that service; so the ads that you have active no longer display, or if they do, they display with errors.

Unless you've changed your mind about having ads on your blog or in your RSS feed, you shouldn't adjust the status of these hosts. Allow them to have the access they need to ensure that your ads continue to display properly.

You can't add multiple users to an AdSense account. You can share your username and password with others but you can't physically add an additional user to your account. If you have an account that you want to share with your spouse or partner (or some other member of your staff), he must use your login.

When you allow someone to use your username and password to access your AdSense account, she has all the same privileges that you do, meaning she can change your account in any way she chooses. She can change ad types and placement, she can change reports, and she can even change your password and lock you out of the account.

Use caution if you plan to share your account with someone. Make sure it's someone you trust. Better yet, don't share. I know, you've been told all your life that sharing is good. In this case though, go ahead and share reports and information gleaned from your AdSense account, but keep actual access to the account to yourself, just to be on the safe side.

Reading your payment history

The Payment History section of the My Account tab is where you can see what your current balance is or what payments have been made to you in the past. AdSense doesn't send out payments until you reach $100, so if you're below that level, the balance carries forward each month until you hit the $100 level. Payments can then be issued through check or direct deposit.

The View drop-down menu in the Payment History section lets you change the months for which you're viewing your payment history. Your options are Last 3 Months, Last 12 Months, or All Time.

You should've set up your payment method on the Account Settings page when you first opened your AdSense account. If you didn't, AdSense can't pay you, but you can't change those details on this page, either. This page is strictly a reporting page. You have to go to your Account Settings page to make changes to your payment method and information.

Next to each month listed on the Payment History page is a blue Details link. Click this link to go to a page that details how your earnings are categorized (AdSense for Content, AdSense for Search, and so on), what the subtotal is, and how much your monthly earnings are. You can also download this information to a CSV file by clicking the Download CSV File link at the top of the Details report (or next to the View drop-down menu on the previous page, as shown in Figure 15-8).

Farther down the Payment History page, you also see a payment schedule. AdSense payments are sent at the end of each month and are sent either by Electronic Funds Transfer (EFT), Express Secured Delivery, or Standard Delivery. The Account Settings area is where you make changes to your payment delivery method and account numbers if you're having payments delivered via EFT.

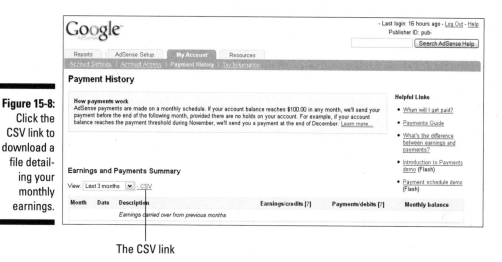

Figure 15-8:
Click the
CSV link to
download a
file detail-
ing your
monthly
earnings.

The CSV link

Giving Uncle Sam his due

I don't know about you, but I hate paying taxes. I could get on a major soap-box about the whole tax system, but this isn't the forum for it. Unfortunately, AdSense income, like every other type of income, is taxable. That means Google has to have tax-withholding information for you, so before you can be paid, you have to fill out an IRS Form W-9.

The first time that you log in to the Tax Information section of the My Account tab, you're prompted to fill out a Form W-9. After you fill it out and submit it, you need to worry about it only if there are major changes in your life (such as a name change caused by getting married or a change in with-holding status).

I'm no accountant, so I can't tell you exactly how you should fill out this form, but I can tell you that any time you need to update it, log in to your account, go to the Tax Information page, click the blue Change Your Tax Information link, and you're taken to the Tax Information Wizard.

The wizard asks questions about your citizenship, your filing status, and your personal information. It's really a simple process and not nearly as confusing as filling out a Form W-9 for your employer.

Walk through the wizard, answer the questions, and then click Finished. Your information is updated automatically, and you'll stay on Uncle Sam's good side, at least where AdSense is concerned. Easy-peasy-lemon-squeezy.

Chapter 16

AdSense Revenues

- -

- -

*A*dSense is all about the money, right? As far as I know, that's the only reason to lease advertising space on your Web site or blog. Because that's the case, it'd be nice if you could get paid.

Assuming you're generating enough income from your AdSense ads, payments should be sent to you on a monthly basis — after you've set up your account to receive payments, that is.

Setting Up AdSense Payments

Setting up your AdSense payments is easier now than it used to be. In the bad old days, you couldn't effectively set up your AdSense payments until you reached $50 or $100 in revenues. Now, you can set up your payment account and payment type almost immediately after you create your AdSense account.

Everything you need to do is found on the My Account tab in your AdSense account. The first thing you need to do is set up your payment account, so follow these steps:

1. **Point your browser to the AdSense Web site at** www.adsense.com.

2. **Sign in to your AdSense account and then click the My Account tab.**

   The tab should open to Account Settings, but if it doesn't, select Account Settings from the links below the tab.

3. **In the third section of the Account Settings page — the Payee Information section — as shown in Figure 16-1, click the Edit link next to the Payee Information title.**

   You're taken to a page where you can change or update account information, such as your name and address. (See Figure 16-2.)

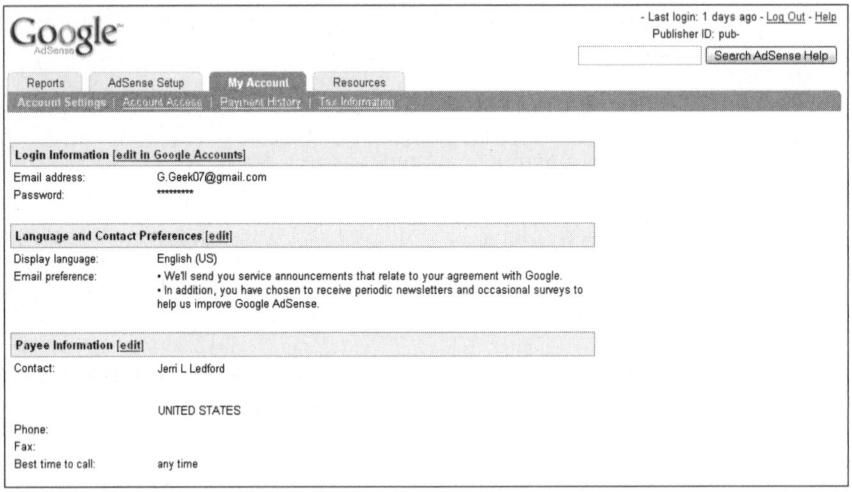

Figure 16-1:
Payment details are set using the Account Settings page.

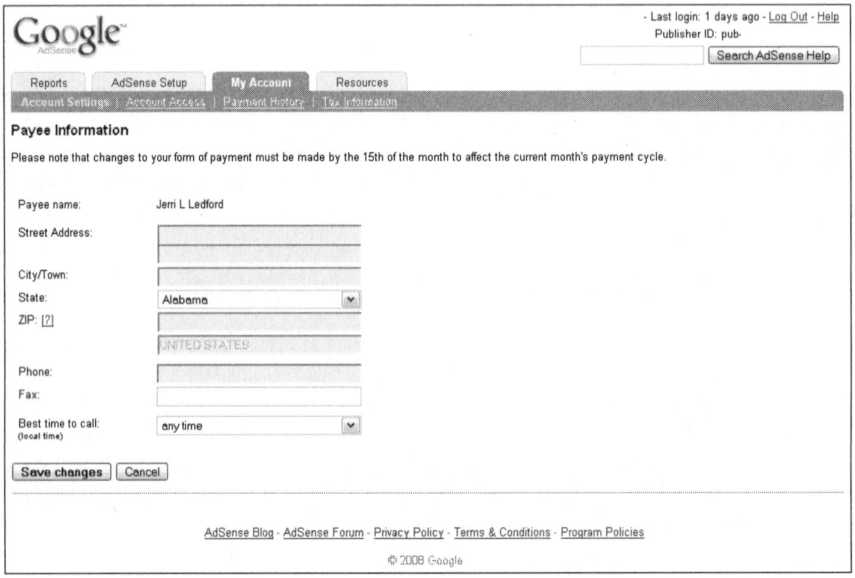

Figure 16-2:
If necessary, edit the address and phone number for your payee information.

4. **Enter your information or make changes to the existing information.**

   You're asked to provide your name, address, phone, and fax information. You can also choose the best time for someone from AdSense to call you. AdSense employees don't usually call, but this information is requested in case a situation develops where the company needs to contact you fast.

5. **When you're finished entering your contact information, click the Save Changes button.**

After you set up your payment account, you still have to verify the account. For that, you need a PIN (personal identification number) from AdSense, which isn't sent out to you until you have at least $10 in AdSense revenue. (AdSense used to send the PIN out when an account reached $50, but the process struck AdSense users as a tad slow — hmm . . . maybe AdSense wanted to keep the money for as long as possible? — so the company reduced the amount to $10.) When you reach the $100 level, use the PIN to authorize a payment to you.

I hear the grumbles already. You have to wait until you make $100 to get paid? Yep. The cost of processing payments is pretty high, and in an effort to make it less costly, AdSense doesn't process smaller payments. Think of it this way: If they were sending out checks to everyone who made under $100 each month, the cost of issuing those checks would explode exponentially. To cover the cost, AdSense would have to cut the percentage that you receive for showing their ads, which means you'd make less money.

 Rather than being aggravated because you aren't getting paid immediately, work to optimize your site and your AdSense income so that you're generating enough revenue to actually get paid as quickly as possible. If you're not sure what you need to do to optimize your Web site to gain the most traffic, flip to Chapter 4. I provide a thorough explanation of optimization there.

Selecting how you get paid

Setting up your account for payment is only half of what needs to be done. You also have to choose *how* you want to get paid. With AdSense, you have three choices:

✔ **Electronic Funds Transfer (EFT):** Your AdSense payments can be directly deposited into your (U.S.) bank account — after you're set up to receive electronic payments, of course.

✔ **Check-Standard Delivery:** Standard delivery checks go out around the 15th of the month and could take two to three weeks to arrive in your mailbox.

✔ **Check-Secured Express Delivery:** Checks sent Secured Express Delivery go out about the 15th of the month, but they're guaranteed to arrive at your doorstep within a week. The rub? It costs you $30 for the privilege.

No matter which form of payment you receive, you still have to make $100 in revenues before the payment's sent to you. If you select EFT, however, you can set that up before you reach the $100 cut-off point.

If you're an International user, you may have two options for payment. AdSense will send checks to all supported countries — if you're not in the U.S. and you can use AdSense, then you're in a supported country — or in some countries you can receive an EFT payment. The countries in which EFT is available are

Australia	Mexico
Austria	The Netherlands
Belgium	New Zealand
Canada	Norway
Czech Republic	Poland
Denmark	Portugal
Finland	Slovakia
France	Spain
Germany	Sweden
Ireland	Switzerland
Israel	Turkey
Italy	United States
Japan	United Kingdom

In all of the countries, payment is available in that country's national currency.

Setting up the EFT account is pretty simple. Follow these steps:

1. **Point your browser to the AdSense Web site at** www.adsense.com.

2. **Log in to your AdSense account and go to the My Account tab.**

   If you're not automatically taken to the Account Settings page, select that link below the My Account tab.

3. **Scroll down to the Payment Details section of the page and click the Edit link.**

4. **In the new page that appears, choose the Add a New Bank radio button and click Continue.**

   You are taken to the Bank Account Information page, as shown in Figure 16-3.

5. **In the Bank Account Information page, enter your bank account information and then click Continue.**

   Your account information is checked automatically to ensure that it's accurate. If everything is correct, you receive a confirmation message.

6. **Wait.**

   You have to wait a few days — four to ten days to be exact — for AdSense to make a small deposit — the amount varies, but it could be anything up to about $1 — into your account.

7. **After you receive your initial deposit, log back in to your account and return to the Payment Details section of the Account Settings page.**

8. **Enter the deposit amount in the Deposit Amount field and then click the Confirm button.**

   That last click does it; you're set up for direct deposits.

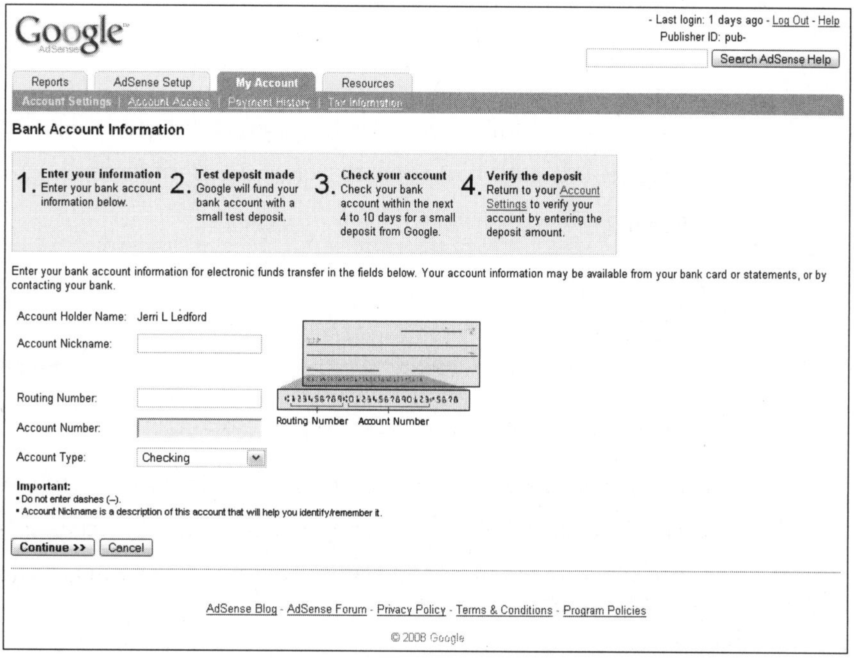

Figure 16-3:
To add a new payment account, supply the requested information on the Bank Account Information page.

If you prefer to have your payments made the old-fashioned way — by check — all you have to do is log on to the Payment Details section of the Account Settings page and select one of the check options. If you happen to live outside the U.S., you don't have any choice but to receive your payment by check.

Hold, please . . .

My life is nuts. I've moved every couple years for most of my life, and even as an adult, I still find myself moving more often than anyone I know. We're not talking little moves, either. If I'm moving, it's across state lines.

Moving across state lines means things have to change — addresses, telephone numbers, and even bank accounts. When it's time for me to make these kinds of moves, I have to put direct payments on hold. My agency is accustomed to it, but sometimes I have to juggle other payments (or bills). AdSense isn't one of those companies that I have to worry about.

AdSense gives you the ability to place your payments on hold indefinitely. "Indefinitely" could mean a lot of different things to you, but during that time you don't have to worry about your payments bouncing around cyberspace while you're getting your banking details under control (or while you're on vacation or whatever).

To put your payments on hold, do the following:

1. **Log in to your Account Settings page.**
2. **Click the Edit link next to the Payment Holding section of the page.**
3. **On the new page that appears, select the Hold Payment check box.**
4. **Click the Save Changes button.**

Now your payments are on hold until you return to the page and deselect the Hold Payment check box.

Your money doesn't disappear into no-man's land, either. While on hold, payments simply accrue. Then, when you reactivate payments, you're paid the full amount during the next regular billing cycle.

The exception to how these holds and payments work (there's always an exception, isn't there?) is around the 15th of the month. If you make changes to your payment status, payment account, or payment type around the 15th of the month, everything gets a little squirrelly.

According to the AdSense Web site, holds placed or released *around* the 15th of the month may or may not process that month. The best thing you can do is try to make adjustments to your payment details around the beginning or end of the month. If you have to make adjustments after about the 10th or before the 20th, watch your account to make sure the changes take effect.

Changing your payment account

Changing your EFT payment account, unlike changing your underwear, isn't something that you'll do every day. However, you will have situations (like getting a new account or getting married) when you'll need to change the account that your deposits are made to. Changing the account is easy:

1. **Log in to your AdSense account and go to the My Account tab to be taken to the Account Settings page.**

2. **Scroll down to Payment Details.**

3. **Click the Edit link, enter the details for your new account, and then click the Save Changes button.**

   You're good to go.

You have to go through the same verification process — waiting for a deposit from AdSense and then entering the deposit amount on the verification page — but then your account will be active, and you can delete the old account. Just like setting up your first account, though, the process can take four to ten days.

To delete an account:

1. **Log in to your AdSense account and click the My Account tab to be taken to the Account Settings page.**

2. **On the Account Setting page, scroll down to Payment Details and click the Edit link.**

   This will take you to the Choose Form of Payment page.

3. **Select the radio button next to the account that you want to delete and click the Continue button.**

   Doing so takes you to the Account Editing page.

4. **On the Account Editing page, click the Delete this account button.**

   You may be prompted to confirm your desire to delete the account. Then the page reloads and you see a confirmation message.

That's all there is to it. Just remember that if you delete an account that you don't really want to delete, you have to go through the confirmation process all over again.

Adding Sites to Your AdSense Account

As uptight as Google can be about the sites that display AdSense ads, you'll find this next little bit hard to believe — I did.

Many people (myself included) have more than one Web site or blog. Because AdSense only allows you to have one account, if you want ads on all your sites, you need to have multiple sites listed on your AdSense account, right? Wrong. You only need to have the one site that you listed when you first created your AdSense account.

Then, all you have to do is create your ads and copy and paste the code onto whatever Web site you choose. Really. Of course, that makes it a little confusing if you want to track your earnings by site, but AdSense even has an answer to that conundrum.

Use channels. (If you read Chapter 15, you might remember the details I gave you about channels.) Well, this is where channels are really the most useful. When you have multiple Web sites that you want to place AdSense ads on — but you want to be able to track them all separately — use different channels for each site.

Creating channels is easy:

1. **Log in to your AdSense account and go to the AdSense Setup tab.**

2. **Select Channels and then select the type of ad that you want to create a channel for (AdSense for Content, Search, Referrals, and so on).**

3. **Click the Add New Custom Channels link, type the desired name for your channel, and click Add Channel.**

See? I told you it's easy.

After you have channels set up and you create an ad, choose the channel that you want to use to track it, and then that linkage is built into the code. When you're ready to track your ads, you can view reports by channel.

Don't feel compelled to add multiple Web sites to your AdSense account to keep your revenues separate. All you have to do is create channels that let you track which site generates which revenue. To make it a little easier, you can also track everything together so you have a consolidated view of how much you're making.

Sharing AdSense Revenues

People who publish AdSense ads on their Web sites are always working to find new ways to increase their earnings from AdSense ads. Usually, that means creating new Web sites and blogs and then populating them with content. That's followed by upkeep on those sites, and over time it becomes a full-time j-o-b.

Not everyone has time to keep up with all that, so some people who publish AdSense ads on their Web sites have come up with an innovative way to show AdSense ads without investing so much time and effort. This innovative way is AdSense Revenue Sharing, and it's just this side of legal, according to the AdSense Program Policy.

AdSense Revenue Sharing is usually accomplished by setting up a forum in which different people from around the world can contribute. _Forums_ are the message board systems you find all over the Web, and they tend to rank pretty well in Google search results because they're usually very narrowly focused, and they change their content often, which is why so many sites now have them.

The forum owners set up the forums so that users who also publish AdSense ads can enter their AdSense account number to show their AdSense ads — based on the number of times that the person wanting to publish their AdSense ads starts and responds to threads within the forum.

For example, if you were to sign up to participate in the forum on Flixya. com — a video-, photo-, and blog-sharing service — you could include your AdSense Publisher ID during the sign-up process. Then, each time you post on the site, AdSense ads could potentially be shown in association with your post. The percentage of times your ads are shown is usually determined by the forum owner and is dependent upon how you post — meaning how relevant your posts are to the topic that you're posting in — how often you post, and what your status is — or how much you contribute to the community.

When your ads are shown on these sites, and other site visitors click through them, you receive either a percentage of the earnings or all the earnings, depending on how the site is set up. Flixya.com actually allows AdSense publishers to keep all their AdSense revenues.

Of course, if you're using this method to show your AdSense ads, you're also showing them against the site owner's ads. The site owner will most certainly run her own ads the majority of the time. If you're looking for a way to boost your income though, this might help — a little.

Your earnings from these types of AdSense Revenue Sharing schemes aren't high. The earnings might be enough to buy you a sandwich from the Dollar Menu now and again, but you certainly won't get rich with ad-sharing programs. For starters, posting often enough to keep your ads in front of visitors is a full-time job. Second, you're not the only person showing ads at any given time, so the competition for visitors' clicks is pretty high.

The thin, red line

Another small problem with the AdSense Revenue Sharing scheme is the whole concept of *you scratch my back, I'll scratch yours* that comes along with it. What I mean is that, in most of these forums, it's implied that if you click my ads, I'll click yours. That's skating very close to the thin ice warnings that Google puts out about enticing others to click your ads.

Google expressly forbids in their program policies asking other people to click your ads or anything on your site that could be construed as trying to coerce others to click your ads. Placing your ads in these forums could be construed as that kind of activity.

Google doesn't have any policy about your ads not appearing on other people's Web sites, though. As long as nothing's implicit on the site that instructs users to click ads, you're safe.

Participating in revenue sharing

You can participate in revenue sharing in two ways. You can sign up with a site that already offers a revenue sharing program and then provide your AdSense Publisher ID and start posting to forums, or you can create your own site and revenue sharing program that other people sign up for.

Option A is a cinch. All you have to do is sign up. Option B, however, is another matter, which is why I spend a bit more time discussing it. Option B requires that you first create the Web site and then add forums to that site. If you're a Web site designer, it might not be as difficult for you as it'd be for me because I'm no Web designer. I can do just enough to get me by.

If you're like me, you're best served by hiring someone to create the forums for your site. In the process of designing them, you need to put into place an AdSense serving application that rotates through the Web sites of people who publish AdSense ads according to how they post on your site.

If you're creating this type of site, I suggest saving your AdSense ads for the main body of your site. Include them in your site content but keep them off the forum, which is where your posters' ads are running.

After you have the forum up and running, get word out. Plenty of other people who publish AdSense ads are all too happy to post in your forum for the chance to have their ads shown. Just make sure you have your program policies, outlining how and when ads are shown, posted clearly for publishers to find. If you're not sure what to include, check out some of the other AdSense Revenue Sharing programs on the Web. A quick Google search turns up hundreds of them.

Just remember that the point of having forums isn't necessarily just to publish your AdSense ads or to allow others to publish theirs. It's to provide a place where your site visitors can go to find the answers they seek on a specific topic. Set up your forums with that goal in mind, and you'll be able to create a whole new way to generate income.

In general, though, what should be included in your program policies are guidelines on how often forum posters need to post, where and how they should post, and how long they must be a member or how many posts they must have before their ads start showing. Spell out these policies very clearly. For example, some forum owners require that forum posters who want to have their AdSense ads shown should have been a member of the forum for three months or have at least 50 high-quality posts — posts that were on-topic and that provided useful information to a majority of the users for that message board — before their ads are shown. These owners also divide (by percentage) how much of a chance posters have of their ads showing if they start a thread, end a thread, or are topic administrators.

In general, the AdSense Revenue Sharing plan could be a good idea for driving traffic to your site, but I don't see it as being a good way to generate a lot of AdSense revenue. I really think it's a waste of time for you to spend that much time either building a forum and drawing publishers to it or participating on message boards where your ads may or may not be shown.

Personally, I spend more of my time generating great content for my own sites, building a community of users who know they can find what they need on my site, and tweaking my AdSense ads on my own site. That's my personal preference, but if you prefer to participate in an AdSense Revenue Sharing program, I wish you luck. I hope that it turns out to be lucrative for you.

Part V
The Part of Tens

The 5th Wave   By Rich Tennant

"We have no problem funding your Web site, Frank. Of all the chicken farmers operating Web sites, yours has the most impressive cluck-through rates."

In this part . . .

This part is everyone's favorite part of a *For Dummies* book. The Part of Tens includes lists that give you short, easy-to-digest bits of information that you can take in quickly when you don't have a lot of time to devote to reading.

This part gives you a list of ten (plus two) tools you can use to improve your AdSense ads and increase your AdSense revenue. To help you avoid making mistakes and to ensure you're generating the most revenue possible, I also added a list of AdSense things you should definitely *not* do. Lastly, I give you a list of suggestions to improve Web site traffic, which translates into dollars in your bank account. Enjoy!

Chapter 17

Ten (Plus Two) Must-Have Tools for AdSense

*E*ven though AdSense can be a pretty complicated application, you can probably find your way through it all on your own, given enough time. Why would you want to though? You have dozens of great tools available to you that can help shortcut the learning process and jumpstart the earning process.

What follows are just a few of the tools that I find useful. Many others exist, so if something here doesn't meet your needs, use your favorite search engine to scour the Web for more. You'll probably have no problem finding what you're looking for.

AdSense Sandbox

```
www.labnol.org/google-adsense-sandbox
```

The AdSense Sandbox is a great preview tool. If you want to see what types of Google AdSense ads will appear on a page — based on the type of content on that page — this tool does a pretty good job of showing you, even if it's not 100 percent accurate.

To get AdSense Sandbox to work for you, go to their Web site and enter the URL of the page you want to see ads for. Alternatively, you could just enter specific keywords that you have in mind.

The result is a list of up to 20 AdSense ads that relate to that URL or keyword.

AdSense Preview Tool

```
www.google.com/adsense/support/bin/answer.
            py?answer=10005&topic=160
```

AdSense Sandbox (see the preceding section) is third-party software, unaffiliated with Google AdSense. The AdSense preview tool, however, is an official Google application that, like AdSense Sandbox, allows you to see what types of ads might appear on new Web pages that you've created. You can then use this information to decide whether you want to add AdSense to that page.

With the AdSense preview tool, you can also check the destination of ads that are on any of your Web pages, view how the formats and colors of ads will appear on your page, and see what ads users in other countries will see.

The preview tool requires that you install a registry file on your computer. To do so, follow these steps:

1. **Go to the Web page listed at the beginning of this section and find the AdSense Preview Tool link.**

2. **Right-click the link and choose Save Target As from the menu that appears.**

3. **Save the registry file to a location where you can find it on your hard drive.**

   I suggest saving it to your My Document file or to your Desktop.

4. **Double-click the file after the download completes.**

   A confirmation window appears.

5. **Select Yes in the confirmation window to update the registry.**

   The registry file is a self-installing file, so you don't have to search for the correct place in the registry to place the file.

6. **After the installation is complete, restart your Internet Explorer window so the installation can take effect.**

That's all there is to installing the preview tool. After the tool's installed, you can use it by right-clicking in any Web page. From the menu that appears, choose Google AdSense Preview Tool to launch the preview tool. When it's launched, you can see the ads in the new window and even click your own ads without fear of inciting Google's ire. As long as you're in the Preview window, clicks don't count.

Note, however, that should you ever decide to uninstall the preview tool, the best way to do it is with the AdSense Preview Tool Uninstaller, available through the AdSense Help Center (www.google.com/adsense/support). Also note that the AdSense preview tool only works with Microsoft Windows Internet Explorer 6.0 and higher.

AdSense Calculator

www.seochat.com/seo-tools/adsense-calculator

If you've ever wondered how statistics, such as daily page impressions, click-through-rates (CTR), or cost-per-clicks (CPC), affect the amount of your AdSense earnings, here's a tool that helps you figure it all out.

To use the AdSense Calculator, enter any or all of the values and then click Calculate. For example, I entered the following values:

Daily page impressions: 1000

Click-through-rate: 1.5%

Cost-per-click: $.06

These are numbers that I mostly pulled from the air for an example. The exception is the 1.5 percent click-through-rate. Experts estimate that 1.5 percent is the average CTR for AdSense ads.

My results are

Daily earnings: $.90

Monthly earnings: $27.00

Yearly earnings: $328.50

Daily clicks: 15

Monthly clicks: 450

Yearly clicks: 5,475

In other words, if I have an average of 1,000 daily impressions and an average cost-per-click of $.06, I would see the results in this list as the average amount of clicks and earnings that I could receive in the given amount of time. Figuring this out isn't an exact science, but it gives you a pretty good idea of what you could earn on your Web site if certain conditions are met.

AdSense Notifier

```
https://addons.mozilla.org/en-US/firefox/addon/500
```

The AdSense Notifier is for those who use the Firefox browser instead of Internet Explorer. The *Notifier* is an add-on that shows your AdSense stats on the status bar of your browser and updates those stats automatically.

To install the Notifier, go to the Web address in the beginning of this section and click Install Now. A software installation dialog box pops up. Allow the dialog box to load completely and then click Install Now. The installation takes a few seconds and then you're prompted to restart your Firefox browser. Select Restart Now, and the browser closes and then re-opens. You're logged in automatically, and your stats display in the bottom-right corner of the browser.

AdSense Heat Maps

```
www.google.com/adsense/support/bin/answer.
            py?answer=17954&topic=8970
```

Heat maps, like the one shown in Figure 17-1, are maps that show the best placement for your ads on a given Web site. The link here leads to Google's suggested best placement. However, it only takes certain factors into consideration. For example, this site has no consideration for scrolling Web pages.

Another resource for heat maps that might be more useful is

```
www.vaughns-1-pagers.com/internet/google-heatmap-2.htm
```

These heat maps show some of the different variations that you might need to take into consideration due to the unique nature of your Web pages — variations like scrolling pages and different navigational structures. Just remember, this isn't an exact science. Test everything before you make any final decisions about what works best on your particular site for your particular audience.

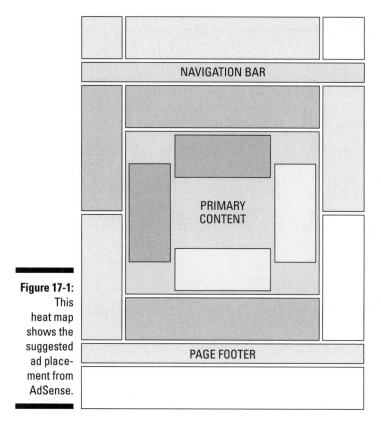

NAVIGATION BAR

PRIMARY
CONTENT

PAGE FOOTER

Figure 17-1:
This
heat map
shows the
suggested
ad place-
ment from
AdSense.

AdSense Accelerator

www.adsenseaccelerator.com

This is the first tool featured here that's not free. At $47 a month, this may be more than you're ready to invest in if you're just getting started in AdSense. However, if you're looking for ways to build a Web site based on high-paying keywords, you may want to make the investment.

The AdSense Accelerator shows the bids for the top-ten placement ads on Google. You can then use this information to ensure that you're targeting the right keywords — which aren't necessarily the top ten. Keep this in mind: Just because a keyword is in the top ten doesn't mean that it's the right key-word for you to target.

Basing your Web pages on the highest-paying keywords is a constant frustration because those keywords change daily. However, you can use the AdSense Accelerator to figure out which keywords consistently pay out at higher rates.

No contract's involved, so I suggest trying it out for at least a month to discover more about what you could do to improve keyword targeting for the ads that you want to display on your Web pages.

AdWords Traffic Estimator and Bid Tool

`https://adwords.google.com/select/trafficEstimatorSandbox`

Remember AdWords? That's the advertising side of AdSense. AdWords is the program that advertisers use to place the ads that you show on your Web site using the AdSense program. The AdWords Traffic Estimator and Bid Tool is actually an AdWords tool, but because AdSense *is* the other side of AdWords, you may find it useful to help determine which high-paying keywords you should be targeting with your Web site.

It works simply enough. Enter a few bits of information into the form provided — information like keywords, bid amount, and targeting location — and then the program generates a report that shows you how much traffic can be expected for an ad based around the keywords you provided. Here's how to use it:

1. **Log in to the Web site listed at the beginning of this section.**

2. **Enter a list of keywords that you want to target in the text box provided, as shown in Figure 17-2.**

3. **Enter a maximum cost-per-click in the Choose a Currency section.**

   You may have to use your imagination here, but don't choose a cost-per-click that's too low or too high. Instead, think in terms of an average cost. There are no averages for what users can expect to pay for the use of a keyword, but my suggestion is to use a figure that's no less than $1 per click and no more than $10 per click. You want to keep your options as wide open as possible, but you can also experiment with the numbers to see what you find.

4. **(Optional) Enter a daily budget.**

   I don't usually bother with this. I leave this blank so that I'm not limited by the hypothetical budget because a daily budget is really only relevant if you're planning to use the AdWords service where you pay to have your ads placed on Web sites.

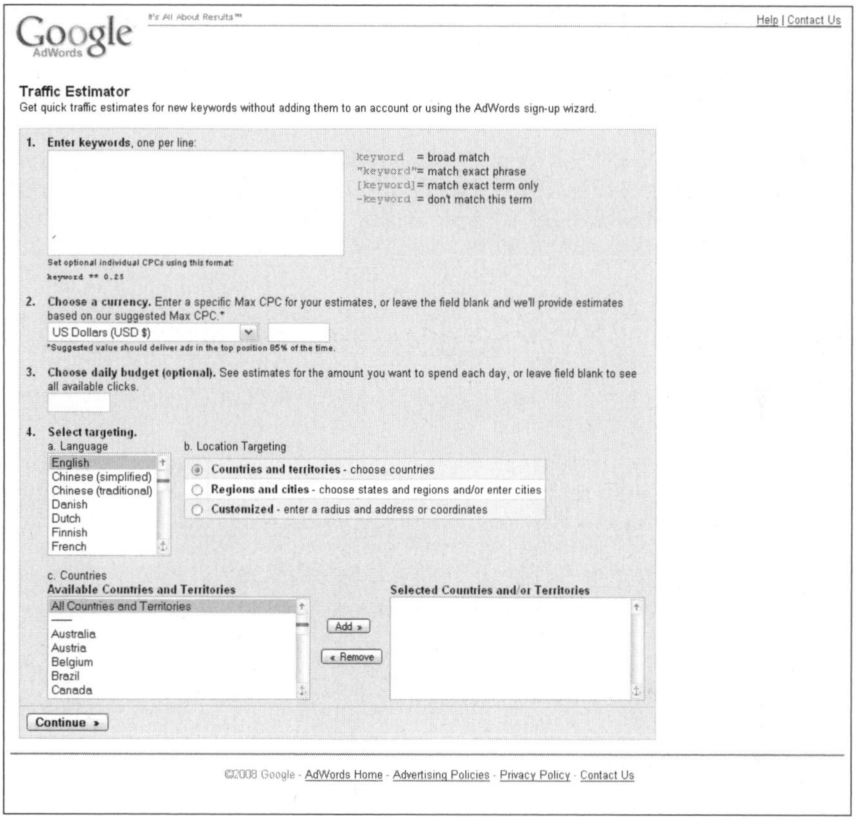

Figure 17-2:
Use the
AdWords
Traffic
Estimator
and Bid Tool
to discover
the poten-
tial of the
keywords
you're
targeting.

5. **Select your regional targeting — language, location, and countries — and then click Continue.**

   A new page appears, displaying stats for the keywords that you selected. You'll see Average CPC, Estimated Clicks Per Day, and Estimated Cost Per Day.

Use the statistics that are returned to get a feel for which keywords you have under consideration that will pay the highest in terms of CPC and cost-per-impression. Again, it's not an exact science, but getting a feel for what advertisers are paying helps you better understand what you can expect (very roughly) as far as earnings are concerned.

Keyword Tools

```
https://adwords.google.com/select/KeywordToolExternal
```

The AdWords Keyword Tool is designed to help you generate new keywords, based on the words or phrases that you enter into the keyword generator. This is another of those tools that, although it was built specifically with AdWords in mind, might also prove useful for AdSense types as well.

One particularly useful feature of the Keyword Tool is that it lets you enter the URL of a specific Web site to see what keywords are generated, according to the content of the site. With it, you can enter the URL of the page you're optimizing for AdSense ads to see what keywords are being recognized on that page.

The Keyword Tool is a great way to make sure that your page is being recognized for the keyword ads you're targeting. As an added bonus, it has a neat little progress meter at the bottom that processes while it's examining the page that you entered. I know . . . small things for small minds, which mine definitely is at times!

The results that are returned when the page is finished processing are pretty comprehensive. You'll probably see the keywords you're targeting as well as some that you hadn't thought of. All in all, a very useful tool.

Keyword-Ranking Tools

```
http://freekeywords.wordtracker.com
```

If you're looking for something to complement the Google AdWords Keyword Tool, try the keyword-ranking tool from WordTracker. This keyword-ranking tool works much like the Google tool with a few minor differences.

The most noticeable difference between the WordTracker version and the AdWords Keyword Tool are that WordTracker only lets you generate keywords by plugging in a word or phrase — it doesn't allow you to generate keywords based on a Web site URL, in other words. WordTracker does, however, show you the estimated daily search volume for the keywords shown.

Oh, WordTracker also doesn't offer a cool progress meter. WordTracker makes up for this, though, by knowing how many times each day a certain keyword is searched for because the number of daily searches is a clear indicator of what's popular. If your site's based on a set of keywords that ranks low in the results, a simple change of keywords might bring more success for your AdSense ads.

Sitemaps

```
https://www.google.com/webmasters/tools/docs/en/
              sitemapgenerator.html
```

The Google *sitemap generator* is an application that examines your Web site and creates a sitemap based on the structure of the site. "But why do I need a sitemap?" you ask.

Simple. A sitemap is the easiest way to get Google to crawl all the nooks and crannies of your site. The problem is that the sitemap generator is a little difficult to use.

First, you have to download the sitemap generator from the Web site listed at the top of this section, and then you have to create a configuration file for the sitemap. After that, you need to upload specific files to your Web site, run the sitemap generator program, add the sitemap to your Google Webmaster account, and set the process up to be repeated.

Those steps are a tough process to get through. If you're really relying on Google when it comes to your search engine ranking, though, this sitemap generator is worth the time and effort.

If you're okay with using a different sitemap generator, however, you might find the XML Sitemap Generator (`www.xml-sitemaps.com`) a little easier to use.

All you have to do with the XML Sitemap Generator is enter the URL, wait for the program to process, and then download the resulting file to your computer. After that's done, log in to your Google Webmaster account, add the sitemap URL, and you're good to go.

The sitemap is a tool — not a requirement. If you have a large site, you may find that your AdSense results for deep pages are much better if you have a sitemap in place to lead search engines to the pages.

AdSense Blog

```
http://adsense.blogspot.com
```

If you want to stay on top of what's happening with AdSense, the AdSense blog is the place to do it. This blog is updated a couple times a week (sometimes more) with tips about using AdSense smarter or with news about AdSense that might affect you.

Several people from the AdSense team work on the blog, so the voices are as varied as the information that you get.

Add it to your RSS — this usually requires adding the blog URL to your RSS reader, but the steps vary depending on the reader that you're using — because it's always nice to know what's going on in AdSense Land.

AdSense Help Group

```
http://groups.google.com/group/adsense-help
```

The AdSense Help files add up to a pretty comprehensive document. Like other aspects of Google Help, the Help files can be a little circular at times, and it's certain that it won't answer all your questions. When you need an answer that you can't find, the AdSense Help Group — through Google Groups — is a useful list to be involved in.

Post your questions to the list, and other listers — or sometimes the moderators themselves — provide answers if they're out there to be had. Don't be discouraged if it takes a little time to get an answer, though. Everyone on the list seems a little busy, so answers can occasionally take days or even weeks to come by. Most of the time, though, you'll have your answer in a much shorter time.

Chapter 18

Ten AdSense Don'ts

The list of activities that you can use to improve your AdSense revenues is long and involved, but so is the list of strategies that you should avoid. In that list, however, some stand out far more than others.

What follows is a list of the top-ten practices that you should avoid when creating your Web site and implementing your AdSense ads. Somewhere along the line someone likely told you that you should try one of the practices listed here.

Don't do it. The results might be nice for a while. You could temporarily bump up your AdSense revenues. However, over time, the risks become much higher, and ultimately, you'll probably end up getting caught by Google, which results in losing the privilege to show AdSense ads — and the right to earn AdSense revenues.

Ultimately, it's just not worth the risk.

Don't Build Your Web Site for AdSense

If I've said it once, I've said it a dozen times in this book: Don't build your Web site for AdSense. AdSense is about getting advertisements in front of *users*. Google has to get those ads out there because the advertisers that are using AdWords — the advertising arm of Google, where advertisers can place their ads to be shown on Web sites like yours — are paying the company to do so. If you build your Web site exclusively for AdSense, the only thing that sees the ads is the crawler that periodically takes stock of your pages.

Build your site for actual, real, live visitors instead. You know, those people sitting on the other side of the computer screen? They play with the keyboard and mouse, and they're looking for something that they hope to find on your Web site. They're *visitors,* and they're your site's target. The more specific the type of visitor, the better.

When you build your site for visitors, you have to put serious thought into how the visitor will use the site. Think about what draws him to your site first. If he's searching for information or products, what keywords will he use to search? If he's randomly typing in a Web address, what address will he use? (Don't laugh. It happens. I usually try the direct URL method of searching before I go to a search engine.)

After you get the user to your site, the next consideration is what he'll do while he's there. This is where your AdSense considerations come into play, because when the user's on the site, you want AdSense to be a natural part of the site for him. Only when you build a site this way — for the visitor first and foremost — will you find that you have success with AdSense.

When you build the site exclusively for AdSense, you're also in the position of being banned from the AdSense program. Google wants visitors to click ads. Your job, as someone who publishes AdSense ads, is to ensure that AdSense ads are displayed to as many potential clicks — that would be *visitors* — as possible. That means putting visitors first, always.

Don't Cut Corners

This rule is sort of a fall-back to *don't build your site for AdSense.* When you cut corners on your site, you take out all the elements that make people want to visit the site. For example, cutting a corner would be using the same tired articles that many other Web site owners are also using. Don't do it. Users quickly figure out that your site doesn't contain quality content, and they'll move on to the next site.

Instead, take your time to create the best possible Web site to meet the need your site was designed to meet. If you're peddling information about kangaroo farms, be the most comprehensive site on the Web about the topic. If you're selling pogo sticks, not only should you include a variety of different models, but you should also include information that's of value to your customers, including how to care for the pogo stick, what types of tournaments there might be, what associations there are, and what kind of creative activities involve pogo sticks.

Give your visitors everything they're looking for. This creates return visitors and great word-of-mouth traffic (or *buzz*), which work together to increase the amount of exposure for your AdSense ads. The more times people look at those ads, the more likely they are to click them and increase your revenue stream.

Don't Hide Your Ads

I know it sounds crazy, but some people do hide their ads. What they do is hide the text of the ad, leaving only the URL visible in an attempt to make visitors think that the URL is part of a list of links or a *blog roll* — the list of links to other blogs that you (as a blog owner) recommend. Do I need to tell you that Google frowns on this practice?

You might think hiding the nature of your links sounds like a great idea, especially in the context of blending your ads into your Web pages as much as possible, but it's not. Don't be fooled if someone tells you she's done this and it worked well for her.

If you try it and Google catches any indications that you're doing something deceptive like this, you'll be banned from the AdSense program. What's more, you could also be excluded from search results generated by the Google search engine.

If you intend to show AdSense ads on your Web site, let them be seen. You can blend them with the other text on the page or even make the backgrounds the same color as your page background. Don't hide the text leaving only the link visible. It might garner you a few clicks in the beginning, but the end results could be disastrous.

Don't Click Your Own Ads

Of all the no-nos you hear about AdSense, this is the most important one. *Don't click your own ads.* Clicking your own ads might seem like just the thing to do. After all, you don't want ads on your site that you don't know where they lead, and it wouldn't hurt to bump your income just a touch.

Hold it just a minute! That's completely the wrong way to think about it. If everyone could just click their own ads and run up their profits, life would indeed be grand, but clicking your own ads is a form of click fraud. *Click fraud* is when you fraudulently drive up the number of ad clicks from people (yourself included) who aren't actually interested in whatever the ad promises.

See, AdSense only works if AdWords works, and AdWords only works if people are truly interested in the ads that AdWords users create. AdWords users place their ads for people to see, and Web site owners who use AdSense then publish the ads for their Web site visitors to view and (hopefully) click. If no one clicks the ads, AdWords users aren't charged a fee for placing the ad and AdSense users aren't paid for placing the ads. If someone *does* click through the ads but never makes a purchase or completes a transaction with the advertiser, advertisers will quit using AdWords and people like you who want to make money from showing ads will have no ads to display. Make sense?

When you click your own ads, you're not usually interested in the content of the ad. That said, I admit that I've clicked one of my own ads because I truly was interested in what it was advertising. Of course, I realized my mistake almost instantly, and I never clicked one again. If I see an ad I'm interested in, I go directly to the URL that's provided.

I understand that you probably want to know where your ads lead. I don't blame you, and neither does Google. That's why there are tools, such as the AdSense preview tool — the AdSense extension for Firefox that lets you preview how ads appear on your page and where those ads lead to. (For more on the AdSense preview tool, see Chapter 17.)

The AdSense preview tool is a free tool, and when you use it as directed, you can click the ads on your own pages without fear of repercussions. What repercussions you might ask? Getting banned from AdSense, of course!

Don't Change the AdSense Code

This one is right up there with the AdSense Don't in the preceding section. Don't change the AdSense code. Google takes creating AdSense code very seriously. Although a program generates the code for your Web site, that program is constantly tweaked and improved (just like everything Google).

The code AdSense generates for you is exactly what Google needs to provide the ads that will appear on your Web page as well as to track the results to those ads, which are important factors.

Keep in mind that AdSense works only because AdWords works (or it could be that AdWords works because AdSense works; which came first, the chicken or the egg?). The only way to prove that either one of them works is in the tracking that Google does. For that tracking to be accurate, the code provided to make ads appear on your Web site must remain intact, as written.

The only exceptions to this are changing style elements of the code, such as colors, and that should be done only with the AdSense code generator. If you create an ad and then re-design your site to have different colors, you can always go back to AdSense and edit the ad that you've created. If you're thinking of messing with anything that's not style related, however, don't — it's just not worth the grief that you get.

What is that grief? Say it with me: Getting banned from the AdSense program.

Don't Use Clickbots

Remember click fraud from a few paragraphs ago? Clickbots are another way to commit click fraud. A *clickbot* is a script or program that's designed to click the ads on your page, and they're readily available on the Web, usually inexpensively.

Just because clickbots are there doesn't mean you should use them, though. Clickbots do the same thing that you'd do if you were clicking your own ads, except on a much larger scale. They inflate the revenue that's generated without increasing the interest in the product or service that's being advertised.

Now, a common misconception is that people only use clickbots to click their own ads — not true. Some people have been caught using clickbots to click *other people's ads,* too. These people are usually AdWords advertisers who are trying to push their competition out of the way.

See, each time someone clicks an ad, it costs the advertiser a set amount of money. A clickbot can click an ad dozens, hundreds, or even thousands of times, driving up the cost of the ad. This can affect how many times an ad is shown in a given period of time, and it can also cost an advertiser a large amount of money. After the budget limit is reached, that advertiser is out of the way until the next billing cycle, allowing the next highest bidders to have their ads shown more often.

Clickbots form a vicious cycle that can be very costly for the person or company that falls victim to this type of click fraud. If you're the one committing it, both AdSense and AdWords will ban you from their programs.

Don't Get Banned for Taboo Content

Taboo content — content that Google's deemed inappropriate for all audiences — is another way to end up on the bad side of AdSense. Examples include content that refers to

- Certain weapons, including guns
- Illegal drugs
- Alcohol
- Tobacco
- Pornography
- Designer knock-offs

If your Web site contains these types of content, AdSense doesn't want ads displayed on it for one simple reason — image. Google, AdWords, AdSense, and all the other arms of Google have an image to uphold. Placing ads for goods or services on inappropriate sites isn't the way to do that.

Google has to screen some of the Web sites on which AdSense ads will appear. If you have a site that's likely to be offensive to a large number of people because it contains any of the content listed earlier, AdSense denies your request to put ads there.

Some folks think it's smart to put the ads on their site and then later change the site and add disagreeable content to it — bad move. If you're using AdSense and the crawler finds this type of content on your site, you're asked to remove the content, and if you don't, you can be banned from the program.

If your site contains any of the topics listed in this section, you might want to look to other affiliate and advertising programs for ways to generate a revenue stream.

Don't Hold Clicking Contests

Here's another facet of click fraud. *Clicking contests* are conducted when someone who publishes AdSense ads creates a contest for which site visitors must click an ad to qualify. The contest is usually monitored with a secondary script that the Web site owner creates.

This artificially inflates the number of clicks that you receive on your AdSense ads, driving up the revenues that your site generates. This is bad for two reasons.

First, you're creating an artificial bump in revenues. That means to maintain that level of revenue, you have to come up with increasingly creative ways to get people to click your AdSense ads until you've reached the point of outright fraud. Never good.

Second, artificially inflating the number of times that someone clicks one of your ads causes the system to be skewed on the Google side, too. The advertisers have to pay more for advertising. Even more troublesome though is that your site could be taken as a site that generates a lot of traffic and so might benefit from a cost-per-impression ad.

Great news for you *if you have a ton of traffic,* but if you don't, you could end up on the losing end of that proposition. Being limited to cost-per-impression ads also means that the advertisers that are specifically targeting your site lose out. In turn, Google loses out on potential revenues.

Now, you may not give a flying flip about the other people and companies in the mix, but you should care that if you get caught using this kind of tactic to increase your AdSense revenues, you'll lose your AdSense privileges.

Don't Pay Others to Click Your Ads

Here's another one that falls into the same category as not using clickbots or holding clicking contests. Don't pay other people to click your ads.

These kinds of programs are sometimes billed as affiliate programs. People who put them together offer a portion of their revenues to a person or group of people who in turn click their AdSense ads. That's all great, and it might even work for a little while, but eventually someone will squeal or Google will catch on.

The penalties for falsely inflating your AdSense revenues can be stiff. You can (of course) possibly lose your AdSense privileges, but there's a darker side to click fraud if you get caught with your hand deep enough in the cookie jar. Google has been known to prosecute people who commit click fraud, especially in cases that are considered extreme.

The best strategy for increasing your AdSense revenue and maintaining that revenue long-term is to do it by-the-book. Use the strategies I talk about in this book — all the chapters include some kind of strategy that should help you increase your revenues — and avoid anything that can get you into hot water with Google. Because you've gone about building your AdSense business the right way, you'll continue to see returns on your AdSense efforts for a long time to come.

Don't Use Any Other Underhanded Methods

Click fraud is just one of the underhanded methods that some people use to increase their AdSense revenues. Whether you're using click fraud or some other deceptive practice doesn't matter though. If you're trying to get the upper-hand on Google, you'll probably fail.

That doesn't keep some people from recommending the wrong methods of increasing Web site traffic and therefore increasing AdSense revenues. What do these people care if you're kicked out of the AdSense program? You getting kicked out doesn't affect them at all.

It's much smarter to avoid *anything* that seems less than honest. I talk about some of the methods that you might see recommended — but that you should never try — in the list here:

- **Cloaking:** By putting one set of content in front of a search engine crawler and then presenting users with another set of content, cloaking deceives potential site visitors into believing they're entering one type of site when in fact they're entering another.

  Cloaking can apply to AdSense, too. If you're using cloaking techniques, you could be baiting AdSense ads for extremely high-paying keywords, but the content on your site doesn't relate to those keywords at all. Site visitors click into your site, but because they don't find what they're looking for, they often click the ads that are displayed instead.

  Cloaking is a bad practice that Google figures out very quickly. When they do, you pay the price for your deception — as in, kiss your membership in the AdSense program goodbye.

- **Duplicate content:** No one wants to see the same boring stuff all over again — just like no one wants to watch reruns on TV — which is why I'm always recommending that you use as much unique, fresh content as you can generate, rather than loading up your site with content found elsewhere.

  What makes duplicate content so troublesome for AdSense is that if dozens of sites all carry the same content, a limited number of relevant ads can be shown on those sites. Duplicate content can also indicate that a Web site isn't regularly updated, meaning that it won't have as much traffic as a site that maintains dynamic content.

  Google wants AdSense (and AdWords) to be successful. So, naturally, the more diverse the sites are within a topic, the more ads that can be shown. Although duplicate content probably won't get you banned from AdSense, it certainly reduces the effectiveness of your site and value of the ads that are shown on the site. You know what that means: less revenue.

- **Hidden text:** This is yet another "helpful hint" you may have suggested to you in the context of improving the AdSense ads that appear on your site. Hidden text involves text that, while present on your site, is colored the same as the background so that it blends into the site and isn't *seen* by site visitors — only Web crawlers can read the text.

  Most of the time, hidden text is used to target a specific keyword that's unrelated to the actual content of the site. People use this tactic to draw ads for higher-paying keywords because these ads are likely to pay better than the ads that appear based on the actual content that the visitor sees.

The problem here is that the ads that can be influenced by hidden text aren't likely to be as relevant to your site visitors, which means that they're likely to get clicked less. That means a reduction in your revenue volume, even if the payment-per-click is higher. In the end, hidden text doesn't work because it's usually more effective to have more clicks at a slightly lower payout than it is to have fewer clicks at a higher payout.

Having relevant ads also means that your site will be more useful to your visitors, making it more likely that they'll come back in the future and click your ads again.

✔ **Spreading malware:** Malware involves applications that are created specifically for some malicious intent. These days, most malware is created to help the process of identity theft. It's not at all uncommon for criminals to pay Web site owners to spread malware, even though it's not exactly a nice thing to do. If you're distributing that malware on your Web site, Google wants no part of your activities.

Besides, spreading malware is illegal, and the pay-off could be jail time. Is it really worth the risk?

✔ **Using false tactics:** Any kind of false tactics that you might employ to trick users into clicking your AdSense ads is forbidden. I know, when you're looking at click revenues of pennies a day, a lot of different strategies look appealing — especially if they increase the amount of money that you're making.

Just remember, it's only more profitable if it helps you to build a long-term AdSense revenue stream. If not, and if it seems even the slightest bit out of line, don't do it. Any risk to your good standing with AdSense means that you could lose whatever revenue stream you've legitimately created.

Chapter 19

Ten Ways to Improve Web Site Traffic

*I*mproving your Web site traffic is a tricky business. You can take advantage of quite a few different strategies — many won't cost you much whereas some won't even cost you a dime. The trick is to find the right balance of strategies and then be consistent in your efforts to draw people to your Web site.

Consistency is also a very important factor in improving the traffic to your Web site. Every day you should be plugging away at your marketing efforts, in whatever form works best for your site. Web site marketing does require constant attention, however. Pushing for a short period of time to improve your traffic but then letting the efforts fall by the wayside does no good. Doing so might get you a temporary increase in traffic, but as soon as you stop your efforts to bring people to your site, you'll see your traffic statistics begin to fall again.

What follows are some of the strategies that you can use to improve your Web site traffic. No single strategy works by itself, but a combination of those shown here — and others that you figure out on your own along the way — gets you moving in the right direction.

Great, Dynamic Content

Everyone seems to be seeking the key to more Web site content. In today's information-driven society, great, dynamic content is the key. People are usually online because they're looking for something — relationships, information, products, or services. Content is the way they find what they're looking for.

Think about it. A decade or so ago, if you wanted to find information on anything, you had to go to the library or the bookstore to find that information. Today, finding what you seek is as close as your computer. Just open a Web browser, type a few words, and what you're looking for is sitting right in front of you. Very little information can't be found online these days.

Here's what makes one site better than another though. When I'm looking for information online, I click into and out of a site in the time it takes most people to take a sip of coffee. That's because I know exactly what I'm looking for, and when I don't see it, I move on to the next search result.

When I do find what I'm looking for, though, I tend to stick around. I'll read the article that brought me to the site and then I'll click through all the articles that are linked to it, and I might even click some of the ads shown on the page if they seem interesting. When I'm done, I bookmark the page to come back later and see what's new.

That is what good content does for a Web site — it buys you time with your site visitors and it buys you return visits. If you don't have content with that kind of stickiness, the first thing you can do to improve your Web site is to create that content. Just remember, don't try buying it from a content *broker* — someone who commissions content from writers and then resells it to Web site or publication owners — if you really want something fresh and new because everyone else in your area is using the same content broker.

Referral Programs

Referral programs have a couple different sides. One side of a referral program is the side on which you make money. That's for putting referral buttons on your Web site.

What if you flip that around and create your own referral program where you pay visitors to share your site with others? You can do that — and should — if you really want to build a sizable flow of traffic to your site.

Creating a referral program isn't too difficult. The first thing you need to do is determine what you can afford to invest in the program. Typically, those who refer your site are paid anywhere from about a penny-a-click to as much as $5 per click or more. Some referral programs promise a flat fee for any referral that results in a purchase.

Your budget is the determining factor here, but remember this: The more you pay, the more likely others will want to refer your site to their site visitors. They're sending traffic away from their site to yours, so you must make it worth the referrers' efforts.

Remember that for a referral program to be effective, it should also be simple. If you're telling people you'll only pay them a referral fee if they send someone to your site who then makes two purchases over a 60-day period, unless your site is truly amazing or the products that you offer are completely unique, not too many people will refer their visitors to you. It's just too hard for them to earn a reward for that referral.

A referral program also has to make it easy for referrers to be connected to the people that they refer. A simple form that includes a Referred By box is okay, but it's only as effective as the memory of the person filling out the form. A link that connects referrers to your referral program so that you can track who they refer is much more effective for the people who are spreading your name around.

Setting up an easy-to-use referral program might be more difficult on your end, but it's worth the investment. The less work that someone has to do to refer people to you and collect a reward for that referral, the more likely he'll use your referral program.

Amazon.com has a referral program that's an excellent example of what really works. They provide all the tools that users need to refer others to Amazon products. All the user has to do is plug a piece of code into her blog or Web site. Amazon and the visitors clicking through the referrals do the rest of the work.

Now, I know you don't have the budget that Amazon has, but you should be able to get the technology you need without having to break the bank. A quick search on Google turns up referral marketing systems that are fairly cost effective. For example, ReferralBlast (`www.referralblast.com`) is an easy to use program that offers four different levels of referral programs — from a basic program to a highly customized program — that range from $99 per year to $999 per year. Another program that's available, and that is fairly easy to use, is ReferralSoftware.com (`www.referralsoftware.com`). This software — unlike ReferralBlast — allows you to set up referral programs for a one-time fee of $299, after which you never pay another fee.

Links and Linking Strategies

You wouldn't think that the links on your site would make too much difference to the traffic on your site, but they do. The Web is an interconnected group of pages. The connection from one page to another comes in the form of a link. So, both on your site and from others' sites, links are an essential part of drawing people in.

One of the easiest ways to begin building a linking strategy is to contact the owners of Web sites that you like and ask them for a reciprocal link. *Reciprocal links* are when you put a link to that site on your page in exchange for a link back to your Web site. Reciprocal linking strategies are very common on the Web.

Another way to get people to link to you is to offer something completely unique on your Web site. For some, that means adding a special download to the site that's not available anywhere; for others, it means adding videos, podcasts, or some other element that's completely unique. Whatever your draw is, keep it unique and fresh. A podcast or video can be effective for a few days, but after a while, it loses its effectiveness and needs to be replaced with something new.

When you have an intricate linking strategy in place (one that leads to other sites of interest and back to you from other sites), you start seeing the results of the strategy — more traffic. The linking strategy takes a little time to create, but it's well worth the effort.

Advertisements

If you haven't already done it, check out AdWords. AdWords is the advertiser's arm of AdSense. With AdWords, you can bid to show your advertisements based on keywords that you select. **Remember:** Although AdWords is an advertising program, it's not good just for products. You can use AdWords with your services or even content Web sites, too. The point of using AdWords is to advertise your site to users who might not otherwise find you. What you sell or provide on that site is up to you.

The cool thing about AdWords is that you can set a budget that keeps you from spending way more than you have available to spend on advertising your site.

Of course, AdWords isn't the only game in the advertising world. You can also consider banner ads or even other pay-per-click advertising options. What's important is that you get your Web site in front of as many people as possible.

Advertising probably isn't the most effective method of getting your name out there — positive word of mouth and great content are your best shot — but if you have some cash to spend on getting your name known, it's definitely a strategy that you should consider.

Blog Promotions

If you have a blog, you simply have to have a blog promotion (or 12). Really. Blogs are cool, but if you're not out there promoting your blog every single day, your numbers will suck pond scum. One of the most effective types of blog promotion is simply to read and post on other people's blogs. When you post on other people's blogs, their readers see your post. They can click through any links that you have connected to your display name or within your comments to see your blog — in fact, you have the opportunity to include your blog URL when you post on most blogs, and you should always include it. Including your blog address gives you free exposure, just for sharing your opinion.

Blogs have become so popular that even corporations now use them to advertise products, services, and events or just to keep readers updated on what's happening with the company. The downside though is that blogs have become so popular that every person who even thinks they might possibly have something of interest to say has a blog.

Making your blog stand out from the rest of the pack is a very difficult process. Start with a truly interesting blog — will it captivate every person on the Web? No. If you can make your blog fresh though, you can potentially gain a huge mindshare in the area in which you specialize.

After you come up with that perfect blog, you have to get the word out. Start by posting comments on other blogs, but don't stop there. Spread the word through your friends and ask them to spread the word, too. Join mailing lists and make sure your blog address appears in the signature line for every post that you make to the list (and you *do* have to post to the list — preferably interesting, useful posts).

Consider other promotions, such as *blog tours* (where a blog author appears on several different blogs as a guest blogger), giveaways, and other contests.

Be creative, but also think in terms of what appeals to potential blog readers. If your blog is about a group of teens that are band groupies, a contest where the giveaway is a copy of *War and Peace* might not be the best idea. If the prize in your contest is a $25 iTunes card, the response could be much more than you even dare to hope for.

As with all types of promotions, think outside the box. Better yet, think of a way to create a whole new box.

Publicity and Public Relations

All too often, publicity and public relations are all lumped into the same category of advertising. From where I sit, publicity and public relations are two different things. Publicity is free, and it includes coverage from other media sources, including newsletters, newspapers, radio stations, television, or whoever else may pick up word of what you're doing.

On the Web, publicity usually takes the form of word-of-mouth type publicity. Someone sees your Web site and then tells someone else who happens to have a blog, so that person writes a blog post about it, which is then picked up by other bloggers, and it then catches the eye of some radio host or newspaper journalist who then runs a brief article or makes mention of your site to their audience.

You get the picture — and that's really a best-case scenario.

Did you know that you can influence publicity, too? You can — by getting the name of your Web site in front of as many people as possible. One way to do that is to write articles that are complete and ready to run, and then distribute them to news outlets, newsletter owners, other Web site owners, or anyone else who has a publication and might be interested in your site. The catch is that to run the article you provide (for free), the publication must also run a short blurb about you, including your Web site address.

That takes care of publicity. *Public relations,* on the other hand, deals with how you handle people, especially in a public setting. You can put that to work for your Web site, too. Public relations can be the donations that you make (in the name of your Web site) to charity organizations, or it can be you taking the time to teach about your topic within your community. Guess what? Just putting your knowledge to use by answering questions posed by folks in search of answers can count as public relations.

Creating a relationship with the public is what public relations is all about. When you use public relations — along with publicity — to get your Web site in front of people, you're building your traffic levels (which in turn helps build your AdSense revenues). Creating public relations and publicity is a time-consuming process, though, so don't make the mistake of thinking that you can spend ten minutes here and there and immediately see results.

Professionals set aside several hours each week to devote to public relations and publicity efforts. You should do the same if you're truly serious about creating a real brand with your Web site that people will think of and recognize when they consider topics related to your site and products. (Creating a *brand* simply means making your Web site or blog immediately recognizable, just like other products [Pepsi, Kleenex, Saran Wrap] are immediately recognizable. The goal is to be the first site or blog that comes to mind when your topic or product is considered.)

Lead Generation and Follow-Up

One thing that Web site owners don't often think of in terms of driving traffic to their sites is lead generation. *Lead generation* in this context is nothing more than the process by which you gather the names and e-mail addresses of people who may be interested in your Web site or blog — these are all potential visitors. And following up on those leads is how you convert those potential visitors into actual visitors. Lead generation takes place in several different ways. For some sites, it's a newsletter sign-up, but for others, it's a contest or promotion that you e-mail to a mailing list you purchased from a marketing company.

How can generating leads help you build traffic on your site? It's easy, really. If you're collecting leads, you can keep your site in front of potential visitors more often.

That does require follow-up, though. Although some Web site owners are great at collecting leads, they don't do much with them — you should. If you have a collection of people who have willingly given you their e-mail address, you should be using that address as often as you can to keep in touch with those potential visitors.

Many Web site owners do collect e-mail addresses (which in this case are your leads). Having folks sign up for a newsletter is one of the most popular *harvesting* methods out there. You can also collect the e-mail addresses of visitors when they register for your site or when they purchase goods or services from you.

However you collect the addresses, they're no good to you if they just sit on a list doing nothing. After you have your e-mail addresses, use them to put your name in front of those people — and the more helpful you can be in the process, the better it is for your Web site.

Here's an example: One Web site owner collects people's e-mail addresses for a newsletter. The newsletter goes out without fail (consistency is key with newsletters) every two weeks. That same Web site owner also sends out a message about once a month that contains tips that the readers can use immediately to improve their business.

This type of extra information — service above and beyond the call of duty — is what helps build traffic for the Web site. When potential visitors turn to the area that the site addresses, that site is of course the first site to come to mind because the Web site owner has kept the site's name in front of them as often as possible.

Keep in mind this fact though: It's absolutely essential that the communications you have with your potential visitors be useful. Sales, extra information, even contest announcements are useful. Just sending a note to say hello? Nothing useful about that at all, and users won't appreciate it.

The idea is to create a feeling of appreciation so that you're first in the visitor's mind when she thinks of the area that you serve. Being first means more Web site traffic for you.

Contests

I briefly mention contests a little earlier in this chapter. I bring them up here because contests are a great way to bring traffic to your Web site. Everyone loves a good contest, especially when the prizes are neat.

Deciding what the prizes are for your contest is very important. Think of what appeals to people who would be interested in your site. I mention earlier in the chapter that if your site's about music, giving away copies of *War and Peace* just won't cut it because such a contest wouldn't target the specific people that you want to see your site.

When you're considering the prizes that you should give away, consider what type of prize would draw the kind of person that would be interested in your site. If the purpose of the contest is to draw visitors to your site, the wrong prizes won't help you at all.

Devising the type of contest to have is the next step. What is it people need to do to get the prize? One thing that many Web site owners do is require that users register for a newsletter, and then the winner is drawn from those who signed up for the newsletter. Bloggers often run contests where visitors are required to leave a comment on the blog.

After you create your contest, all you have to do is get the word out. Announce the contest on your Web site, blog, and any mailing lists that you have. Tell your friends and ask them to tell their friends. If the contest's good, word gets around quickly.

You'll see a spike in the amount of traffic that you have to your site during the contest period, but if you conduct it right, an overall increase will remain after the contest is over. Take the time to design your contest to meet the specific goal of creating traffic (especially return traffic) to your site, and you'll see the benefits of this strategy the first time you try it.

Social Media Marketing

Social marketing is a relatively new concept that's based on a phenomenon that's grown despite the fact that no marketing experts saw it coming, and it's all based on social networks, such as those brought into being by MySpace and Facebook.

The idea with social networks is that you have an online community where you can connect and share with people who have the same interests that you do. For some, that might be an interest in specific people or hobbies. For others, the interest could surround employment or education. What's important is that a social network lets you create a circle of like-minded friends and acquaintances — also called a *community*. For example, with MySpace, the concept is to build a home page where you and your friends can connect. You can also connect with others who are potential friends because they can view your MySpace page and learn about you and your interests.

If you're marketing with social networking, create your network, and as you have something to market, share it with that group of friends in your community. They then share it with their friends, and before you know it, a network that's far beyond the group you could reach on your own knows what you're doing.

Here's the catch with social media marketing though: If you develop a social network specifically to sell something to the people in that network, you'll fall right on your face. Really. Social networks are created by people who have something to share with other people who think like them. If you barge into the network with a sales pitch and nothing more, you'll be completely ostracized.

To be truly effective, you have to actually participate in the communities that you join. That means interacting with people and offering up something that others can use most of the time without expecting anything in return.

If you really want to see how social media marketing works, check out some of the organizations that have successful sites on MySpace or Facebook — Christian bands like Three Days Grace, for example. To get to the point where a social media marketing strategy is successful requires a lot of effort and attention, but the results can be very much worth the time you put into developing your place on the network.

Offline Marketing Strategies

Offline marketing strategies are probably the last type of marketing you'd expect me to address when it comes to Web sites, but sometimes the offline strategies can really work — it does depend on how you go about it, though.

Offline marketing strategies can be anything from press releases to T-shirts to direct mailings. Think about all the commercials that you see during the Super Bowl. How many of those commercials had Web site addresses attached to them? Did you know that those companies paid millions of dollars to have those commercials shown?

You may not be in a position to pay millions of dollars to have your Web address plastered all over the television, but that doesn't mean you should avoid offline advertising methods. Some of the things that you can do on a very small budget include putting magnetic signs on the side of your car, wearing T-shirts with your Web address on them, doing radio interviews, sending out press releases, sponsoring a little-league sports team, and the list goes on nearly forever.

The trick with making offline advertising work is to make sure that you're not investing too much into it, and that it appears in front of the widest audience possible. I wouldn't suggest that you spend thousands of dollars on offline advertisements, but spending a few hundred here and there could increase your traffic in small, but valuable increments.

Ultimately, the best way to draw more traffic to your Web site isn't a single way but is more a combination of all the ways listed here. You have to work to find the right balance of what works, but with enough time and effort, you can get the word out there and draw in visitors.

Index